Plight in Common

American University Studies

Series XXIV
American Literature

Vol. 34

PETER LANG
New York • San Francisco • Bern • Baltimore
Frankfurt am Main • Berlin • Wien • Paris

Elżbieta H. Oleksy

Plight in Common

Hawthorne and Percy

PETER LANG
New York • San Francisco • Bern • Baltimore
Frankfurt am Main • Berlin • Wien • Paris

Library of Congress Cataloging-in-Publication Data

Oleksy, Elżbieta.
Plight in common : Hawthorne and Percy / Elżbieta H. Oleksy.
p. cm. — (American university studies. Series XXIV, American literature; vol. 34)
Includes bibliographical references and index.
1. Hawthorne, Nathaniel, 1804-1864—Criticism and interpretation. 2. Percy, Walker, 1916-1990—Criticism and interpretation. 3. American fiction—History and criticism. I. Title. II. Series.
PS1888.O47 1993 813.009'1—dc20 92-4487
ISBN 0-8204-1848-X CIP
ISSN 0895-0512

Die Deutsche Bibliothek-CIP-Einheitsaufnahme

Oleksy, Elżbieta H.:
Plight in common : Hawthorne and Percy / Elżbieta H. Oleksy.—New York; Berlin; Bern; Frankfurt/M.; Paris; Wien: Lang, 1993
(American university studies : Ser. 24, American literature ; Vol. 34)
ISBN 0-8204-1848-X
NE: American university studies/24

A portion of Chapter 4 of this book appeared in a slightly altered version as "Walker Percy's Demonic Vision" in *Walker Percy: Novelist and Philosopher*, ed. Jan Nordby Gretlund and Karl-Heinz Westarp, Jackson: University Press of Mississippi, 1991, pp. 199-209.

Contents

Acknowledgements

I am grateful to Lewis P. Simpson for his encouragement in the initial stages of this project and to Louis J. Budd for his help in the final stages. Helena Goscilo, with a busy pencil, read the entire manuscript, an act of supererogation that passes praise. Her ability to curb my writing and her many insightful comments have helped me improve this book in countless ways. A fellowship from American Council of Learned Societies in 1983-84 and grants from the University of Pittsburgh and the Kosciuszko Foundation in 1989-90 are also gratefully acknowledged. Thanks are due to Piotr Walczak for meticulous copy-editing. My biggest debt is to my mother Helena, husband Wiesiek, and son Mateusz for patience and emotional and intellectual support. To them I dedicate my work.

Elżbieta H. Oleksy

The common denominator, I think, between Southern writing of this century and Northeastern writing of the last is a certain relation of the writer to a shared body of belief. . . . The vocabulary remains intact; there is a common universe of discourse. It is shared by believer and scoffer, even when the scoffer is like Melville or Joyce and cannot relax in his unbelief. Take these factors, a shared belief or a shared warfare against belief, a major talent like Melville's, a community of one's peers, and a common universe of discourse and you've got the makings of a major literature.

Walker Percy, "Herman Melville"

The modern literature of alienation is in reality the triumphant reversal of alienation through its re-presenting. It is not an existential solution . . . but is an aesthetic victory of comradeliness, a recognition of plight in common. . . . As a mode of deliverance from alienation, experiencing it directly is no different from experiencing it through art.

Walker Percy, *The Message in the Bottle*

Introduction

I

The first impression of Walker Percy shared by his interviewers, including the present one, was of "a quiet man, spare, courtly," "lean and graying . . . [with] milky blue, transparent eyes that, if not sad, seem[ed] somehow inviolably internal," "a white-haired Southern gentleman . . . tempered by the shy, awkward uncertainty of a child eager for reassurance."[1] That portrait evokes the image of another American writer from whom Percy was temporally and geographically distanced, yet with whom he has strong psychological and spiritual affinities—Nathaniel Hawthorne.

Hawthorne's biographers draw a direct connection between several events, including some traumas, in Hawthorne's life and the focal thematic concerns of his fiction. They invariably single out the death of his father when Nathaniel was not quite four years old, his injury when he was nine and his house-confinement for two years, when he developed a habit of intensive reading, his highly ambivalent feelings for the paternal, and patriarchal, figure of Uncle Robert Manning, his twelve lonely years in Salem, his marriage to Sophia Peabody, his seven years in Europe, and his fascination with Catholicism.

Percy's biographers likewise focus on such significant aspects of Percy's life as the death of his father when he was thirteen, followed two years later by the death of his mother, the influence of Uncle Will, who adopted the three orphaned Percy boys, two bouts of tuberculosis, which terminated his medical career, two years (and then another year) of seclusion in sanitariums, during which he read incessantly and decided upon his vocation as a writer, his marriage to Mary Townsend, and their conversion to Catholicism. Even these rudimentary "snapshots" reveal striking similarities between the two writers.

Walker Percy's indebtedness to existentialism is an indisputable fact, acknowledged by Percy in a number of interviews, demonstrated by his fiction and miscellaneous non-fictional writing and analyzed in innumerable articles and several book-length studies. For over two decades (the 60s and the 70s), Percy was almost invariably discussed in the existentialist context. As Thomas D. Young remarks, "Most of Percy's critics write . . . as if he were born at age thirty with an M.D. degree, reading Kierkegaard while recovering from tuberculosis at a sanitarium in upstate New York."[2] The 80s ushered in a change of emphasis, which is reflected already in Panthea Reid Broughton's collection of essays *The Art of Walker Percy. Stratagems for Being* (1979). A year later Jac Tharpe issued a book of essays on Percy, followed by his monograph *Walker Percy* (1983), which combines the various facets of Percy's heritage and training. I owe a special debt to Tharpe for basically three of his insights. In his listing of the philosophers and writers who exerted influence over Percy's work, Tharpe mentions the New England authors of the nineteenth century, Melville, Hawthorne, and Emerson, though he does not explore this debt at any length. Likewise, in his study of Hawthorne in a separate book, Tharpe notes that Hawthorne's writing needs reinterpretation in the context of both Western thought and contemporary writing of the American South. This latter gap has been filled since the publication of Tharpe's book (1967), notably by such learned studies as, for instance, Marion Montgomery's *Why Flannery O'Connor Stayed Home* (1981), which pursues the affinity between Hawthorne and O'Connor, and a number of articles on Faulkner's debt to Hawthorne.[3] Yet despite occasional mentions of Percy's possible indebtedness to Hawthorne, until now no one has undertaken a comprehensive analysis of this influence.

Where my analysis in this study directly intersects with Tharpe's insights is in our discussion of Hawthorne as an essentially existentialist thinker. Tharpe never as much as mentions the term "existentialism," possibly convinced, like Percy, and in Percy's words, that "existentialism has gotten a bad name."[4] Nor does he refer to any of the thinkers who, in my opinion, "modified" his reading of Hawthorne, to use Borges' term. Nevertheless, his analysis of what he considers to be a *leit motif* in Hawthorne's work, "the odyssey of life," contains a strong existentialist component. That "odyssey," in Tharpe's view, presupposes the existence of a goal that vanishes in proportion to the character's proximity to it. Tharpe's analysis is so reminiscent of Sören Kierkegaard's concept of the *telos* that it deserves to be quoted at length:

> [the odyssey of life] of course derives from Homer's epic, and the connotations are intended specifically to include the account of the vicissitudes that occur during the lifetime of man. The suggestion is certainly of a life of difficulties. Included too is the idea of erratic wandering with but a vague goal, if there is one at all. If home is the goal, as with Odysseus, the emphasis nevertheless is on the process, on the incidents, the adventures and the episodes that affect the character involved. In Hawthorne's work, the goal appears to be almost nonexistent; thus, there is a special emphasis on the process. The lack of goal leaves little hope, and the lack of hope makes the wandering to

> avail nothing for Hawthorne's characters, whereas Odysseus was at least going home.[5]

Kierkegaard's usage of the term *telos* emphasizes not the structure of the goal but the movement toward it. According to Kierkegaard, the goal is practically unattainable. It is thus a "vanishing" goal, a notion articulated in *Concluding Unscientific Postscript*: "For the absolute goal has vanished, and the dim sight of the individual has lost its vision."[6] The movement toward the "vanishing" *telos* determines the narrative structure of Hawthorne's first romance *The Scarlet Letter*, the point that I also argue for Percy's National Book Award winning *The Moviegoer*.

It may seem odd that ideas like Kierkegaard's should turn up in America in the middle of the nineteenth century, as if blown across from some central philosophical nursery in the Atlantic. Yet Hawthorne is not the only writer whose ideas seem to coincide with Kierkegaard's. Melville's *Pierre*, for instance, has clear-cut connections with Kierkegaard's *Fear and Trembling*. Plinlimmon's discourse on Chronometricals and Horologicals seems remarkably akin to Kierkegaard's contrast between the Knight of Faith and the ordinary Christian, and the novel raises a similar question about the "teleological suspension of the ethical," the possibility of an individual law higher than a social law. A reader who harbors misgivings about seeing Hawthorne's works in existentialist terms, most likely does so because of the conservatism of Hawthorne's political thought. Such a reader would probably argue against placing Hawthorne in the vanguard of religious speculation when he seems so much at home with the Puritan vocabulary. But Hawthorne was keenly interested in the psychological dimension of the religious mind. His pervasive concern that art not become a science, that it always remain fundamentally imaginative rather than analytical, springs from his fear of violating the integrity of the individual conceived in religious terms.

Tharpe's analysis promotes two leading themes in Hawthorne's works, which he labels "seeing" and "being":

> Seeing refers to observation and to the mental processes, such as cognition and reasoning, that follow observation. Being refers to human existence and to enigmas regarding its source, specifically to the essence that may be related to being, either preceding or deriving from it. The enigmas make being itself the more mysterious. Thus, any one person is a miracle and a mystery.[7]

On close inspection, "seeing" and "being" are, in fact, Gabriel Marcel's categories of "ontological problem" and "ontological mystery," or "problem of being" and " mystery of being." Essential to the idea of the "problem" is that it is conceived to be solved. Conversely, "mystery," in Marcel's words, "applies to what cannot be conceived as a problem, to what is repugnant to problematizing."[8] Tharpe likewise argues:

> Hawthorne apparently was very much aware of the problems and of the unlikelihood of their being solved. For him, then, particularly in view of his knowledge of Puritanism, human motives and human acts were fascinating and quite as enigmatic as being itself. In having these interests, Hawthorne anticipates the widespread speculation about being that has arisen in recent years following the development of psychology and the decline of moral codes.[9]

Generations of Hawthorne critics have searched for some covert principle that would give unity to Hawthorne's vision. Several confess to having encountered a stumbling block in Hawthorne's last finished novel, *The Marble Faun*. Some have attempted to justify their failure by suggesting that their reading of

The Marble Faun is confusing because the book reflects, in Agnes M. Donohue's words, "a serious derangement, a muddle, a chaotic disturbance in the mind of Hawthorne himself."[10] Donohue criticizes the book's "circumspect and unsatisfying" conclusion, which, unlike other ambiguous endings of Hawthorne's novels, does not lend itself to explication through the theory that has informed Donohue's reading of Hawthorne's works—Calvinist-ordained irony. Donohue's book on Hawthorne makes for a delightful reading, and though my own reading is generally at odds with her interpretation, I agree with Donohue on various specific points. I cannot share, however, her condescension towards *The Marble Faun*, the book which, I think, anticipates several personalistic theories. In no other text is the word "mystery" used as obsessively and as consistently as in this novel. It is used in both the Pascalian and the Marcelian sense, and it not only gives the book its unity, but may, in fact, provide a rationale for our understanding of Hawthorne's vision.

A question suggests itself at this point: can we legitimately speak of the precursors, or pioneers, of literary existentialism in the nineteenth century? If we answer this question affirmatively, we must search for some common principle that would unite the several isolated figures who addressed the recurrent existentialist themes in the nineteenth century with a host of twentieth-century authors. The vision of a disjointed, purposeless world that haunts twentieth-century man finds its echoes in major dislocations of the nineteenth century: divisive individualism, the collapse of religion, the new position of man vis à vis nature, and the breakdown of the traditional concepts of personality. American Romanticism, and specifically Transcendentalism, addressed several concepts, which later became associated with existentialism: denial of materialism, emphasis on self-reliance and independence, and radical individualism. The qualification is on the "radical." For, as Joyce W. Warren pertinently remarks, Americans "took the concept of individualism—in Europe, a negative concept connoting selfishness and social anarchy—and transformed it so that it . . . came to represent the positive qualities of freedom and self-determination." This preoccupation with the importance of the self, which dates back to Benjamin Franklin's maxims, and which has guided generations of Americans, finds its most succinct expression, reports Warren, in the statement on the "individual man in himself as an independent end" incorporated in the 1839 issue of the *Democratic Review*.[11] Any student of Kierkegaard can recognize in this statement the great Dane's central idea.

Sidney Finkelstein traces the roots of American existentialism to several transcendentalists who, like Kierkegaard, "preached" the regeneration of their society. Though Finkelstein pertinently acknowledges the difference between the rebellion and the questioning of the American authors and those of Kierkegaard, he perhaps too automatically includes Hawthorne in the group. He says that the American rebels of the nineteenth century sought "the regeneration of a democracy in which, as they saw it, capitalistic greed was an alien and diseased growth."[12] To illustrate his argument, Finkelstein mentions Hawthorne's Brook Farm episode, Emerson's hope and optimism in advocating his readers to "study nature," Thoreau's "experiment" at Walden Pond, where he lived by his own hands in an attempt to prove the futility of materialistic greed, etc. But he fails to mention that Hawthorne's "experiment" was a fiasco. Hawthorne's Brook Farm episode was not prompted by any transcendentalist or socialist convictions; its express purpose was to secure a place to live for him and Sophia after their marriage. Neither does Finkelstein mention that Hawthorne's stand on reform was marked by suspicion, to say the least. What Finkelstein says of Kierkegaard—"He does not flee from society but is engaged in society as a self-proclaimed outsider"—applies more to Hawthorne than to any of his *frère de plume*, and it adequately sums up Hester Prynne's predicament in *The Scarlet Letter*.

The situation of the twentieth-century existentialist writer is, one could contend, more fortunate because he is not a loner, he has a community of other writers who share his vision and ponder the same incongruities. It was definitely different for the nineteenth-century writer. All the pioneers of literary existentialism were lonely figures who fought depression or insanity, or both. When Henry James, Senior, first met Hawthorne at a Saturday Club dinner, he labelled him a "quiet desperado." Several critics attribute Hawthorne's death-wish, towards the end of his life, to his nascent agnostic mood.[13]

Certainly some passages from his last letters to friends and publishers, as well as from his last abortive romances, seem to support this view, as when, for instance, in "Study 4" of the "Ancillary Documents" Hawthorne writes that "the shortness &c. of life shows that human action is a humbug," and that death "so breaks off and brings to naught all human effort; so as to make man a laughing stock to whoever created him." But we have other testimony in Hawthorne's desperate struggle, in the last four years of his life, to bring "full wisdom about matters of life and death" into creative writing. A year before his death, he writes to James Fields, "I am not low-spirited, nor fanciful, nor freakish, but look what seems to be realities in the face, and am ready to take whatever may come."[14] Hawthorne does not lament, like a Miniver Cheevy, or like Hölderlin, "But, friend, we have come too late." The reality that Hawthorne faced was that he had come too early. His vision was shared by only a few and, among American authors, by Melville alone. But Melville's pessimism is total, all-encompassing. Hawthorne dreaded Melville's nihilism, which he saw as destructive of the self. The only refuge for Hawthorne lay, it seems, in the sphere of interpersonal relations, which surfaces in the romances written after *The Scarlet Letter*.

Hawthorne's link with existentialism is not as accidental as those critics who acknowledge this aspect of his work make it out to be.[15] Hawthorne was acquainted with Blaise Pascal's thought; he checked the *Oeuvres* out of the Salem Athenaeum in the summer of 1829.[16] Pascal's image of a man in a cell must have appealed to Hawthorne, particularly at this time in his life. Significantly, this image, which had its counterpart in Hawthorne's solitary chamber in Salem, made its way into several novels. We find it in Hester's cottage, Clifford's arched window, and Donatello's tower in his ancestral home. Interestingly, a parallel image recurs in Percy's novels that evokes his solitary years spent at sanitariums, where Percy was treated for tuberculosis: Will Barrett's room at Macy's, Lance Lamar's pigeonnier, and Allison Huger's greenhouse.

In Pascal Hawthorne found what was to become the central dichotomy in his own work: the impotence of "reason" in dealing with the human condition. Of all Pascalian concepts, the notion of the heart that "has its reason which reason does not know" was to be elaborated repeatedly in Hawthorne's writing. What makes it difficult to attribute Hawthorne's concept of the "heart" solely to "coeur Pascalien" is the fact that the "heart" and "head" (Pascal's "reason") dichotomy was widespread not only in Romanticism generally but also in Puritanism. The "head" versus "heart" clash and its corollary in self-deception (Pascal's "être imaginaire") was of vital importance for the Puritans in estimating one's prospects for salvation.[17] Nevertheless, the similarities, which I hope will become apparent, between Hawthorne's "heart" and the "coeur Pascalien" are what gives a peculiarly existentialist flavor to Hawthorne's contribution to what Norman S. Fiering calls "the universal clashing motifs" in American literature.

There has been much controversy as to the interpretation of "coeur Pascalien," which possibly results from Pascal's inconsistent usage of the word. In several studies of existentialism, Pascal's "heart" is associated with feeling or emotion. James Collins discusses the term as parallel to Kierkegaard's "passion" and Rousseau's "instinct."[18] In fact, Rousseau uses the terms "instinct divin" and "coeur" synonymously, and part of the confusion derives from the fact that, like Pascal, he juxtaposes the "heart" to "reason." The "heart," for Rousseau, is man's innate ability to grasp the basic truths without reason, hence instinct. One of Pascal's *pensées*, however, contains this exclamation: "How hollow and foul is the heart of man!", which parallels Hawthorne's, "In the depth of every heart, there is a tomb and a dungeon" (9: 306). Jan Miel gives us the most satisfactory definition of the "coeur Pascalien," saying that it is neither emotion nor instinct, but rather it "designates the seat of all the faculties of the soul."[19] Thus, Pascal uses the word "heart" as it is used in the Bible, and even if the word "soul" seems impossibly vague to us today, it was not vague for Pascal, and surely not for Hawthorne. Hawthorne uses the words "heart" and "soul" synonymously. The "soul," to Hawthorne, is an empty space which, without grace, fills itself with dross. He says that "the soul may pollute itself even with those crimes which we are accustomed to deem altogether carnal" (9: 220). Pascal has a corresponding passage: "Man is therefore nothing but disguise, falsehood and hypocrisy, both in himself and with regard to other . . . all these tendencies, so remote from justice and reason, are naturally rooted in his heart."[20] Hawthorne has allegorized the heart as the cavern that houses gloom and monsters, which make it seem like hell. Yet for both Pascal and Hawthorne, the heart may be the seat of grace, as in Pascal's, "That is what faith is. God perceived by the heart, not by the reason," and in Hawthorne's, "There are the depths of the heart or of human nature . . . the gloom and terror may lie deep; but deeper still is the eternal beauty" (9: 309).

They differ, however, on one point. Pascal ascribed sin to man's nature, Hawthorne to man's will. To Pascal, man's freedom is a limited one; man cannot freely will his salvation unless God predestines him to do so. And divine predestination is entirely beyond our grasp. This belief puts Pascal at variance with the existentialist tradition because to believe in predestination is to lose the vision of man's freedom. To regard guilt solely as the inescapable consequence of being human inexorably leads man to the conviction that he cannot do anything for himself and that his life is entirely in the hands of God, regardless of his freedom. It would deny the individual's responsibility for himself and for others. As Hawthorne says:

> In truth, there is no such thing in men's nature as a settled and full resolve, either for good or evil, except at the very moment of execution. Let us hope, therefore, that all the dreadful consequences of sin will not be incurred, unless *the act have set its seal upon the thought.* (9: 226)

Pascal attributes all existing human evils to three impulses: *libido sentiendi, libido sciendi,* and *libido dominandi.* Hawthorne, likewise, centers his analysis of sin on these three impulses. The sinners of the flesh, like Hester Prynne, who work toward their salvation, undoubtedly earn Hawthorne's sympathy. His attitude as regards the sin of the intellect seems to vary in accordance with the sinner's motivation. Critics usually group together such characters as Rappaccini, Ethan Brand, Aylmer, Chillingworth, and even Wakefield, as the ones who inhumanly probe the psyche of others and thus violate the sacredness of the human heart. But there is a vast difference between Rappaccini and Chillingworth, and Ethan Brand and Aylmer, not to mention Wakefield, whose sin, I think, Hawthorne unreservedly condemns. As one critic observes, Rappaccini "does the wrong thing for the right motive," i.e., his fanatical love for Beatrice, and in this he differs from Baglioni, who "does the wrong thing for the wrong motive."[21] Chillingworth is another case in point. He of course does the wrong thing for the wrong motive, but in the early sections of *The Scarlet Letter* the narrative voice carries a note of sympathy for him that gradually fades. Through this modulation in tone Hawthorne develops the contrast between the kind of man Chillingworth was prior to the narrative and what he becomes after he learns of Hester's adultery. He used to be "kindly" and "calm in temperament," and in his relations with the world he was a "pure and upright man." When he visits Hester in prison and recalls the early stages of their marriage, Hawthorne endows his confession with warmth and genuine affection. The reader tends to forget those reminiscences as gradually Chillingworth's "better nature" becomes compromised by his demonic quest for vengeance.

Conversely, Aylmer and Ethan Brand are depicted in consistently negative terms. Of Aylmer, Hawthorne says at the beginning of the tale that "he had devoted himself, however, too unreservedly to scientific studies, ever to be weaned from them by any second passion" (10: 36). And Ethan Brand, who "had lost his hold of the magnetic chain of humanity," was "no longer a brother-man, . . . he was now a cold observer, looking on mankind as the subject of his experiment, and, at length, converting man and woman to be his puppets, and pulling the wires that moved them to such degrees of crimes as were demanded for his study" (11: 99). For both Aylmer and Brand intellect becomes a false idol that they worship unreservedly. Their sins are "unpardonable" to Hawthorne, for they are committed for no human motives, be it even hatred, but for the sake of mastery over Mankind and Nature. Their transgressions comprise *libido sciendi* and *libido dominandi.*

The same applies to Wakefield, who, however, has no intellect to sustain him. If at times he is akin to J. Alfred Prufrock and would admit with Prufrock: "I have measured out my life in coffee spoons," the questions of identity that surface in the tale are posed not by Wakefield himself, but rather by the narrative voice. It is the narrator who addresses queries to Wakefield; Wakefield asks no questions, he is no Prince Hamlet, nor meant to be. He is, indeed, a fool, as Hawthorne intimates, "In Wakefield, the magic of a single night has wrought a . . . transformation, because, in that brief period, a great moral change has been effected. *But this is a secret from himself*" (9: 135). And, later, he says that Wakefield "had contrived," and immediately corrects himself, "or rather he *had happened*, to dissever himself from the world" (9:138).

Jorge Luis Borges' reading of "Wakefield" is through both ethics and rhetoric *created,* as Borges insists, by Kafka. Even though Borges adds that he means no "discredit" to Hawthorne, he in fact weakens Hawthorne's merit in this remarkable tale, especially by comparing Hawthorne and Kafka with Marlowe and Shakespeare. He says:

> The circumstance, the strange circumstance, of perceiving in a story written by Hawthorne at the beginning of the nineteenth century the same quality that distinguishes the stories Kafka wrote at the beginning of the twentieth must not cause us to forget that Hawthorne's particular quality has been created, or determined, by Kafka. "Wakefield" prefigures Franz Kafka, but Kafka modifies and refines the reading of "Wakefield." The debt is mutual; a great writer creates his precursors. He creates and somehow justifies them. What, for example, would Marlowe be without Shakespeare?[22]

Andrew Shiller's estimation of the same tale gives Hawthorne due credit, even though his initial assumption is similar: "We have had to learn to read Joyce, James and Kafka before we could read Hawthorne." He importantly adds, however, that "just as in the plastic arts we needed sophisticated imitators to teach us to feel African sculpture, so we have been a long time coming to understand that in Hawthorne's work we have un ur-form of modern fiction, and in him an original."[23]

We frequently encounter this discussion of anteriority and posteriority in Hawthorne criticism. Jean Normand is one of those critics who maintain that if Hawthorne's position is clearly existential, it is "not out of any intellectual conviction, but instinctively."[24] We may deduce that Normand believes that Hawthorne was not, as Percy says of himself, "equipped as a philosopher to express [his] ideas." But if it is true that, as Mary Warnock remarks, "existentialism, as a way of thinking, is . . . naturally suited to express itself in novels, plays, films, and other unargued statements of how the world is,"[25] we have certainly seen characteristic features of such expressions in Hawthorne's work.

Hawthorne read Pascal's works during the most formative years of his life, the twelve lonely years at his Salem house. Of the room in which he spent these years he writes: "Here my mind and character were formed." There has been abundant speculation among critics as regards these lonely years. Some perceive this seclusion as manifesting Hawthorne's neurotic, almost morbid, nature. Others tend to give his estrangement a dramatic function in the evolution of Hawthorne's character, an argument also raised in reference to Emily Dickinson's compulsive reclusiveness. Still others point to the fact that although Hawthorne preferred his own company during this period, he made several trips, which took him into society, walked at night in the neighborhood, mixing anonymously with unnamed people, and wandered on the seashore near Salem. These critics invariably attempt to somehow *justify* Hawthorne's reclusiveness. Hawthorne, however, was convinced that his calling required an unusual degree of self-discipline, reflection, and even private risk. He regarded his own vocation as similar to that of a spy or a lonely sentry, occupations which tend to emphasize the independence and importance of a single individual. The picture of a writer that emerges from Hawthorne's miscellaneous works recalls a Kierkegaardian ironist, whose "intercourse" with the world makes him acutely aware that inauthenticity manifests itself in the language people use—that in their discourse the significant matters so often lie "undisturbed beneath a heap of superficial topics." Hawthorne's "silences" puzzled his contemporaries. William Dean Howells, who visited Hawthorne in 1862, commented on "a great deal of silence" about Hawthorne, which made Howells' "spirits sink." Hawthorne's notion of language as superficial camouflage recalls Heidegger's concept of inauthenticity. According to Heidegger, inauthenticity arises in man's relation to the crowd and to the requirements of daily life rather than to himself. In both situations, he substitutes curiosity and calculative thinking for genuine understanding, just as he substitutes "prattle" for genuine discourse. Conversely, to live authentically is to be capable of genuine understanding and original thinking, expressed in genuine language.

Any reader of the *Pensées* has no difficulty recognizing in "Wakefield" such familiar concepts as routine (Pascal's "coutume"), self-love (Pascal's "amour propre"), which invariably expresses itself in egocentricity and vanity, and self-deception (Pascal's "être imaginaire"). The great paradox of the tale, however, consists in Hawthorne's creation of the archetypal isolate without endowing him with any degree of self-consciousness. Even Roderick Elliston, a clinical exemplification of egocentricity, in the end is allowed to "forget [himself] in the idea of another." Similarly, Clifford Pyncheon, who is initially characterized in a somewhat similar fashion to Wakefield, ultimately also awakens from his torpor. But not Wakefield, whom Hawthorne, at the end of the tale, describes as having "become, as it were, the Outcast of the Universe" (9:140). Hawthorne ends his tale with these illuminating words:

> Amid the seeming confusion of our mysterious world, individuals are so nicely adjusted to a system, and systems to one another, and to a whole, that, by stepping aside for a moment, a man exposes himself to a fearful risk of losing his place forever. (9:140)

Hawthorne anticipates here one of the central themes of his fiction. He maintains, with Kierkegaard, that the formation of personality is a solitary venture, but he also demonstrates deftly that excessive internalization may lead to indifference, or to what Percy calls "death in life." Hawthorne's *The Marble Faun* and Percy's *The*

Second Coming reveal that both writers perceive intersubjective communion as the alternative to radical subjectivity.

Hawthorne's Pascal-indebted fiction gave vent to the mood of crisis that had begun to spread throughout America of the late nineteenth century. Another forty years or so, and American literature would boast Richard Cory, Miniver Cheevy, and J. Alfred Prufrock, to name but a few archetypal isolates. That type, however, originated with Hawthorne, whose fiction explored its dilemmas even before Melville, one of the few contemporaries who could truly appreciate his vision. Like Melville, Hawthorne was convinced of the essential mystery surrounding human life. He was frankly annoyed by his contemporaries' demand that he explain the ambiguities of his plots. He recognized that man must abandon any ideas of a "final solution" to his problems, as well as to his longing for truth. There are no "final" solutions, he says, and adds that we should refrain from staying content with pre-fabricated answers, as well as past accomplishments, but rather fill our lives with a genuine search. We must accept responsibility for our acts, and we must seek truth without any guarantee that "the great Sphinx will ever speak."

II

One of the commonest criticisms of existentialism has been its narrow focus on individualism and subjectivity. Though personalists have taken pains to remedy this situation by focusing on two human subjects engaged in an interpersonal bonding, most existentialists, by promoting excellence and depreciating the mass, posit the ideal of a kind of superman.[26] That superman is inevitably always male. One can hardly imagine woman as a subject in existentialism. Existentialism from Kierkegaard and Dostoyevsky to Sartre and Camus was typically male-oriented. Would Kierkegaard, for instance, conceive of woman as a Knight of Faith? Had he read Hawthorne, he surely would have been surprised to see how many characteristics of the true Knight of Faith, that solitary quester embarked on what he calls "existential pathos," lingered in the portrayal of Hawthorne's woman with the letter.

Consider, for instance, Albert Camus, whose fiction not only idealizes the fraternity of men, male bonding in sports, journalism, and politics (*à la* Hemingway, the most phallocentric of American writers), but repeatedly excludes women as characters except when they assume the symbolically phallocentric role of mother or lover.

In his imaginary interview with Camus, Robert C. Salomon asks the writer-philosopher the question that, I believe, was never posed in Camus' lifetime:

> **RCS**: I must ask, for you speak continually of "man" —man's fate, man's happiness, man's responsibility—what about *women*? What, if I may ask, about *Missus* Sisyphus?
> **CAMUS**: [a quick smile, then very serious] Well, in French as in English, the word "man" is a general term including both men and women.
> **RCS**: Yes, but you seem to evade the point. All your characters, for example, are men. Your women are silent.
> **CAMUS**: As my mother was silent, but no less significant for that.
> . . .
> **RCS**: But the mother in *The Stranger* is dead when the novel begins. Meursault's girlfriend Marie is little but a pretty face, a warm body; we know her only by her smell, her giggle, her laugh.
> **CAMUS**: Meursault isn't much more.
> **RCS**: Yes, but Meursault is a least a character; Marie isn't even a foil.
> **CAMUS**: That's true, but the mother's presence is what defines the novel.

> **RCS**: It's true, that's so, but the point is, again, she isn't a *character*. And *The Plague*: it's all men. *The Fall*, a man; *The Myth of Sisyphus*, all about the absurd *man*, the absurd hero, Don Juan, Kafka, all men, often womanizing men.
>
> **CAMUS**: I'm guilty, I suppose. There is Martha in my play *Malentendu*, but yes, you're right, and I admit, I distrust women. I am thoroughly dependent on them, but they do not share my world.
>
> **RCS**: Would you say that existentialism is primarily a male philosophy?
>
> **CAMUS**: That isn't my concern. But you might ask Simone.[27]

And Simone de Beauvoir, prompted by the sexist existentialism of her contemporary compatriots, argued for the concept of the *other*, which sees woman not as an end in herself but as an auxiliary in man's important quests. De Beauvoir derives this function of woman from *Genesis*, where woman in the form Eve was created not as a separate entity, but complementary to man and from the body of man.[28]

Recent feminist criticism takes pains to identify Simone de Beauvoir as the foremother of feminism, but not without reservations. According to Janet Todd, de Beauvoir's *The Second Sex* is not very useful for feminist theory on account of its tendency to "universalize as nature rather than historicize as culture the distinctions of men and women." De Beauvoir is trapped, Todd contends, in a "rationality defined by and for men," whereby *consciousness* is conceived as *maleness*. De Beauvoir, Todd aptly concludes, cannot "appropriate for feminism the Sartrean notion of free *subjectivity* and self-defining agency without becoming 'contaminated' by the profoundly sexist ideology of objectivity to which this notion is inevitably coupled."[29]

Viewed from this perspective, the development of Hawthorne and Percy, which coincides in other respects, substantially differs on the question of gendered otherness. Percy begins in *The Moviegoer* by defining consciousness as exclusively male, Hawthorne in *The Scarlet Letter* as almost exclusively female. Nina Baym and Louise DeSalvo have respectively made strong cases for Hawthorne as a feminist writer and as a militant sexist.[30] Paradoxically of course, they are both right. If, as Baym argues, Hawthorne is acutely sensitive to the oppression of women, and knows exactly "what this sort of behavior [the rejection of women] means and depicts it as stupid, ugly, and evil," he at the same time repudiates any "aspirations" of women to public pronouncements in defense of the feminine gender.[31] The same dichotomy is encountered in Percy. If Hawthorne wrote tales and novels about women who are "mistreated" and "injured," in Baym's words, so did Percy. If Hawthorne pleaded ignorance on issues that have become identified with feminism, so did Percy. Moreover, if we survey both writers' works, we realize that they connect the rejection and victimization of women with men's fear of their sexuality.

In an early tale, "The Shaker Bridal," Martha Pierson literally wastes away from unfulfilled sexual desire ("her heart could endure the weight of its desolate agony no longer" [9: 425]). Mary Goffe suffers under Richard Digby's adamant coldness, and also dies. Hester is rejected by Dimmesdale after she demonstrates her physical desire for him, and Miriam Shaefer is shunned by Donatello after the consummation of their union. *The House of the Seven Gables* likewise contains a number of victimized females. Similarly in Percy's novels: In *The Moviegoer*, Binx shies from Kate's "not whorish bold but theorish bold carrying on" to the point of impotence. Will Barrett in *The Last Gentleman* can "hardly" consummate his union with Kitty. In *Lancelot*, Lance Lamar disintegrates under the sexual demands of his second wife, Margot. And the later Will, fresh from discovering the joy of love and sex combined, repeats his old cliché, musing about Kitty's "special boldness" and concluding that "women grow more lustful as they grow older."

In Percy's fiction, as in Hawthorne's, sexual women are punished in a number of ways for the sexuality that misogyny has conventionally stigmatized. Kate loses all "self" by becoming witlessly integrated into the paradigm of male authority: she has to be told what to do and say to the point where her individuality gets totally erased. The metaphor of silence and self-annihilation becomes literalized when Margot and Raine are murdered by Lance, thereby *losing* themselves in all senses. Even mothers, female children and "good" wives (that is, those who are neither "theorish" nor "whorish" bold) are depicted in stereotyped misogynistic images; Lance uses the sexist attributes of "scissoring legs" and "boring fists" for his mother, his first wife Lucy, and his daughter Siobhan alike.

By any feminist standards, this would suffice to ban Percy's works from the feminist syllabus on the grounds of sexism. Or, on the contrary, one might join the scholarly chorus of those who still think that gender issues are not of vital importance to Percy's worldview. Adopting either of the two attitudes, however, means confusing the identities of author and character in Percy's fiction. Percy's male protagonists (the epithet sounds tautological, for prior to *The Second Coming*, *all* of Percy's protagonists are male) fail, if not in their quests, then surely in their relationships with women. And their failure in forging and developing relationships with women stems not only from their incomprehension of the women in their lives, but also from the nature of their goal: a unique (read: performed solitarily) quest for faith the realization of which could be threatened by a relationship with a "separate" female individual. Or it may well be that both arguments are mutually conditioning. Binx exemplifies what Northrop Frye calls a "stylized figure," a carrier of Kierkegaard's notion of the Knight of Faith. The younger Will wavers among several contending forces in a fashion reminiscent of Jake Horner in Barth's early novel, sooner resembling an allegorical agent than a flesh and blood man. And Lance, likewise embarked on a quest of sorts, epitomizes the characteristics of Percy's earlier protagonist in his incapacity to understand, let alone love, *any* woman.

Nonetheless, it would be a gross exaggeration to say that the extreme case of Lance or Percy's other male protagonists voice their author's convictions about women. If such were the case, why did Percy make of Lance such a pitiful, if not revolting, figure? Why, in the final episode of *The Moviegoer*, do we come to pity not only Kate, whom Binx "hands along" her journey downtown, but also Binx himself? If Binx's role in their marriage amounts to just this "handing along," then he surely picked up the right profession (he becomes a medical student). And why, in *The Last Gentleman*, did Percy make Will miss the import of the crucial scene of Jamie's baptism, just the way Kate missed a parallel event in *The Moviegoer*? Why, in other words, does the Percy protagonist almost invariably fail?

Percy provides the answer to these questions in an interview with Bradley R. Dewey on the subject of his debt to Kierkegaard's thought, where he confesses his unease with Kierkegaard's notion of subjectivity. What he finds lacking in subjectivity is, in Percy's words, an "understanding or an explanation of intersubjectivity —caring for the other person."[32] He goes on to explain that the discovery of this gap took him to the two philosophers Martin Buber and Gabriel Marcel, and to the concept of *I and Thou.* Of course, *I and Thou* has its less celebrated counterpart: *I and It.* The first presupposes the relationship between two subjects or, in terms of gender relations, reciprocity and partnership. The second defines the relationship between a subject and an object, hence a quintessence of any story of privation. Both philosophers consider the relationship with another person a passport to freedom. Marcel is the best-known representative of the personalistic tendency of existentialism. Sartre's and Camus' compatriot, Marcel counterbalances their pessimism with a "metaphysic of hope" that is based on a theistic conception of the universe and a sense of human community. This is the hope of a man who is always on his way, man the wayfarer, the *homo viator*.

Whereas Percy acknowledged his debt to Marcel's philosophy on many occasions, it may seem problematic to discuss Hawthorne's views on religion in Marcelian terms. For one thing, a whole century divided them. Moreover, Hawthorne, unlike Percy, who made a commitment to Catholicism at the age of thirty one, did not sort out his religious beliefs until almost the end of his life. Speculations about Hawthorne's religious views have always been subject to the critical fray. Various critics claim that Hawthorne was a Unitarian, a Calvinist, a Catholic convert, etc., and there are others who easily repudiate each of these assertions. However, Hawthorne eludes us here as in no other sphere of his personal life. It still appears that he experienced two rather serious religious "temptations": one, when he was still a young man, and the other towards the end of his life. Shortly after his graduation from Bowdoin, he gave some thought to a possibility of joining a sectarian group known as the Shakers or the Millennial Church. To what extent Hawthorne was familiar with the Shakers' dogma is hard to determine, for his impressions amount to brief mentions after each of his visits at various Shaker settlements. James Mellow reports that Hawthorne studied the Shakers' documents, and thus was quite possibly acquainted with the sect's emphasis on confession.[33] The importance of this hypothesis will become clear once we remember that Hawthorne's later attraction to Catholicism was most pronounced in relation to the sacrament of confession. The fact, however, remains that Hawthorne's fascination with the Shakers spent itself, and the venom, which we find in his ultimate criticism of the sect, anticipates the austerity of his views on Catholicism. The latter influence was, however, much more profound in Hawthorne's life and can be best captured by that trite epithet, ambivalent. During his one-and-a-half-year sojourn in Italy Hawthorne experienced as profound an agony of religious doubt as this afflicting Hilda in *The Marble Faun.* "One day," writes Donohue, "Hawthorne saw much to be admired in Catholicism; the next day he was revolted and all of his hidden Calvinism surfaced as disgust."[34] It seems, however, fair to say that just as the vicissitudes of Hilda's attraction to Catholicism resemble Hawthorne's own, so Hilda's determination to remain the "daughter" of her Puritan forbears, also parallels Hawthorne's decision. Hawthorne was as much opposed to proselytizing as he was to any institutionalized religion, resembling in this respect, and in many others, his Danish contemporary, Kierkegaard. His miscellaneous writings indicate, however, that Hawthorne was a consistent theist. He time and again articulates his belief in God, with whom an individual may possess a permanent personal relationship. But, most importantly, this relationship, emphasize both Hawthorne and Percy, fulfills itself in a personal encounter with another person approached as a *Thou.*

Critics have traditionally looked for intersubjective bonds in almost every novel Percy wrote. Linda Whitney Hobson perceives such a union in several odd couples: Binx and Kate, Binx and Lonnie, Will and Sutter, Lance and Percival, and Tom and Ellen.[35] If Percy indeed approached intersubjectivity in each of his novels, he never fully explored it before *The Second Coming.* Percy defines intersubjectivity as "that meeting of minds by which two selves take each other's meaning with reference to the same object beheld in common."[36] In each of these novels the subjectivity explored is invariably that of one person, and invariably male. In three of the five "couples" Hobson lists, the second "self" (Lonnie, Sutter, and Percival) is entirely, or almost entirely, absent from the narrative as the subject. The unique character of intersubjectivity is trans-personal togetherness, reciprocity, if you will. We cannot really judge if the intersubjective communion has taken place if we do not witness it in the "presence," in Marcel's understanding of the word, of the other. As one commentator of Marcel's thought notes, "intersubjectivity, or being in the presence of *one another*, involves an event articulated by *freedoms* and grace" (emphasis added—note the plural in "freedoms").[37] It is not until *The Second Coming* that two consciousnesses, female and male, are developed along parallel lines until they meet in intersubjective communion. And it is Will Barrett, in *The Second Coming*, who ultimately understands, if not women, then a woman.

Although neither Hawthorne nor Percy examines the social status of women, both evidence interest in gender and are acutely conscious of men's dependence on women. This awareness leads Hawthorne and Percy to define the "New Woman" of their fictions in terms usually associated with the Savior. In the often dissected penultimate paragraph of *The Scarlet Letter*, Hawthorne speaks of "some brighter period . . . in Heaven's own time" when "a new truth would be revealed, in order to establish the whole relation between man and woman on a surer ground of mutual happiness." That woman is defined as "the angel and apostle of the coming revelation," who will show how "sacred love should make us happy, by the truest test of a life successful to such an end" (1: 263). He returns to this image in *The House of the Seven Gables*, where Phoebe becomes religion incarnate, "warm, simple, true, with a substance that could walk on earth, and a spirit that was capable of Heaven" (2: 168). And in *The Marble Faun*, we see this image articulated overtly in the description of Hilda as a "household Saint," whose "white wisdom" "clothes" her "as a celestial garment" (4: 460-61). If the trite discussion of Fair Maiden versus Dark Lady in Hawthorne's writing will come to mind here, it should, for even if we do not always benefit from perceiving Hawthorne's "women" as stereotypes, the practice that prevents us from seeing them as separate individuals, Hawthorne's last finished novel puts a seal on this dichotomy. However, it is important to realize that Hawthorne (and also Percy) uses a mythical source in his definition of the woman just described.

As already mentioned, Hawthorne was for a period of time attracted to Shakerism. Recent concern in redefining women's history has generated new interest in Shakerism by feminist theologians. Though they are far from reaching a consensus on whether or not Shakerism is feminist (one of the main obstacles seems to be the Shakers' traditional division of labor), they still seem to concede that Shakerism, in the words of one commentator, was "the only female-led religion that developed a consistent system of equal empowerment of women."[38]

Although Hawthorne ultimately criticized Shakerism in terms reminiscent of his condescension toward Catholicism (criticism that surfaces in the two tales concerning this sect), the image of a dual Godhead stayed under his pen, if you will, throughout his literary career. In "The Shaker Bridal" he conceives two characters, Adam and Martha, as the ones who are to "renew, in their persons, the primitive form of Shaker government, as established by Mother Ann" (9: 422). This "form," of course, was meant to reflect the Shakers' belief in a dual Godhead, dual leadership, and equality of rights between men and women. Similarly, in "The Canterbury Pilgrims" two characters, a man and a woman, retreat from the Shaker settlement to "mingle in an untried life." Many a Hawthorne work concludes with such a retreat: for example, that of the two "couples" in *The House of the Seven Gables*, or Hilda and Kenyon's return to America at the end of *The Marble Faun*. Such a resolution also closes Percy's fifth novel, which, as I will demonstrate, offers an eloquent context for the analysis of this mythical source. Furthermore, in the novels discussed in the last part of this study Hawthorne and Percy use Shakerism as a broad analogy to their fictional strategy. While neither Hawthorne nor Percy directly tackled the woman question, both of them approached that question in an unprecedented way, notably through the application of the Shakerist symbol of liberated womanhood, which is the story of Mother Ann.

III

This study is divided into three main parts: *Renunciation*, *Catharsis*, and *Intersubjectivity*. Each of the three sections treats a book each by Hawthorne and Percy, so that the study examines six texts in all. By following this structure, I attempt to demonstrate parallel developments in Hawthorne's and Percy's craft and vision. My presentation of this development benefits from Peter Brooks' insightful "Freud's Masterplot," which examines the relationship between Freud's structuring of life's trajectory in *Beyond the Pleasure Principle* and the narrative dynamics in several nineteenth-century texts.[39] Susan Winnett, pointing to differences in the dynamics of beginnings, middles, and ends between texts created by men and women, observes that Brooks' model describes essentially "male narratology." Winnett contends that the movement of plot charted by Brooks, with what he calls its "motor force in human desire," pertains to male, and not female, sexual experience.[40]

While Brooks is hardly the first to discover the connection between art and the erotic, what Robert Scholes calls the "orgastic rhythm of tumescence and detumescence, of tension and resolution, of intensification to the point of climax and consummation,"[41] he importantly notes that most nineteenth-century novels register the narrative of the "attempted homecoming: of the effort to reach an assertion of origin through ending." That ending (what Brooks after Freud calls "significant discharge") is reached, argues Brooks, through the "chain of metonymies," or "the vacillating play of the middle, where repetition as binding works toward the generation of significance [*anagnorisis*], toward recognition and the retrospective illumination that will allow us to grasp the text as total metaphor." "Significant discharge" (the point at which clearly male, though not female, pleasure ends) is followed, needless to say, by what Freud calls "quiescence" and Brooks "nonnarratability."

I will argue this model not for individual novels (interestingly, most of Percy's novels are open-ended, which Winnett considers generally more characteristic of female rather than male narrative), but for sequences of novels by each of the two writers. The "total metaphor" (homecoming), I contend, is what structures *The Marble Faun* and *The Second Coming*. The "significant discharge" furnished by two highly symbolic scenes, the hurling of the Model over the Tarpeian Rock in *The Marble Faun* and the flinging of the guns over the gorge in *The Second Coming*, is illuminated through what Brooks calls return and repetition, that is, "partial recognitions of the middle." Both writers return to their middle texts—Hawthorne to *The House of the Seven Gables* and Percy to *Lancelot*—in the sense that they repeat the scenes that served there only as "partial revelation" (I will note here, as a subject for later exploration, that considering Hawthorne's reluctance to talk directly of matters pertaining to sex, and Percy's criticism of pornography in literature, the middle novels, *The House of the Seven Gables* and *Lancelot*, reverberate with sexual overtones). The "chain of metonymies" from these middle novels enhances our understanding of the ending. The sense of closure that we experience in both *The Marble Faun* and *The Second Coming*, or what William R. Allen calls "a feeling of the rounding off of an imaginative world," is not accidental. Although my conclusions differ from Allen's, I fully share his insight that "Percy's early critics suffered under the disadvantage of not being able to see his first three or four novels in the light of *The Second Coming*."[42]

The Second Coming, which I perceive as simultaneously Percy's final confrontation with existentialism and his dramatic liberation from existentialism and stoicism alike (as love triumphs), grows out of, yet also outgrows, Percy's earlier fiction. During my interview with him, Percy searched for a phrase that would succinctly define the dominant theme in his fiction, and ultimately came up with the French "solitude à deux." His formulation essentially duplicates Hawthorne's phrase, "solitude of a united two," in his letter to Sophia. At the conclusion of *The Marble Faun*, Hilda uses these words after Kenyon's declaration of love and dependence on her, again almost *expressis verbis*. Both Hawthorne and Percy embraced a view of life as something transcendently enigmatic, subject to inexplicable forces. For Hawthorne, "the actual experience of even the most ordinary life is full of events that never explain themselves, either as regards their origin or their tendency" (4: 455). Similarly Percy asserts: "Life is a mystery, love is a delight. Therefore I take it as axiomatic that one should settle for nothing less than the infinite mystery and the indefinite delight, i.e., God. In fact I demand it. I refuse to settle for anything less."[43] What links the two writers, then, is a shared body of belief, or—a plight in common.

NOTES

1. See Introduction to *Conversations with Walker Percy*, ed. Lewis A. Lawson and Victor A. Kramer (Jackson: Univ. Press of Mississippi, 1985), pp. vii-xii.

2. Thomas Daniel Young, "A New Breed: Walker Percy's Critics' Attempts to Place Him," *The Mississippi Quarterly*, vol. XXXIII, no. 4 (Fall 1980), p. 491.

3. See, for instance, Richard Bridgman, "As Hester Prynne Lay Dying," *English Language Notes*, vol. II, no. 4 (June 1965), pp. 294-96.

4. See Jo Gulledge, "The Reentry Option: An Interview with Walker Percy," in *Conversations with Walker Percy*, p. 300.

5. Jac Tharpe, *Nathaniel Hawthorne. Identity and Knowledge* (Carbondale and Edwardsville: Southern Illinois Univ. Press, 1967), p. 16.

6. Sören Kierkegaard, *Concluding Unscientific Postscript*, trans. David F. Swenson (Princeton: Princeton Univ. Press, 1941), p. 364.

7. Tharpe, p. 6.

8. Gabriel Marcel, *The Existential Background of Human Dignity* (Cambridge: Harvard Univ. Press, 1963), p. 82.

9. Tharpe, p. 6.

10. Agnes McNeill Donohue, *Hawthorne. Calvin's Ironic Stepchild* (Kent: The Kent State University Press, 1985), p. 266.

11. Joyce W. Warren, *The American Narcissus. Individualism and Women in Nineteenth-Century American Fiction* (New Brunswick: Rutgers Univ. Press, 1984), pp. 4-5.

12. Sidney Finkelstein, *Existentialism and Alienation in American Literature* (New York: International Publishers, 1965), p. 32.

13. See, for instance, Donohue, pp. 309 and 310-39, and Tharpe, p. 149.

14. A letter to James Fields (February 25, 1864), in *The Centenary Edition of the Works of Nathaniel Hawthorne*, ed. William Charvat, Roy Harvey Pearce, Claude M. Simpson, Thomas Woodson, Fredson Bowers, L. Neal Smith, and James Rubino, 18 vols. (Columbus: Ohio State Univ. Press, 1962-87), vol. 18, p. 641. All parenthetically-enclosed volume and page numbers throughout this study refer to this edition. All emphases in the quoted material are mine.

15. See Jean Normand, *Nathaniel Hawthorne. An Approach to an Artistic Creation* (Cleveland and London: The Press of Case Western Reserve Univ., 1970), pp. 332-33; Henry Fairbanks, *The Lasting Loneliness of Nathaniel Hawthorne. A Study of the Sources of Alienation in Modern Man* (Albany: Magi Books, Inc., 1965), pp. vii and 51; and Edgar Dryden, *Nathaniel Hawthorne. The Poetics of Enchantment* (Ithaca and London: Cornell Univ. Press, 1977), p. 85.

16. Most studies of existentialism at least mention Pascal as a kind of proto-existentialist thinker. Emmanuel Mounier (see *Existentialist Philosophies. An Introduction*, trans. Eric Blow [London: Rockliff, 1948], p. 4) says that "with the advent of Pascal, we come right up to modern Existentialism. He blazed all the trails and he shaped almost every theory."

17. For the discussion of "head" and "heart" dichotomy and self-deception, see Kenneth Marc Harris, *Hypocrisy and Self-Deception in Hawthorne's Fiction* (Charlottesville: Univ. Press of Virginia, 1988), pp. 12-14.

18. James Collins, *The Mind of Kierkegaard* (Chicago: Henry Regnery Company, 1965), p. 115.

19. Jan Miel, *Pascal and Theology* (Baltimore and London: The Johns Hopkins Univ. Press, 1969), p. 158.

20. Blaise Pascal, *Pensées*, trans. A. J. Krailsheimer (New York: Penguin Books, 1987), p. 350.

21. See Nicholas Ayo, "The Labyrinthine Ways of 'Rappaccini's Daughter'," *Research Studies* 42 (1974), p. 61.

22. *Borges. A Reader. A Selection from the Writings of Jorge Luis Borges*, ed. Emir Rodrigues Monegal and Alastair Reid (New York: E. P. Dutton, 1981), p. 224.

23. Andrew Shiller, "The Moment and the Endless Voyage: A Study of Hawthorne's 'Wakefield'," in *Casebook on the Hawthorne Question*, ed. Agnes Donohue (New York: Thos Y. Crowell, 1963), pp. 111-12.

24. Normand, p. 333.

25. Mary Warnock, *Existentialist Ethics* (London: Macmillan St. Martin's Press, 1970), p. 57.

26. Warren argues a similar point for American individualism in general. See Warren, pp. 4-17.

27. Robert C. Solomon, *Introducing the Existentialists. Imaginary Interviews with Sartre, Heidegger and Camus* (Indianapolis and Cambridge: Hackett Publishing Company, 1981), pp. 80-81.

28. Contemporary feminist theologians introduce the figure of Lilith, Adam's first wife, as a viable archetype of a liberated woman. See, for instance, Barbara Hill Rigney, *Lilith's Daughters. Women and Religion in Contemporary Fiction* (Madison: Univ. of Wisconsin Press, 1982), pp. 93-94.

29. Janet Todd, *Feminist Literary History* (New York: Routledge, 1988), p. 18.

30. See Nina Baym, "Thwarted Nature: Nathaniel Hawthorne as Feminist," in *American Novelists Revisited: Essays in Feminist Criticism*, ed. Fritz Fleischmann (Boston: G. K. Hall & Co., 1982), pp. 58-77, and Louise A. DeSalvo, *Nathaniel Hawthorne* (Brighton, Great Britain: The Harvester Press, 1987).

31. This is apparent in Hawthorne's criticism of "scribbling women" and such historical figures as Anne Hutchinson. Hawthorne's condescension, however, appears mild in comparison with that of his wife, who, for instance, wrote of Margaret Fuller that "if [Fuller] were married truly, she would no longer be puzzled about the rights of woman."

32. Bradley R. Dewey, "Walker Percy Talks about Kierkegaard: An Annotated Interview," in *Conversations with Walker Percy*, p. 119.

33. James R. Mellow, *Nathaniel Hawthorne in His Times* (Boston: Houghton Mifflin Company, 1980), p. 40.

34. Donohue, p. 352.

35. See Linda Whitney Hobson, *Understanding Walker Percy* (Columbia: Univ. of South Carolina Press, 1988), pp. 41, 53, 108, and 146.

36. Walker Percy, *The Message in the Bottle* (New York: Farrar, Straus and Giroux, 1975), p. 265.

37. Katharine Rose Hanley, *Dramatic Approaches to Creative Fidelity. A Study in the Theater and Philosophy of Gabriel Marcel (1889-1973)* (Lanham: Univ. Press of America, 1987), p. 67.

38. Mary Farrell Bednarowski, "Outside the Main Stream: Women's Religion and Women Religious Leaders in Nineteenth-Century America," *JAAR* XLVIII (1980), p. 225.

39. Peter Brooks, *Reading for the Plot. Design and Intention in Narrative* (New York: Alfred A. Knopf, 1984), pp. 90-113.

40. Susan Winnett, "Coming Unstrung: Women, Men, Narrative, and Principles of Pleasure," *PMLA*, vol. 105, no. 3 (May 1990), pp. 505-19.

41. Robert Scholes, *Fabulation and Metafiction* (Urbana: Univ. of Illinois Press, 1979), p. 108.

42. William Rodney Allen, *Walker Percy. A Southern Wayfarer* (Jackson: Univ. Press of Mississippi, 1986), p. xii.

43. Walker Percy, "Questions They Never Asked Me," in *Conversations with Walker Percy*, p. 17.

PART I

RENUNCIATION

One: Existential Pathos

The Scarlet Letter

There is no way of proving Hawthorne's intellectual debt to Kierkegaard. However, the fact that the two great minds arrived at similar conclusions at almost exactly the same time makes the hypothesis of influence attractive.[1] To claim that existentialism was "in the air" in the latter half of the nineteenth century would be a gross exaggeration. Although Kierkegaard formulated its ideology in the 1840s and 1850s, existentialism did not become really influential until a century later. The fact remains, however, that Hawthorne thought along the same lines as his Danish contemporary, and the primary aim of this chapter is to demonstrate this affinity.

Subjectivity, which, Kierkegaard maintains, is "truth and reality," calls for commitment and brings responsibility with it. Even a cursory reading of *The Scarlet Letter* reveals that these ideas occupy an important place in its narrative. At various points in the book Hester speaks or thinks of her responsibility in connection with Pearl, Dimmesdale, her community, even Chillingworth. She conceives of responsibility and guilt as inseparable. For example, she feels responsible for Chillingworth when she reflects upon the change in the doctor caused by the seven years of his preying on Dimmesdale ("Here was another ruin, the responsibility of which came partly to her" [1: 170]). Earlier in the narrative, she feels compassion for Dimmesdale after his first attempt at public confession ("The Minister's Vigil"), and similarly she assumes responsibility for the minister's mental torment. These convictions are occasioned by Hester's awareness that she is a "law unto herself," an idea that has affinities with Kierkegaard's views on the individual's ethical sovereignty.

Any consideration of Kierkegaard's thought necessitates a discussion of the stages of existence that are basically three: the aesthetic, the ethical, and the religious.[2] Some commentators maintain that these stages, or modes, are neither temporally successive nor mutually exclusive. In other words, they argue, the life of the existing individual may be dominated by one way of life over the others, rather than be characterized by the exclusive presence of one.[3] However, various innuendoes present in Kiekegaard's discussion all point to the irreconcilability of these modes. As James Collins writes:

> We may indeed *consider* these conflicting modes of existence together, but it is impossible to *live* them together. In the order of choice and existence, there is no straddling and no compromise between these mutually exclusive outlooks. From this standpoint, one does leave the other stages behind in consenting to some particular mode of existence, although there is no special order which must be preserved in making the transition or in consolidating one's original position.[4]

In mentioning both arguments as regards Kierkegaard's stages of existence, I want to draw attention to the fact that much of Percy criticism suffers from following the first of these interpretations—namely, that the modes are temporally successive and mutually inclusive. Critics assign to Binx, in *The Moviegoer*, the position of Kierkegaard's ethical *and* religious man or, even more erroneously, of the one who, having made the leap of faith, "will no doubt slip back into the aesthetic from time to time."[5] Since the discussion of Kierkegaard's stages of existence is focal in my analysis of both *The Scarlet Letter* and *The Moviegoer*, it is necessary to begin by elucidating them here.

Kierkegaard associates the aesthetic mode with three figures: Don Juan, Faust, and Ahasuerus, the Wandering Jew. In the first illustration he follows the romantic tradition, represented by Mozart's *Don Giovanni*, and he recognizes both positive and negative aspects of the aesthetic ideal, though he emphasizes its weaknesses. Don Juan incarnates sensuality in both its exuberance and its primitivism. "Naive" sensuality thus conceived posits ignorance of the ethical and religious principles of a higher order. Don Juan embodies the first form of the aesthetic mode of existence, with its tendency to make aesthetic values principal, even exclusive. Such a mode of life is limited by the absence of reflection which could modify sensuous desire, and in this context Kierkegaard paradoxically comments on Don Juan's innocence, which he views as a mark of ignorance bordering on stupidity.

The second form of the aesthetic mode of life is represented by Faust, who substitutes reflection for the direct pursuit of pleasure. At one point, Kierkegaard compares Faust to Socrates in that both figures repudiate the claims of society, with the crucial difference between them lying in their respective attitudes to God. Socrates does not break with the divine, whereas in Kierkegaard's version of the Faustian myth authority is furnished by neither God nor Mephistopheles. On the other hand, the element of pride, which Kierkegaard conceives as a moral category, prompts Faust to search for preternatural aid in the fulfillment of his life-plan. Hence, he falls victim to superstition and diabolism, maintains Kierkegaard and launches into a discussion of daimonia, which he distinguishes from ordinary philosophical doubt. A daimonic life is based on the principle of *idée fixe*, and a daimonic person becomes subordinated to his all-encompassing idea to the exclusion of all ordinary relationships with human society. However, Kierkegaard does not convey this form of the aesthetic life in utterly negative terms because, after all, it marks the search for truth, the exploration of the mystery of sin and of the whole range of human possibilities. Yet he asserts that such an exploration may be overcome—though Faust's is not—by faith and a consequent turning to God.

Ahasuerus, or the Wandering Jew, represents the third form of the aesthetic mode of life. Kierkegaard perceives this form, with its silent despair and loss of hope in either God or man, as the symbol of his age. He then proceeds to elaborate on diverse ways individuals attempt to escape despair. These "exits" have been so often articulated by various existentialists that they function as existentialist categories: diversions, acknowledged by Pascal, the inauthenticity of everyday life, voiced by Heidegger, irony, and the repetition of happy events. The two latter categories occupy a special position in Kierkegaard's thought, but since they apply more to Percy's writing than to Hawthorne's, they will be treated further in the following chapter.

Arguably, the second form of the aesthetic mode of life is exemplified by several characters in Hawthorne's fiction. The tales furnish the earliest examples: Wakefield, who heartlessly spies on his wife, Roderick Elliston, who explores the mystery of sin in himself and others, Aylmer, who relinquishes love to dream of mastery over Nature, Rappaccini, who sacrifices his beloved daughter on the altar of pride and vanity, and Ethan Brand, who embodies the "sin of intellect," which makes him lose hold of the "magnetic chain of humanity." *The Scarlet Letter* features Chillingworth, who represents a synthesis of all these early characters and is, moreover, a clinical exemplification of daimonia. The pursuit and "systematic exercise of revenge" constitutes his *idée fixe*: "he chose to withdraw his name from the roll of mankind, and, as regarded his former ties and interests, to vanish out of life" (1: 118-19). Since he has neither man nor God to cherish or fear, Chillingworth sucks his life's blood from the torment of another. In Hawthorne's scheme of values, he commits the worst possible sin against a fellow human: the violation "in cold blood" of "the sanctity of a human heart." Consequently, he is conceived in daimonic terms as "the Black Man" (so perceived by Hester and Pearl), a devil ("Roger Chillingworth was a striking evidence of man's faculty of transforming himself into a devil" [1: 179]), and a fiend ("the hatred that has transformed a wise and just man into a fiend" [1: 173]). To Hester's suggestion that he "purge" his guilty emotions and thus recover his humanity, Chillingworth responds, "It has all been a dark necessity. Ye that have wronged me are not sinful, save in a kind of typical illusion; neither am I fiendlike, who have snatched a fiend's office from his hands. It is our fate" (1: 174). Hawthorne's formulation again reflects Kierkegaard's conviction that a Faust is a man caught by a ruse of fate and incapable of reflection upon the moral or religious aspects of existence.

It should be pointed out, however, that Hawthorne's and Kierkegaard's views on the daimonic principle differ in some respects. Kierkegaard recognizes the moral danger of what Collins calls "a deliberately fostered concealment," which parallels Chillingworth's concealment of his real motive in his relationship with Dimmesdale, but at the same time he refutes the intrinsic evil of the daimonic principle. Hawthorne, by contrast, attributes the worst evil to persons who embody indifferent theorizing and inhuman probing into the psyche of others. Which is not to say that Hawthorne is utterly unsympathetic to sinners of Chillingworth's type, excepting perhaps Wakefield, whom Hawthorne ridicules mercilessly. But Wakefield, apart from other affronts to humanity, is also characterized by ignorance bordering on stupidity (hence he bears some resemblance to Kierkegaard's first form of the aesthetic mode of life, though obviously with no sexual implications); he remains faithful to his wife because of "a certain sluggishness," is intellectual "but not actively so," plain, cold, selfish, and vain. But it must be also remembered that Wakefield abandons wife and home, the pleasures of domestic life, of his own volition, and, for Hawthorne, nothing compensates for this offence. The sentence Wakefield receives is that he "must never feel the warmth of the one [home], nor the affection of the other [wife]" (9: 138). By contrast Chillingworth, for all his daimonic traits, manifests a longing for the once cherished and now irrevocably lost happiness of domestic life:

> My heart was a habitation large enough for many guests, but lonely and chill, and without a household fire. I longed to kindle one! It seemed not so wild a dream,—old as I was, and sombre as I was, and misshapen as I was,—that the simple bliss, which is scattered far and wide, for all mankind to gather up, might yet be mine. And so, Hester, I drew thee into my heart, into its innermost chamber, and sought to warm thee by the warmth which thy presence made there!! (1: 74)

The domestic bliss painted in this passage is in fact voiced by several characters in Hawthorne's fiction. Hawthorne critics tend to hold conflicting views on the subject: Some maintain that Hawthorne valued his family life to such an extent that he posited it as an ideal.[6] Others point to Hawthorne's attraction to the sexual heroine of Hester's type, who is never associated with conjugal love, and they suggest that Hawthorne was compelled to conceal this fascination only because of the traditional clichés regarding womanhood, and the example set by his wife Sophia.[7] Although both arguments are tenable, we have to remember that the allusion to the restorative qualities of domestic life (the hearth) and the wife who kindles the fire appear as early as "Wakefield," published in 1835, seven years before he married Sophia.

The problem of conjugal love leads quite naturally to the next mode of existence defined by Kierkegaard because he conceives of the ethical mode primarily in terms of marriage. Most interpreters of Kierkegaard's thought comment on the inconclusiveness of this aspect of the ethical mode. The ethical viewpoint is clarified through juxtaposition with the aesthetic mode, for the concealment of the latter contrasts with the openness of the former. Concealment stems from ambiguity, the ability to deceive and to follow one's personal whim, whereas the ethical mode advocates frankness, openness, and sincerity in dealing with others. In other words, it counsels a moral standard in the life of the existing individual. Viewed in light of this duality, Hawthorne's characters of the Wakefield type may be said to embody concealment whereas Hester is a forerunner of the latter category.

According to Kierkegaard, two elements foster the individual's personal rebirth in the ethical mode: the conquest of selfhood and moral choice based on an awareness of the absolute distinction between good and evil. The awareness of this irreconcilable dichotomy necessitates the admission of sin, which, in turn, brings about repentance. But it must be pointed out that Kierkegaard's understanding of guilt and repentance within the ethical mode of life substantially differs from what he calls the aesthetic view of guilt. The aesthetic view of guilt implies a dialectics with the world rather than with oneself and assumes that the only kind of guilt is one which violates the accepted social or legal standards of behavior. Accordingly, as long as the individual acts in harmony with the accepted norms he is not guilty.[8] Consider, for example, Kierkegaard's criticism of bourgeois ethics as "a short summary of police ordinances; for them the most important thing is to be a useful member of the state."[9]

To Kierkegaard, one individual cannot be morally judged by another who "cannot understand him except as a possibility. When therefore anyone attempts to judge another, the expression of his impotence is that he merely judges himself."[10] Similarly, the individual cannot atone for his guilt by publicly acknowledging it in the form of fine or punishment:

> One reads in the older works of theology a defence of eternal punishment in hell which affirms that the magnitude of sin requires such a punishment, and that the magnitude of sin is determined in turn by the fact that it is sin against God. The *naiveté* and outwardness of this is that it makes as if it were a law, a tribunal, a third party which deliberates and votes upon the cause which is between the man and God. Thus there is always something *naive* and outward when a third party talks about that which essentially concerns the individual precisely in his isolation before God. The *naiveté* and outwardness disappear entirely when it is the individual himself who puts the conception of God together with the conception of guilt.[11]

Hawthorne seems to be acutely conscious of this problem when he says of Hester that she was "little accustomed, in her long seclusion from the society, to measure her ideas of right and wrong by any standard external to herself" (1: 159). This idea is extended when Dimmesdale intimates that in his interpretation of the Scripture the intended "retribution" does not call for "the disclosure of human thoughts and deeds." And he adds: "That, surely, were a shallow view of it" (1: 131). True repentance, or ethical repentance, does not occur when the individual, conscious of his guilt, is willing to acknowledge it, and thereby atone for it, but it begins with the recognition of the independent individual—that is, in relation to himself—as absolute. This idea will receive more attention later in this chapter.

But what of marriage as the center of ethical life? Here the moral category issues from the fact that man makes the choice only once, but its consequences last throughout his life. Kierkegaard comments on the risk of routine and boredom inherent in marriage but deems it advantageous over the purely aesthetic life insofar as the progress made by the ethical individual is realized in a lifelong attachment rather than in a series of momentary attachments. Moreover, marriage resolves tensions inherent in the aesthetic life, brings security and, while sharing some principles of the aesthetic life, for example, eroticism, it simultaneously puts an end to selfishness and despair. Kierkegaard says:

> Marriage I regard as the highest *telos* of the individual human existence, it is so much the highest that the man who goes without it cancels with one stroke the whole of earthly life and retains only eternity and spiritual interests—which at the first glance seems no slight thing but in the long run is very exhausting and also in one way or another is the expression of an unhappy life.[12]

However, we should not be led astray by Kierkegaard's depiction of marriage as "the highest *telos.*" It is the highest *telos* only of the ethical life, and as such is not the absolute *telos*. The absolute *telos*—the individual himself—is to be realized in an absolute relation to God. This relationship marks the third, the religious mode of existence, and Kierkegaard gives no clue as to how conjugal love might be incorporated into the religious sphere of life. Conversely, he says that marriage constitutes a self-sufficient and independent sphere and, as such, prevents further progress and the full development of the existential dialectic. It is in later existentialists, specifically, Buber and Marcel, that love will be assigned a religious attribute.

The religious mode of existence fulfills itself in man's lonely encounter with God. No norms or standards apply to this unique condition. Progress within this mode is achieved through suffering, the *telos* is striven toward, though never fully attained, in what

Kierkegaard terms “fear and trembling.” He illustrates this mode of life with the figure of Abraham, who decides to sacrifice his son if that be the demand of God. Abraham faces a task that is horrifying from an ethical viewpoint, and he could naturally yield to the temptation of judging this task hostile to his paternal feelings and morally inconceivable. But recognizing that the word of God is to be respected above all else, Abraham deceives his wife and son and wrestles with his moral scruples in solitude before God. Kierkegaard focuses on two problems. First, Abraham’s decisions, though unacceptable from an ethical viewpoint, can be conceived as driven by piety and religious sacrifice. Kierkegaard’s line of reasoning is this: If we consider Abraham not a pious man but a murderer in intent, than we must assign to God the role of a wicked tempter. Consequently, Kierkegaard maintains, we attribute divinity to ethics and forbid man to enter into a personal relationship with God. Kierkegaard advances this point of view only to dismiss it and to interpret Abraham’s decision as the enactment of the famous “leap of faith.” Secondly, what does Kierkegaard make of Abraham’s plan to conceal his intentions from his wife, his son, and his servant? What Kierkegaard thinks of this kind of concealment is very much in keeping with what has been said about his concept of guilt and repentance. The secrets of the heart are inviolable: one’s moral state is beyond the judgment of another human being and can be revealed only to God in a personal and lonely encounter. We can thus see the substantial difference in Kierkegaard’s scheme between the concealment of the aesthetic mode of life and the concealment resulting from religious choice.

Hawthorne’s tale “Roger Malvin’s Burial” bears a close resemblance to Abraham’s story. In it, however, concealment takes place prior to the climactic event of the latter part of the tale. It concerns Reuben’s decision to abandon a dying friend, a decision that Hawthorne conceives in ethical terms, as evidenced by the passage: “concealment had imparted to a justifiable act, much of the secret effect of guilt; and Reuben, while reason told him that he had done right, experienced, in no small degree, the mental horrors, which punish the perpetrator of undiscovered crime" (10: 349). To understand the affinity between the two texts, let us consider the following passages, from Kierkegaard's and Hawthorne's versions, respectively:

> It was early morning; everything was ready for the journey in Abraham's house. He bade farewell to Sara. . . . Sara kissed Isaac, who . . . was her pride, her hope in all posterity. So they rode in silence along the road and Abraham's gaze was fixed upon the ground.[13]

> It was early in the month of May that the little family snapped asunder whatever tendrils of affections had clung to inanimate objects, and bade farewell to . . . their friends. . . . Reuben, a moody man, and misanthropic because unhappy, strode onward, with his usual stern brow and downcast eye. . . . Dorcas . . . felt that the inhabitants of her inmost heart moved on with her. (10: 251-52)

Besides the details of these two descriptions, Hawthorne's direct commentary as to the significance of the tale points to its parallels with Kierkegaard's text. Reuben is discerned as "the father of a race, the patriarch of a people, the founder of a mighty nation yet to be" (10: 352).

Finally, both Kierkegaard's and Hawthorne's versions conclude with the "leap of faith." The Kierkegaardian "leap" projects man into an entirely new mode of being. The significance of Abraham's decision, which gives a new meaning to his life, finds a clear echo in Hawthorne's conclusion of "Roger Malvin's Burial":

> Then Reuben's heart was stricken, and the tears gushed out like water from a rock. The vow that the wounded youth had made, the blighted man had come to redeem.

> His sin was expiated, the curse was gone from him; and, in the hour when he had shed blood dearer to him than his own, a prayer, the first for years, went up to Heaven from the lips of Reuben Bourne. (10: 360)

Yet this passage also reveals Hawthorne's conviction that sin should be confessed or otherwise expiated in order that man recover his lost psychological equilibrium. This credo partly explains why Hawthorne showed a bias toward Catholicism and for a while was attracted to the dogma and rites of the nineteenth-century American communitarian sect known as the Shakers or the Millennial Church to whom confession was an important element of ritual. Hawthorne's Catholic bias, though fully explored in his last finished romance, already manifests itself in *The Scarlet Letter*, where, in the initial pillory scene, he contrasts the moral severity of Puritanism with what he imagines a Catholic would perceive in the figure cut by Hester and her baby: "the image of Divine Maternity . . . of sinless motherhood, whose infant was to redeem the world" (1: 56).

Hawthorne did not support any form of institutionalized religion. He was as strongly opposed to what Kierkegaard termed "objective Christianity" as his Danish contemporary. They both believed that religion concerned the most private sphere of individual life. But they differed in their respective approaches to what may be called the outward manifestation of sin. Hawthorne deemed such tangible proof necessary; it will suffice to remember that Hooper ("The Minister's Black Veil") assumes the veil, Hester wears the scarlet letter, Dimmesdale makes an involuntary gesture of putting his hand on his heart, Elliston clutches at his throat, to mention just a few. Conversely, Kierkegaard believed that a human being cannot communicate to another the uniqueness of his personal condition. Thus, by extension, to confess one's sin to another is not the same as to confess it to God in a personal and lonely encounter. Kierkegaard makes this point clear when he speaks about Abraham's concealment, noting that it is ethics, and not religion, that demands manifestation. Thus ethics condemns Abraham because of his silence. Had he spoken, he would have been the tragic (ethical) hero who is thus defined by Kierkegaard:

> The tragic hero sacrifices himself and everything he possesses for the universal. Everything he does, all his emotions belong to the universal; he is made manifest and in this manifestation he is the well-beloved son of ethics. But this does not fit the case of Abraham, who does nothing for the universal and remains concealed.[14]

These themes, which Hawthorne explored so masterfully in the tales, find their richest synthesis in *The Scarlet Letter*.

Since the narrative of *The Scarlet Letter* is conceived in the form of a movement or progress toward a realization of a single task, it can be argued that the novel's contents fit the pattern of existential pathos. That pathos in turn can be defined, in Kierkegaardian terms, as consisting of several way stations: resignation (or renunciation), suffering, guilt, repentance, and faith.

Emmanuel Mounier uses the term "renunciation" to denote a special faculty resulting from choice.[15] Renunciation is of two kinds: it may be renunciation of diversion, which was also counseled by Pascal (he elaborates at length on "divertissement" in the *Pensées*), and also of consolation, which results from communal involvement. One has to be cautious when accounting for these issues because there is a very thin line dividing the two kinds of renunciation from the individual's relation to what John Elrod terms the "relative matrix of relations."[16] Isolation is necessary for the concentration of thought; in a crowd one's absolute relation to the absolute *telos* cannot be attained. Since the absolute *telos* is the individual himself, to relate oneself to the absolute *telos* means the same as to confront oneself as a task. This is to be done in resignation because only in renouncing the attitude of absolute relation to relative ends, that is, the elements that constitute one's daily routine, can the existing individual relate himself to the absolute *telos*. But while Kierkegaard advocates this essential solitude in performing one's task, he maintains that in the process one must be relatively related to everything else that does not constitute the absolute *telos*. The first pages of *The Scarlet Letter* reveal that these notions had a special meaning for Hawthorne. From the very beginning he characterizes the "desperate recklessness" of Hester's mood, which took her "out of the ordinary relations with humanity", and enclosed her "in a sphere by herself."

Two chapters especially illuminating as regards the progress of existential pathos are Chapter 3, "The Recognition," and Chapter 13, "Another View of Hester." The title of Chapter 3 may signify, of course, Hester's recognition of Chillingworth in the crowd of the Puritan witnesses of her miserable spectacle at the scaffolding. But it can be argued that the title has a more profound meaning. In the focal scene of the chapter Dimmesdale is requested to persuade Hester to break her concealment and reveal her partner in sin. The words spoken by Dimmesdale establish the ethical context of the book: "What can thy silence do for him, except it tempt him—yea, compel him, as it were—to add hypocrisy to sin?" (1:67). But Hester will not reveal her secret, arguing, "my child must seek a heavenly Father; she shall never know an earthly one!" (1: 68). Her words introduce the religious dimension, one that is germane to what has been said in reference to Abraham's concealment. Hester will not speak because she is expected to reveal objective facts rather than her personal subjective motives. Even had she been asked to reveal the latter, she would not have been able to communicate them because they can be expressed only to God. It can be thus perceived that Dimmesdale is locked in the ethical mode, or perhaps more accurately, poised between the aesthetic and the ethical.

Interestingly, Dimmesdale resembles the last phase of the aesthetic mode, with its despair and utter absence of hope, symbolized, in Kierkegaard's scheme, by Ahasuerus, the biblical king of Persia. In the Book of Esther of the Old Testament, and Hester is but a variant of the biblical name, we find these illuminating facts: Esther was a foster-daughter of a Jew Mordecai. The Greek translation of the books of the Old Testament indicates that Mordecai took Esther under his roof for the express purpose of eventually marrying her. This plan never materialized because Ahasuerus (apparently with Mordecai's blessing) made Esther his wife and a queen of Persia. Conceivably, Hawthorne incorporated this theme in the book, which, apart from the allusive name, manifests itself, for example, in Hester's "rich, voluptuous, Oriental characteristic," which finds its only outlet in her artful practice of embroidery.

Towards the end of the chapter, after Dimmesdale's plea that Hester reveal her fellow-sinner, Reverend Wilson adds a new element to the argument. He announces that if Hester manifests her repentance, the letter "A" will be removed from her bosom, a consolation of sorts that elicits Hester's passionate response of, "Never! It is too deeply branded. Ye cannot take it off" (1: 68). As has already been noted in earlier sections of this chapter, Kierkegaard stated that internalization should not be made manifest by what he calls "a foreign mode of dress." Man should be "incognito, but his incognito consists in having an appearance entirely like others" (*CUP*, 367). Hester, for all the modest grays of her daily garb, is far from being "incognito" due to the flamboyance of the letter she is sentenced to wear. Of course, much is made by Hawthorne of the luxurious embroidery that decorates the letter. Three questions suggest themselves at this point: First, why would Hester put so much effort into the embroidery of a token of sin and shame? Second, why should she insist on wearing it despite outright statements made later in the narrative that she relinquish it? And, finally, how does the whole matter relate to Kierkegaard's ideas about the manifestation of sin?

Admittedly, Hester's burden is not self-imposed. The situation here is different from that in "The Minister's Black Veil," even though, at the same time, there is a remarkable affinity between the novel and the tale where Hooper assumes the veil of his own volition. Thus, while the letter is initially imposed on Hester by society, its meaning undergoes a transformation, most importantly in Hester's own perception of it. Hester insists on wearing the letter because it functions as the symbol of her *telos*. This recognition of her *telos* constitutes the essential meaning of Chapter 3 and accounts for its heading, "Recognition." Hereafter, her recognition and her choice to pursue her *telos* cause her to be relatively related to her actuality (Kierkegaard calls it "immediacy," Hawthorne, "daily custom"), and absolutely related to the absolute *telos*. Let us look from this perspective at how Hawthorne formulates her predicament in Chapter 5:

> By now, with this unattended walk from her prison-door, began the daily custom; . . . To-morrow would bring its own trial with it; so would the next day, and so would the next; each its own trial, and yet the very same . . . burden for her to take up, and bear along with her, but never to fling down; for the accumulating days, and added years, would pile up their misery upon the heap of shame. (1: 78-79)

This tragic acceptance of a burden faintly recalls Albert Camus' *The Myth of Sisyphus* and can be summarized in Camus' words, "his fate belongs to him. His rock is his thing . . . The struggle itself toward the heights is enough to fill a man's heart."[17] In both cases the externally imposed burden is transformed into a symbol of victory, not narrowly understood as victory over those who imposed it but rather as victory over the self. In both examples, the burden constitutes the reality of the subject; for Sisyphus, "Each atom of that stone, each mineral flake of that night-filled mountain, in itself forms a world." Similarly, for Hester, "the infant and the shame were real. Yes!—these were her realities,—all else had vanished" (1: 59). While the religious dimension is absent from Camus' existential thought because he preferred to depict the hopelessness and absurdity of man and his world, there is at least one important aspect of his presentation of Sisyphus' task which intersects with Kierkegaard's views, and Hawthorne's as well. Camus' version of the myth focuses on the process of becoming. Thus, the individual is never in a fixed state but, rather, strives to become what he is not. Sisyphus' unceasing effort conveys this idea, but also we should remember that Camus draws from his example of Sisyphus a more general idea—namely, that the task which originally came from the gods is to be approached in human terms and "settled among men."

Conversely, for Kierkegaard man's relationship to the absolute *telos* necessarily must be realized in the God-relationship: "One who distinguishes absolutely has a relationship to the absolute *telos*, and *ipso facto* also a relationship to God." God does not call upon the individual to understand Him, but He calls upon man to understand himself in the process of becoming. Thus the God-relationship comes into being in the process of the individual's struggle with himself as the absolute *telos*. The process entails suffering, whose essence lies in the individual's separation from his happiness, i.e., his *telos*, brought about by his inability to extricate himself successfully from an absolute relation to relative ends. To emphasize Kierkegaard's central principle, the ideal task may be realized only in one's absolute relation to the absolute *telos*, while at the same time one must be only relatively related to relative ends. This is the essence of existential pathos, and we shall see now how closely *The Scarlet Letter* reveals its structure.

Hester's position in the above context is established when Hawthorne reports, in Chapter 5, on her "new birth" and further explains that "the scarlet letter had endowed her with a new sense" (1: 86). He then confirms Hester's position as an existential seeker when he notes, "In all her intercourse with society . . . there was nothing that made her feel as if she belonged to it" (1: 84). She voluntarily accepts suffering, which Hawthorne conveys by such words as "anguish," repeated obsessively in reference to Hester, Dimmesdale, and Pearl, "daily torture," as a way of atoning to God for her sin, and "the torture of her daily shame." Her suffering results from her inability to extricate herself from relative ends. For example, she still relies on the opinion of others, and her mental torment is caused, at least partly, by social ostracism. But she also realizes that she should not subject herself to the ethical judgment of others, that she should stand "apart from moral interests." This division in the structure of her self occasions more suffering:

> But sometimes, once in many days, or perchance in many months, she felt an eye—a human eye—upon the ignominious brand, that seemed to give a momentary relief, as if half of her agony were shared. The next instant, back it all rushed again, with still a deeper throb of pain; for, in that brief interval, she had sinned anew. (1: 86)

This passage underlies two problems relevant to Hawthorne's conception of sin: The individual's sin-consciousness makes him instinctively conscious of his fellow-sinners. However, to base one's self-consciousness on the opinion of another is tantamount to abandoning self-reflection and, consequently, one's freedom. Related to the latter problem is Hawthorne's conviction that excessive preoccupation with sin may result in rationalization or morbid despair, both of which are also critically viewed by Kierkegaard.

The idea of the brotherhood of sinners, which is intimated in the above passage, harks back to several tales. In "Young Goodman Brown" Hawthorne speaks about the "communion" of sinners. Father Hooper's implied sin gave him "power over souls that were in agony for sin" (9: 49), and he, on his death-bed, detected evil in the faces of those who came to mourn him ("lo! on every visage a Black Veil!") Roderick Elliston believes that "there is poisonous stuff in any man's heart, sufficient to generate a brood of serpents" (10: 282). The same idea is conveyed in *The Scarlet Letter* when Hawthorne says that Hester's sin "gave her a sympathetic knowledge of the hidden sin in other hearts," and that, if the truth were to triumph, "a scarlet letter would blaze forth on many a bosom besides Hester Prynne's" (1: 86). But Hawthorne also warns his reader that such a preoccupation with sin is "ever one of the saddest results of sin," and may conduce, as it does for Goodman Brown, to a loss of faith.

Hawthorne's comments about Hester's practise of embroidery convey the same idea. They first suggest that, prior to the narrated events, Hester cherished a passion for the "gorgeously beautiful." In her subsequent solitude as a social outcast, shunned by adults and children alike, her craft of needlework offers her the only possible means for expressing her exuberant nature and finding peace and consolation. Yet even this possibility she "rejected as sin." Therefore:

> This morbid meddling of conscience with an immaterial matter betokened, it is to be feared, no genuine and steadfast penitence, but something doubtful, something that might be deeply wrong, beneath. (1: 84)

For both Kierkegaard and Hawthorne sin-consciousness is the *conditio sine qua non* in the individual's process of becoming. Sin separates the individual from God, but sin-consciousness heals this breach in search of a reconciliation. And such a reconciliation can only be found in faith which is rooted in what Elrod calls "a prior ethico-religious understanding of the nature and purpose of human existence."[18]

Hawthorne criticism has traditionally identified Pearl as the embodiment or symbol of sin and thus, by extension, of the scarlet letter. Indeed, to locate Pearl in the symbolic scheme of the romance is essential for a fuller grasp of Hawthorne's vision, but does her major function reside in her symbolic representation simply of sin? The very first paragraph of the chapter bearing her name depicts Pearl, in fact, as "a lovely and immortal flower," attributes that focus our attention on the atemporal significance of Hester's child. Pearl's symbolic nature may be educed from the following details, which Hawthorne carefully introduces at various junctures of the narrative. First of all, while Pearl's attitude to Chillingworth is consistently negative, she considers herself invulnerable to Chillingworth's power. She warns her mother, "Come away, or yonder Black Man will catch you! He hath got hold of the minister already. . . . But he cannot catch little Pearl!" (1: 135). In Hawthorne's initial characterization of Pearl, the reader learns that "the child could not be made amenable to rules. In giving her existence, a great law had been broken; and the result was a being whose elements were perhaps beautiful and brilliant, but all in disorder; or with an order peculiar to themselves" (1: 91). Hawthorne underscores this characteristic through repetition, as in Chillingworth's perception of Pearl: "There is no law, no reverence for authority, no regard for human ordinances or opinions, right or wrong, mixed up with that child's composition" (1: 134). Furthermore, Pearl's reclusive nature points to her symbolic role in the novel. As Hawthorne observes, she is a "born outcast of the infantile world," endowed with an instinct that enables her to "comprehend her loneliness." Hester intuitively perceives Pearl's unique nature, and with the passage of time becomes increasingly aware of Pearl's function in decoding the meaning of the scarlet letter, "as if the only thing for which she had been sent into the world was to make out its hidden import" (1: 178).

Finally, Pearl's symbolic significance emerges during her three encounters with Dimmesdale. First, in the governor's house, upon the suggestion that the child be taken from her, Hester passionately explodes:

> "God gave me the child!" cried she. "He gave her, in requital of all things else, which ye had taken from me. She is my happiness!—she is my torture, none the less! Pearl keeps me here in life! Pearl punishes me too! See ye not, she is the scarlet letter . . . ?" (1: 113)

The key words here are "torture" and "happiness," and, we remember, suffering and happiness are to Kierkegaard the mutually conditioning elements of man's struggle toward the absolute *telos* or the truly authentic relationship. The second encounter, depicted in Chapter 12, narrates Dimmesdale's first attempt at public confession. The minister invites Hester and Pearl to join him on the scaffold, takes the child by the hand, and feels "what seemed a tumultuous rush of new life, other life than his own, pouring like a torrent into his heart and hurrying through all his veins" (1: 153). The scene takes place in the middle of the night, and Pearl wants to know whether the full light of day could witness their reunion. When Dimmesdale answers negatively ("the daylight of this world shall not see our meeting"), Pearl attempts to withdraw her hand with the words, "thou wast not true." The whole scene may serve as a parable of existentialism, with Pearl as the agent of authenticity. This is the primary meaning of the letter "A," and Pearl's function is to communicate the crucial nature of authenticity to Dimmesdale. Thus in the final pillory scene, which constitutes Pearl's third encounter with Dimmesdale, she kisses the minister, thus breaking the spell of falsehood that bound his former life. It is also the first time that Pearl responds to a situation in human terms:

> . . . and as her tears fell upon her father's cheek, they were the pledge that she would grow up amid human joy and sorrow, nor forever do battle with the world but be a woman in it. Toward her mother, too, Pearl's errand as a messenger of anguish was all fulfilled. (1: 256)

The key word "anguish" marks a mid-way stage *en route* to "authenticity," both being central notions of existentialism. While authenticity denotes the goal of existence, anguish is the process of arriving at it.

Anguish and authenticity likewise play a key role in Hester's and Dimmesdale's process of becoming. Chillingworth is dealt with peripherally in this analysis because, as indicated earlier, he is locked in the aesthetic mode of existence, and thus the above notions do not apply to his development in the narrative. Meanwhile, having established as a working hypothesis that Dimmesdale is poised between the aesthetic and the ethical modes of life, while Hester enacts the genuine process of becoming, we may now turn to Kierkegaard's thought for further elucidation of existential pathos.

The religious, maintains Kierkegaard, preserves the ethical within itself. In other words, the religious must pass through the ethical. In Kierkegaard's example, the religious poet, but we may also add the religious preacher, is in a peculiar situation because he attempts to relate himself to the religious through the imagination. He thus establishes only "an aesthetic relationship to something aesthetic " (*CUP*, 348). Roy R. Male claims that in *The Scarlet Letter*, "significant expression is achieved in art: Hester's needlework, Chillingworth's psychiatric alchemy, and Dimmesdale's Election Sermon."[19] He further argues that Hester finds grace and grasps the truth only through her art. This interpretation, however, fails to acknowledge that Hawthorne has indicated Hester's ambivalent attitude toward her art. While its flamboyance reflects her passionate nature, Hawthorne indicates that, to Hester, it provides primarily a source of support ("She possessed an art that sufficed . . . to supply food for her thriving infant and herself"), and a means of charity:

> Except for that small expenditure in the decoration of her infant, Hester bestowed all her superfluous means in charity, on wretches less miserable than herself, and who not unfrequently insulted the hand that fed them. (1: 83)

As pointed out earlier, Hester repudiates any other significance of her art as sin. Such a distinction reveals Hester's transcendence over the aesthetic mode; whatever ties she had earlier with this mode she left behind the prison door.

Conversely, Dimmesdale's attachment to the aesthetic mode is quite substantial, as attested by the evocative epithets used to characterize him. He is "morbidly self-contemplative" and egotistic (like Elliston), a "subtle, but remorseful hypocrite" who is "trammeled" by the "regulations," "principles," and even "prejudices" of his society (like Wakefield). Even his awareness of his condition, which gives him an edge over Elliston and Wakefield and implies what can be called his higher consciousness, only adds to his miserable predicament. He is, in the words of Murray Krieger, an "excommunicated ethical man" who,[20] at the same time, has transcended the limits of the aesthetic mode. This is the essence of his tragic vision, and the source of his despair. Were he an atheist, he would find strength to confront nothingness and its empty consequences. He, however, is a believer, but, in Kierkegaard's terms, "faith is not faith" for him but "a kind of knowledge."[21] His despair prompts him to assume another persona, but his despair also derives from the fact that he appears to be what he is not. It seems appropriate to account for this phenomenon in

Pascalian terms. Pascal distinguishes two kinds of "being" ("être") somewhat reminiscent of Kierkegaard's modes of existence: "être veritable" and "être imaginaire." The former is our real, i.e., authentic being, which is realized in the process of our opting for God, that is, in the process of our becoming. The latter is the imaginary self or one's narcissistic illusion of oneself. "Être imaginaire" is created by self-love ("amour propre") which is characterized by hypocrisy ("déguisment") and vanity ("vanité").

In the forest episode, where Hester reveals to Dimmesdale Chillingworth's true nature and motive, the minister's reaction is prompted by self-love:

> O Hester Prynne, thou little, little knowest all the horror of this thing! And the shame!—the indelicacy!—the horrible ugliness of this exposure of a sick and guilty heart to the very eye that would gloat over it! Woman, woman, thou art accountable for this! I cannot forgive thee! (1: 194)

These words bluntly reveal Dimmesdale's vanity, hypocrisy, and instability of character. He looks up to Hester, whom he deems strong, for the solution of his dilemma, and their conversation demonstrates Dimmesdale's fear that Chillingworth will reveal his sin. However, his appeal brings Hester's passionate response:

> Leave this wreck and ruin here where it hath happened! . . . Begin all anew! . . . Exchange this false life of thine for a true one. . . . Preach! Write! Act! Do any thing, save to lie down and die! Give up this name of Arthur Dimmesdale, and make thyself another, and a high one, such as thou canst wear without fear or shame. (1: 198)

Following the prompting of her heart, Hester here proposes that Dimmesdale replace one falsehood with another. In the forest episode their long-forgotten emotions are stirred, and Hester yearns for communion with her lover. Thus, for a moment, a new subject is hinted at—namely, a possibility of becoming through true communion with another human being. However, Pearl appears on the other side of the brook, and she puts things back together again. During the last pillory scene, Hester will evoke the episode, but then she will deem it "a delusion."

Nevertheless, Dimmesdale attains a breakthrough, through shock, and what follows testifies to his transcendence of the aesthetic mode. A moment witnesses his enchantment with Hester's bright vision of the future, but it vanishes even as "hope" and "joy" shine out of his face. Chapter 20 relates Dimmesdale's peculiar state, which, to use the existentialists' vocabulary, may be interpreted as "frenzy." This term may signify anything from "mild physical giddiness" to "madness."[22] Feeling as though Hester has "lent him unaccustomed physical energy," Dimmesdale experiences the following:

> Before Mr. Dimmesdale reached home, his inner man gave him other evidences of a revolution in the sphere of thought and feeling. In truth, nothing short of a total change of dynasty and moral code, in that interior kingdom, was adequate to account for the impulses now communicated to the unfortunate and startled minister. At every step he was incited to do some strange, wild, wicked thing or other, with a sense that it would be at once involuntary and intentional; in spite of himself, yet growing out of a profounder self than that which opposed the impulse. (1: 217)

As the chapter closes, however, the minister regains tranquillity and gets ready for his last sermon.

The sermon condenses an entire series of familiar notions: "anguish," "pathos," and "suffering humanity," followed by the final pillory scene when Dimmesdale climbs on the scaffold and invites Hester and Pearl to join him. This episode of course parallels the initial pillory scene, likewise conducted in daylight, with Hester as the main focus, and members of the community convened as spectators. The ethical significance of Dimmesdale's gesture on the scaffold is obvious. What is not obvious, however, is why Hawthorne makes Dimmesdale die the moment he passes into the ethical mode. The only possible answer, if one accepts the present interpretation, is that Dimmesdale's death is symbolic in the sense that the ethical he has attained reveals to him its impossibly paradoxical nature. This idea suggests itself in Dimmesdale's answer to Hester appeal:

> "Hester," said the clergyman, "farewell!"
>
> "Shall we not meet again?" whispered she, bending her face down close to his. "Shall we not spend our immortal life together? Surely, surely, we have ransomed one another with all this woe! Thou lookest far into eternity, with those bright dying eyes! Then tell me what thou seest?"
>
> "Hush, Hester, hush!" said he, with tremulous solemnity. "The law we broke!—the sin here so awfully revealed!—let these alone be in thy thoughts! I fear! I fear! It may be, that when we forgot our God,—when we violated our reverence each for the other's soul,—it was thenceforth vain to hope that we could meet hereafter, in an everlasting and pure reunion." (1: 256)

Dimmesdale gives an ethical answer to Hester's question, whereas Hester performs here the leap of faith. She transcends the ethical, and her question is her passport to the religious. One is tempted to compare this scene with the concluding episode of Dostoyevsky's *The Brothers Karamazov*, where the boy Ilusha has just died, and Kolya Krassotkin asks Alyosha Karamazov, "Can it be true, as they teach in church, that we shall rise again from the dead and shall live and see each other again, all, Ilusha, too?" To which Alyosha answers, "half laughing, half enthusiastic," that indeed it will be so. Even while he laughs, he tells the truth as he believes it. Had he not believed it, he would have dismissed the question, or would have given a casual answer. He says instead, "Certainly, we shall rise again, certainly we shall see each other and shall tell each other with joy and gladness all that has happened."[23] We will have a parallel scene, Percy's acknowledged tribute to Dostoyevsky, at the end of *The Moviegoer*.

Kierkegaard states that the only way the existing individual can live authentically in the world is as a free man. This freedom is to be achieved only through the awareness of the absolute task. So far, I have argued that the absolute task is figuratively represented by the scarlet letter. Hawthorne communicates Hester's awareness of the relationship between the ideal task and freedom in the reflection that "the tendency of her fate and fortune had been to set her free. The scarlet letter was her passport into regions where other women dared not tread" (1: 199). While this passage has frequently been read as suggestive of the book's feminist theme, in this reading it also suggests a symbiosis between the ideal task, *telos*, and freedom.

However, Kierkegaard maintains, the process of arriving at the absolute *telos* is complicated by several obstacles which constitute the structure, as it were, of the process of becoming. Thus, first of all, the existing individual chooses himself as the absolute *telos*. He subsequently renounces the relative matrix of his life (i.e., daily routine). But it should be kept in mind that a difficulty inheres in the act of renouncing because the individual's ties with relative ends are still substantial. In the meanwhile, time has elapsed, and it is no longer feasible to make a choice. Thus, a new beginning must be made. At this juncture the individual realizes the impossibility of unifying himself with his *telos* and becomes guilty. A possibility remains, however, that he will break through time into eternity and find God in the eternal moment. This, roughly speaking, is the structure of Hester's development in the narrative.

Chapters 3, 13, 18, 19, 21, 23, and 24 reveal the structure of Hester's existential pathos. In Chapter 3, she recognizes her *telos* and makes her choice. In Chapter 13, which he significantly entitled "Another View of Hester," Hawthorne focuses on Hester's transformation. He first indicates the society's altered perception of Hester; where she inspired awe and hostility in the past, she has now earned "reverence and affection." The community would now gladly welcome her as a neighbor but, as the chapter unfolds, Hawthorne stresses Hester's utter reclusiveness. For instance, she dismisses any attempt by her neighbors to communicate:

> Meeting them in the street, she never raised her head to receive their greeting. If they were resolute to accost her, she laid her finger on the scarlet letter and passed on. (1: 162)

Hawthorne further registers the change in her physical appearance, "Even the attractiveness of her person had undergone . . . a change. . . . Some attribute had departed from her, the permanence of which had been essential to keep her a woman" (1: 163). The departed attribute is later associated with "passion and feeling," and Hawthorne comments on her "marble coldness." Passion is replaced with thought or "freedom of speculation" which, as Hawthorne says, "sufficed" Hester "without investing itself in the flesh and blood of action." We again find direct parallels in Kierkegaard's ideas, specifically his theory that in human action "passion" must enter as the "over and above" principle. Hester's attitude reminds one of the often encountered warning of existentialists against excessive introspection or inwardization, which likewise harks back to Kierkegaard:

> The more abstract the individual is, the less he is related to an eternal happiness, and the more remote he is from guilt; for abstraction assumes the indifference of existence, but guilt is the expression for the strongest self-assertion of

> existence, and after all it is an "exister" who is to relate himself to an eternal happiness. (*CUP*, 470)

Kierkegaard's text aids in clarifying why Hester views "her own individual existence . . . in the negative," why Hawthorne indicates that she should undergo "a still mightier change," why he says that "her heart had lost its regular and healthy throb," and, finally, why he asserts that "the scarlet letter had done its office." These thoughts are occasioned by Hester's reconsideration of her double concealment: of Dimmesdale's partnership in adultery and of Chillingworth's real nature and motive. She considers both concealments in ethical terms and they now seem to her to have been "a defect of truth, courage, and loyalty" (1: 166). The choice she made in prison, though "she had climbed her way, since then, to a higher point," was "the more wretched alternative," and rendered Hester guilty. Her guilt results from her inability to renounce the appeal made by the universal or ethical principle. In other words, having made her choice (in Chapter 3), she renounces the daily matrix of relations but falls victim to excessive introspection and the demands made by the universal (ethical) principle.

The same structure is revealed in Chapter 18, again significantly entitled—"A Flood of Sunshine." It begins with the above quoted statement of Hester's freedom but, as the chapter unfolds, we see her passionate response to the call of the aesthetic. As she removes the letter and the cap, the symbolic transformation summoned by Hester's gesture is accompanied by a change of weather:

> All at once, as with a sudden smile of heaven, forth burst the sunshine, pouring a very flood into the obscure forest, gladdening each green leaf, transmuting the yellow fallen ones to gold, and gleaming down the gray trunks of the solemn trees. The objects that had made a shadow hitherto, embodied the brightness now. The course of the little brook might be traced by its merry gleam afar into the wood's

> heart of mystery, which had become a mystery of joy. (1: 202-03)

The optimism of this chapter has always vexed Hawthorne's readers. Again, Kierkegaard's thought offers the most satisfying explanation of the initial optimism that immediately cedes to the total pessimism of the chapter. According to Kierkegaard, suffering by definition encourages the sufferer to seek a way out of his condition. This release may be found, for example, in poetic production or the poetic premonition of a happier and less flawed state of things. Such a respite from suffering within the aesthetic mode is reflected in *The Scarlet Letter* in Hester's fantastic plans for the future and in the "exquisite relief" she experiences upon the removal of the letter and the cap. However, Kierkegaard contends that the hope and the optimism of the aesthetic mode precede total pessimism. In this sequence resides the essence of repentance, for Kierkegaard, which entails the existential relinquishment of all hope in realizing one's absolute *telos* exclusively through freedom. Moreover, the final act of freedom is the existential assertion of its nothingness, which accounts for the desperate pessimism voiced in this passage:

> . . . there was a sense of inevitable doom upon her, as she thus received back this deadly symbol from the hand of fate . . . here again was the scarlet misery, glittering on the old spot! . . . Hester next gathered up the heavy tresses of her hair, and confided them beneath her cap. As if there were a withering spell in the sad letter, her beauty, the warmth and richness of her womanhood, departed like fading sunshine; and a gray shadow seemed to fall across her. (1: 211)

The woman we see again in Chapter 21, in Hawthorne's words, sooner resembles a "statue" than a living human being:

> Her face, so long familiar to the townspeople, showed the marble quietude which they were accustomed to behold there. It was like a mask; or rather, like the frozen calmness of a dead woman's features; owing this dreary resemblance to the fact that Hester was actually dead, in respect to any claim of sympathy, and had departed out of the world with which she still seemed to mingle. (1: 226)

It should be noted that between Chapter 19, where Hester replaces the letter and the cap, and Chapter 21, which depicts her as wearing a "mask," Hawthorne excludes her from the narrative. The preceding chapter focuses on Dimmesdale's peculiar state and concludes with Chillingworth's appearance. Therefore, Hester's transformation results not from her knowledge of Chillingworth's Machiavellian plot to thwart their plans of escape, but rather from her own resolve to continue her movement toward the absolute *telos*.

At this juncture in the narrative, then, Hawthorne attempts a psychological justification of Hester's departure "out of the world," attributing it, significantly, to an "inconsistency" in Hester's nature and to a "feeling of regret" that derives from her inability "to win her freedom from pain which had been thus deeply incorporated with her being" (1: 227). The reader cannot mistake this "pain . . . incorporated with her being" as anything other than the most basic existentialist category of anguish or *Angst*, or what Percy terms "malaise," which accompanies the existing individual at every moment. Wishing to avoid this anguish, the individual attempts to cast off his identity and assume a role or, in Hawthorne's vocabulary, a "mask." Or, alternatively, he may try to sidestep the anguish by "rotating," says Kierkegaard, or "lighting out," in Huck Finn's fashion, for new territories. However, as the existentialists tell us, every attempt at avoiding the anguish only further aggravates the condition because the individual's *telos* consists not of avoiding, but rather of choosing himself. That choice cannot be achieved through a single act. On the contrary, one most regain this ground over and over again in passionate living. This existentialist paradigm is precisely what structures the last chapter of *The Scarlet Letter* and offers an interpretive framework for the book's conclusion.

Hester and Pearl "rotate" as they depart for England, but Hester returns to New England to resume her *telos*, the cyclical nature of which Hawthorne conveys one last time by these words, "Here had been her sin; here, her sorrow; and here, was yet to be her penitence" (1: 263). To grasp the meaning of the final paragraphs of the book, within the proposed scheme, we should once again resort to Kierkegaard's philosophy and, specifically, to his concept of an "apostle." Since Kierkegaard couples this concept with that of a "genius," it seems appropriate to examine both terms together. A genius is an individual who arrives at truth *sub specie aeternitatis*, as Kierkegaard has it, objectively, in the manner of a scientist or a philosopher. Chillingworth, in fact, perfectly fits this image, for he combines both roles. His speculative meditations, his methodical discovery of Dimmesdale's secret, and his subsequent manipulation of the minister's psyche clearly indicate his kinship with this Kierkegaardian concept. An apostle, on the other hand, is the one to whom a certain message is communicated, but his task does not consist of "pondering over" this message. As Kierkegaard says, "it is not given him for his own sake, he is, on the contrary, on a mission and has to proclaim the [message] and use authority."[24] Thus, inherent in the notion of an apostle are two faculties, those of hearing the message and of passing the message on to somebody else. Such is essentially Hester's image upon her return to Salem:

> And, as Hester Prynne had no selfish ends, nor lived in any measure for her own profit and enjoyment, people brought all their sorrows and perplexities, and besought her counsel, as one who had herself gone through a mighty trouble. Women, more especially,—in the continually recurring trials of wounded, wasted, wronged, misplaced, or erring and sinful passion,—or with the dreary burden of a heart

> unyielded, because unvalued and unsought,—came to Hester's cottage, demanding why they were so wretched, and what the remedy! Hester comforted and counselled them as best she might. (1: 263)

The book does not conclude with these words, however. We still have the ambiguous passage where Hawthorne speaks of "some brighter period, when . . . a new truth would be revealed, in order to establish the whole relation between man and woman on a surer ground of mutual happiness" (1: 263), and defines "the angel and apostle of the coming revelation," who will be a woman "lofty, pure, and beautiful." Hawthorne had no doubt as to the essential loneliness of individuals. All of his major characters, without a single exception, are fundamentally isolated. But the pessimism of Hawthorne's conviction is counterbalanced by the assertion of a possibility that two lonely persons, a man and a woman, can discover each other and, as Percy has remarked, "out of the existential solitude they can create a new world."[25] A look ahead to Hawthorne's later heroines reveals that the woman as "angel and apostle" enters his subsequent romances, specifically Phoebe in *The House of the Seven Gables* and Hilda in *The Marble Faun*, both books which, significantly, end with marriage. We can thus assume, as a working hypothesis for the subsequent parts of the present study, that the idea voiced in the final sections of *The Scarlet Letter* anticipates the concept that several contemporary existentialists have termed "intersubjectivity."

The Scarlet Letter ends with the heraldic symbol "ON A FIELD, SABLE, THE LETTER A, GULES" as an inscription on Hester and Dimmesdale's collective grave. This final touch is reminiscent of Kierkegaard's statement that on his tombstone he would prefer to have engraved only one word—THE INDIVIDUAL. And although Hawthorne makes it very clear that the future belongs to another woman, Hester remains in the reader's memory precisely that—THE INDIVIDUAL.

NOTES

1. Kierkegaard was born in 1813 and died in 1855. His most important works saw publication before 1850: *Either/Or* and *Fear and Trembling* (both in 1843), *Stages on Life's Way* in 1845, and *Concluding Unscientific Postscript* in 1846. Translations into English started appearing only in the twenties of the following century. Although Hawthorne's only direct link with existentialism is his reading of Pascal's *Oeuvres*, there is a thin chance that he became acquainted with Kierkegaard's thought through the sources other than the original texts.

2. Kierkegaard uses the term "aesthetic" in his own very special way, and its meaning has no bearing whatsoever upon the common notion of aesthetics that pertains to works of art and our responses to them as art. Since the word will be used exclusively in Kierkegaardian sense, it need not be set in quotation marks.

3. See, for instance, Ernst Breisach, *Introduction to Modern Existentialism* (New York: Grove Press, Inc., 1962), p. 21. I use the terms "stage" and "mode" interchangeably for lack of a better word which would contain both meanings.

4. James Collins, *The Mind of Kierkegaard* (Chicago: Henry Regnery Company, 1965), p. 60.

5. See Linda Whitney Hobson, *Understanding Walker Percy* (Columbia: Univ. of South Carolina Press, 1988), p. 29.

6. See, for instance, Edgar Dryden's analysis of the treatment of love in Hawthorne's fiction in: *Nathaniel Hawthorne, The Poetics of Enchantment* (Ithaca: Cornell Univ. Press, 1977), pp. 83-107.

7. See Henry Fairbanks, *The Lasting Loneliness of Nathaniel Hawthorne. A Study of the Sources of Alienation in Modern Man* (Albany: Magi Books, Inc., 1965), pp. 139-45.

8. The personal pronoun used here, and consistently throughout this study, in reference to existentialist thought is not merely a convenience, but reflects the patriarchal quality of this style of philosophizing.

9. *The Living Thoughts of Kierkegaard*, ed. Wynstan Hugh Auden (New York: David McKay Company, Inc., 1952), p. 32.

10. Ibid., p. 75.

11. Sören Kierkegaard, *Concluding Unscientific Postscript*, trans.

David F. Swenson (Princeton: Princeton Univ. Press, 1941), p. 472. Page references for quotations will be placed in the text after the entry "*CUP*."

12. Sören Kierkegaard, *Stages on Life's Way*, trans. Walter Lowrie (Princeton: Princeton Univ. Press, 1944), p. 107.

13. *The Living Thoughts of Kierkegaard*, pp. 104-05.

14. Ibid., p. 107.

15. Emmanuel Mounier, *Existentialist Philosophies. An Introduction*, trans. Eric Blow (London: Rockliff, 1948), p. 41.

16. John W. Elrod, *Being and Existence in Kierkegaard's Pseudonymous Works* (Princeton: Princeton Univ. Press, 1975), p. 148.

17. Albert Camus, *The Myth of Sisyphus and Other Essays*, trans. Justin O'Brien (New York: Vintage Books, 1955), p. 91.

18. Elrod, p. 217.

19. Roy R. Male, *Hawthorne's Tragic Vision* (New York: The Norton Library, 1957), pp. 102-03.

20. The term is borrowed from Murray Krieger, *The Tragic Vision. The Confrontation of Extremity* (Baltimore: The Johns Hopkins Univ. Press, 1973), p. 14. The entire passage deserves quotation:

> . . . our excommunicated ethical man, realizing the complete futility of human existence, cannot find a relationship with anything beyond it. His permanent forsaking of the universal seems to forbid it. This, the essence of the tragic vision, is the "sickness unto death," despair. It is the stage induced by shock; the stage which, beyond the "aesthetic" and the ethical, yet falls short of Kierkegaard's version of the Christian. . . . If one can attain a break-through—a bravely irrational one unmediated by universals—he can reach the glories of transcendence; if he fails, he must live in the contemplation of nothingness.

21. *Sören Kierkegaard's Journals and Papers*, trans. Howard V. Hong and Edna H. Hong, I vol. (Bloomington: Indiana Univ. Press, 1967-70), p. 10.

22. See Mounier, pp. 31-35.

23. Fyodor Dostoyevsky, *The Brothers Karamazov*, trans. Constance Garnett (New York: The New American Library, 1957), p. 700.

24. Sören Kierkegaard, *The Present Age and Of the Difference Between a Genius and an Apostle*, trans. Alexander Dru (New York and Evanston: Harper and Row, 1962), pp. 105-06.

25. These words come from my interview with Percy published in Poland under the title "Ostatni dżentelmen z Luizjany—rozmowa z Walkerem Percy," *Literatura na świecie* 5-6 (maj-czerwiec, 1987), p. 422.

Two: Ironical Consciousness

The Moviegoer

Of differences between *The Moviegoer* and *The Scarlet Letter*, one that most readily comes to mind is the difference in the gender of the focal characters. In *The Moviegoer*, the subjectivity explored is, typically for existentialist writing, that of a man. Furthermore, the moviegoer, John Bickerson Bolling, in short Binx, is initially an unbeliever, whereas Hester's faith is never questioned. Moreover, for all Percy's acknowledged indebtedness to Kierkegaard's thought, *The Moviegoer* shows relatively little interest in the concept of existential pathos, as defined in the previous chapter. In fact, the only character, whose development in the narrative parallels this Kierkegaardian concept, is Binx's half-brother, Lonnie. But Lonnie is a figure only lightly sketched. Nevertheless, the affinities between the two books are most arresting. Both novels depict essentially lonely persons embarked upon a search. Viewed in the larger perspective of the writers' later works, both novels function as negative commentaries on the dangers of excessive introspection. Both books are open-ended in the sense that they address a possibility of more rewarding personal relationships between men and women, to be realized in the writers' later works. And finally, children (Pearl in *The Scarlet Letter* and Lonnie in *The Moviegoer*) function as theological-philosophical foci in the novels.

Walker Percy has abundantly acknowledged his intellectual debt to Kierkegaard's philosophy.[1] His first two novels, *The Moviegoer* and *The Last Gentleman*, carry epigraphs from Kierkegaard, and in the epilogue to *The Moviegoer* there is an explicit reference to Kierkegaard's thought as Binx, the protagonist, says: "I have not the authority, as the Danish philosopher declared, to speak of such matters in any other way than the edifying." The last word has pejorative connotations of which Percy is well aware because he makes Binx add, "it is not open to me even to be edifying, since the time is later than [Kierkegaard's], much too late to edify."[2] In fact, the only character in the book who evidently "edifies" is Aunt Emily, but neither Binx, nor Percy himself, identifies with her views.[3] Instead, Percy's aim, and his indisputable achievement, is his presentation of the individual in his real predicament, a predicament suggested by the flyleaf quotation from Kierkegaard's *The Sickness Unto Death*: "the specific character of despair is precisely this: it is unaware of being despair".

Arguably, despair culminates the aesthetic mode; it is the signal, often unacknowledged, which fact the flyleaf quotation also underlies, that the possibilities of the aesthetic mode have been exhausted. Dialectically speaking, the aesthetic mode progresses from the unreflecting sensual phase, through the modes of grief, cynicism, imagination and, boredom. At the end lurks despair or what Kierkegaard calls "inwardness with a jammed look." This phrase signifies that the self is enmeshed in the infinity of the imagination to the point where it utterly loses its footing in what Kierkegaard calls "immediacy." The individual thus characterized may now reach the demarcation point between the aesthetic and the ethical mode, which is furnished by ironical consciousness. I will argue in this chapter that the bulk of Percy's novel explores Binx's ironical consciousness. I will also attempt to demonstrate that Binx performs two Kierkegaardian "leaps": one to ethical choice, the other to faith.

Considerable confusion in the existing criticism of *The Moviegoer* as regards the book's religious dimension has resulted from the fact that Binx is not a clear-cut embodiment of any Kierkegaardian mode. Lewis A. Lawson and Bradley R. Dewey argue that Binx represents the aesthetic mode and at the end of the book progresses to the ethical choice of marriage and responsibility for Kate.[4] Martin Luschei recognizes the fact that the real Knight of Faith of the book is Lonnie, but he further maintains that Binx's decision to marry Kate parallels the Kierkegaardian leap of faith.[5] This interpretation assigns the leap of faith to the ethical mode, with marriage as its utmost expression. However, the leap of faith marks the transition to the religious mode, and nowhere in the book is it suggested that Binx's decision to marry Kate may be conceived in other than ethical terms. Tracy K. Lischer and Janet Hobbs perceive Binx as the embodiment of all three modes. Hobbs contrasts Binx's position to Emily Cutrer's because she progresses from "aesthetic posing into ethical responsibility," whereas Binx's movement through the ethical mode is only transitional.[6] Ultimately, he becomes Kierkegaard's man of faith. Lischer, in turn, argues that the novel ends with only Binx's "potential . . . leap of faith from the ethical to the religious life."[7] Apparently lost in these interpretations of Binx's position as regards the modes of existence is the fact that the "potential" for Binx's leap of faith occurs midway through the book, in Section Three, which is the most illuminating part of the novel. Most perceptive readers of *The Moviegoer* identify the leap with the episode following Binx's visit to Lonnie's death-bed.

Another apparent difficulty in assigning Binx a position within Kierkegaardian modes of existence is the fact that Binx does not represent a uniform type of any phase of even the aesthetic mode. Inherent in his characterization are aspects of the first phase of the aesthetic mode, but we must remember that, in Kierkegaard's scheme, the eroticism of the first phase is utterly devoid of reflection. Reflection pertains only to the second and third phases.

Following Kierkegaard, one can tropically conceive the potential individual existence as a road with two bridges and an obstacle at the end of each bridge, or as a hurdle race where obstacles have to be overcome by way of jumping. To apply this terminology to Kierkegaard's modes of existence would be to say that the movement within a mode may be smooth, but in order to proceed to a new mode one has to leap. The leap reflects man's free decision, which arises from the conviction that the possibilities of the inferior mode have been exhausted. The demarcation point of the aesthetic mode is furnished by irony. A cynical or despairing irony characterizes the individual who has plumbed the depths of the aesthetic mode and now confronts the possibility of making a leap to the ethical mode. The narrative of *The Moviegoer,* having enacted the possibilities of the aesthetic mode, moves to the ethical choice, which consists in the conquest of selfhood and the acceptance of responsibility for another, and finally opens up possibilities for the religious choice. However, the bulk of Percy's novel explores what Kierkegaard calls ironical consciousness, with its two standard forms: "the despairing irony of the seducer" and "the irony of the true ironist."

The seducer believes that the passage of time, which irrevocably moves one closer to death, can be counteracted by momentary attachments. He thus hopes to find refuge from despair in sensual pleasure. Binx, for example, expects to find such an escape in his relations with his consecutive secretaries:

> They could be called love affairs, I suppose. They started off as love affairs anyway, fine careless raptures in which Marcia or Linda (but not yet Sharon) and I would go spinning along the Gulf Coast, lie embracing in a deserted cove of Ship Island, and hardly believe our good fortune, hardly believe that the world could contain such happiness. (8)

No doubt, such a portrayal of Binx follows Kierkegaard's humorous definition of what he calls the "immediate" man, whose only wish is for "wealth, good fortune and the most beautiful of damsels." Yet Binx's illusion soon gives way to despair, and he recognizes that "whenever one courts great happiness, one also risks malaise," which parallels Kierkegaard's insight that "[the seducer's] love made him indescribably happy for the moment; as soon as he thought of time he despaired."[8] Rather humorously suspecting that his car, a new Dodge sedan, is a generator of malaise, Binx buys a new car, an MG, hoping that it will be "immune to the malaise." But as the novelty of the new car wears off, the MG also becomes infested with the malaise. This transpires on a Sunday, the day when it is most likely that the malaise will strike, as Binx and Sharon Kincaid are returning from the week-end visit at his mother's summer place. Sharon is Binx's third secretary, and the parts of the book depicting the various stages of their relationship function as Binx's own "diary of a seducer." The scene culminates in a Don Juan fantasy when Binx, having been introduced to Sharon's roommate Joyce, hesitates as to which of the two girls he wants:

> A sadness overtakes me. If only—If only what? If only I could send Sharon on her way and go straight upstairs and see Joyce, a total stranger? Yes. But not quite. If only I could be with both of them, with a house full of them, an old Esplanade rooming house full of strapping American girls with their silly turned heads and their fine big bottoms. (123)

As a secretary and a conquest, Sharon is only an "item" on Binx's list of expenditures. Like Camus' Meursault, Binx lives in his body, on the level of sensation. Just like for Meursault, women exist for Binx superficially, to satisfy his physical needs. Unlike Meursault, however, Binx has significant people in his life, and Lonnie Smith is one of them.

Dewey has convincingly argued that children create the "theological foci" in Percy's first three novels. Significantly, these children's untimely deaths convey the idea of posthumous victory in that they "challenge the reader to see through their eyes the vision of an Apollonian world full of God's grace where sorrow and death do not have the last word."[9] Like Jamie in *The Last Gentleman*, Lonnie is afflicted with a lingering disease, and he believes that "he can offer his sufferings in reparation for men's indifference to the pierced heart of Jesus Christ" (137). Binx claims to envy Lonnie his faith because the boy's life is a "serene business." Lonnie's predicament stands in clear contrast to their mother's "instinct for the ordinary," an instinct spotlighted by Binx's comments on the "smell of two thousand Sunday dinners" clinging to her curtains. She seems to belong to the category of females in Percy's fiction whose chief talent lies in "emblematizing" others. Binx reports that in his mother's recollection of his father (she remarried after his death, when Binx was a child), "it is not him she remembers but an old emblem of him." Similarly, as Binx notes, she "made an emblem out of Kate and does not know her at all" (155). To Emily Cutrer, people likewise "become what she sees them to be": Sam Yerger is "only a Cato on long Sunday afternoons," Mercer is "the old retainer," her husband Jules is "the creole Cato," and so on. This tendency, provisionally here called "emblematizing," appears in Percy's theoretical writing under two headings: "the loss of visibility," which harks back to Pascal's definition of the self,[10] and "abstraction," the term Percy borrows from Kierkegaard.[11] The first concept functions in Pascalian vocabulary as "être imaginaire," to be distinguished from "notre propre être" or "être veritable," and it is described as man's existence as conceived by others ("dans l'idée des autres"), which is to say that the individual, who attempts to create his "illusory" existence, assumes the attributes of another person. His loss of visibility signifies that his real self is "covered," and we see not him but his attributes. The second concept is elaborated in the *Pensées*, where Pascal begins by asking "Quest-ce que le moi?" and subsequently demonstrates that man's existence for other people consists purely of the attributes ("qualités") they see in him; these attributes "emblematize" his existence. Pascal illustrates this idea with an example of a passerby (Percy gives an example of a sparrow in an identical context) who is perceived by somebody watching him from the window not as a person but as a symbol of a passerby. Percy adds that not only people, but also objects, lose their visibility and become concealed "under the hardened symbol when the world comes to be conceived as Alice's museum of name-things: shoes and ships and sealing wax."[12] The difference between the two concepts concerns little else than a viewpoint. Man becomes invisible when he assumes the attributes which are alien to his real nature. Thus, he is himself an agent of his invisibility. This concept is invariably identified as role-playing, the heralding form of inauthenticity. Abstraction, in turn, occurs when another person perceives in the individual only the qualities he wants to find. Percy's notion, which echoes Pascal's, has relevance for the passage where Binx for the first time *sees* the objects which have constituted his everydayness:

> They looked both unfamiliar and at the same time full of clues. I stood in the center of the room and gazed at the little pile, sighting through a hole made by thumb and forefinger. What was unfamiliar about them was that I could see them. They might have belonged to someone else. A man can look at this little pile on his bureau for thirty years and never once see it. It is as invisible as his own hand. (11)

Binx's ability to see them for what they are is the passageway to alienation, but it also marks Binx's higher consciousness, which is the starting point for the search.

Percy is wont to convey a crucial difference between authenticity and inauthenticity on a linguistic level. In *The Moviegoer*,

Lonnie incarnates authenticity, which instantly manifests itself in the language the boy uses. Binx believes that Lonnie's speech "gives him an advantage foreigners have: his words are not worn out" (162). Kierkegaard identifies inauthenticity on a linguistic level as "twaddle." This concept is of particular interest here because Kierkegaard uses it in his discussion of irony, which, as has been indicated, is the mode employed by Percy to establish Binx's special position between the aesthetic and the ethical mode. Kierkegaard says:

> An immediate enthusiast assails the world's ears with his twaddle early and late, always on his feet and arrayed in buskins, he plagues people with his enthusiasm, and he does not notice that what he says does not inspire them. . . . If such an enthusiast happens to be contemporary with an ironist, the latter will of course know how to utilize him profitably as comic material.[13]

Eddie Lovell is an example of Kierkegaard's "enthusiast." The humorous encounter between Binx and Eddie early in the narrative clearly conveys the idea of the quoted passage. They are talking about the client Binx sent to Eddie, and Eddie says:

> I'll tell you one thing, Binx. I count it a great privilege to have known him. I've never known anyone, young or old, who possessed a greater fund of knowledge. That man spoke to me for two hours about the history of the crystallization of sugar and it was pure romance. I was fascinated. (20)

He then jumps to another subject, and this transition from topic to topic, with no conceivable connection between them, this inability to concentrate on one idea, is also characteristic of a "twaddler":

> I think more of Miss Emily—and Kate—than anyone else in the world except my own mother—and wife. The good that woman has done. (20)

Binx demonstrates alertness to the fact that Eddie's "twaddle" is meant to fill the void between them and he gives off-hand, casual replies. Kierkegaard has keenly observed that the ironist perceives that "what interests him absolutely does not interest the others absolutely; this discrepancy he apprehends, and sets the comical between himself and them, in order to be able to hold fast to the ethical in himself with still greater inwardness."[14] This aspect of ironical consciousness surfaces in the dialogue between Binx and Walter Wade, who is yet another "twaddler":

> "What's wrong with the goddamn world, Binx?"
>
> "I am not sure. But something occurred to me this morning. I was sitting on the bus—"
>
> "What do you do with yourself out there in Gentilly?" People often ask me what is wrong with the world and also what I do in Gentilly, and I always try to give an answer. The former is an interesting question. I have noticed, however, that no one really wants to listen to an answer.
>
> "Not much. Sell mutual funds to widows and dagos."
>
> "Is that right?" Walter drops his shoulder and feels the muscle in his back. Squatting down on his heels, he runs an eye along the baseboard calculating the angle of settle. (39)

Binx's intellectual Geiger is set to detect inauthenticity in others, and he subsequently ridicules it in his characteristically flippant manner, which he invariably displays in his relations with Eddie and Nell Lovell, Walter Wade, Uncle Jules and, to some extent, also Aunt Emily. Binx views others from a certain vantage point, for he is acutely aware of his own and others' pretensions and he understands that neither his nor their viewpoint is absolute. While this awareness marks the ironist's higher consciousness, its danger lies, admonishes Kiekegaard, in that irony may reduce everything, man and God included, to the status of possibility and, consequently, it may lead to despair. This is probably what Binx has in mind when he says that the search culminates in despair. Characteristically also, the ironist is judged by others as the one who holds nothing important. This aspect is illuminated in Binx's relationship with Aunt Emily.

Emily is Kierkegaard's ethicist who, moreover, will never transcend the ethical and opt for the religious. She represents Binx's statistical American: "an Episcopalian by emotion, a Greek by nature and a Buddhist by choice" (23). Earlier in the narrative, when Binx launches the meaning of his search, he echoes Kierkegaard's criticism of "objective Christianity." Binx considers himself an unbeliever because available to him are patterns of "organized religion," the only exception to which is Lonnie, whose faith Binx secretly envies and becomes an heir to at the end of the novel. He protests that if "98% of Americans believe in God and the remaining 2% are atheists and agnostics," it does not leave a "single percentage for a seeker" (14). Unlike some other questers after faith in Percy's fiction, Binx says bluntly that "the proofs of God's existence may have been true for all I know, but it didn't make the slightest difference" (145). While this statement reveals one of the fundamental characteristics of ironical consciousness (the danger that everything, including God, will be levelled to indifference), it also articulates the problem of the enactment of faith. Four possibilities, technically speaking, are open to the Percy hero. Placing a "wager," as Pascal recommended, on the existence of God is one of them. The wager calls for prudent calculation, and its value lies in the logical analysis of the situation: if man willingly acts on faith in all different areas of life, he cannot rationally justify singling out religion as an exception. In fact, Percy explicitly refers to Pascal and the wager in *The Second Coming*, but, in his view, Pascal trivialized the situation. The second possibility, the familiar leap of faith, suggests a degree of arbitrariness, but its value rests in helping man recognize that faith "in something" is as indispensable to spirit as air is to physical living and that if faith breaks down, man must "leap into uncertainty if [he is] to avoid certain destruction."[15] St. Augustine's obverse claim that evil proves the existence of God marks the third possibility open to the Percy hero. This idea structures Lance Lamar's search in *Lancelot.* Finally, the intersubjective communion with another person is contemporaneous with God-relationship, and this idea surfaces in *The Second Coming.* However, the choice for Binx, as for other focal male characters in Percy's fiction, is not among these four possibilities but between the Christian viewpoint (embodied in the novel in the figure of Lonnie Smith) and the ethical Stoic heritage of the South (represented by Aunt Emily).

A mouthpiece for a traditional Southern viewpoint with its inherent idea of the Götterddammerung voiced by sensitive Southerners ever since the Civil War, Emily says, "The world I knew has come crashing down around my ears. The things we hold dear are reviled and spat upon" (54). The things she holds dear are but echoes of Melanie Wilkes' chivalric code:

> . . . a certain quality of spirit, a gaiety, a sense of duty, a nobility worn lightly, a sweetness, a gentleness with women—the only good things the South ever had and the only things that really matter in this life. (224)

Percy has disavowed the claim that Emily's broadsword virtues represent his own point of view. He nevertheless makes Binx capitulate to Emily's viewpoint. Binx's decisions at the end of the novel stem from the enactment of the possibilities that Emily's ethical viewpoint opens up for him. We have to go back to an earlier exchange between them to realize that she has initially suggested the possibilities which Binx carries into effect as the novel closes. She first indicates his responsibility to himself: "I want you to think about entering medical school this fall. You know you've always had it in the back of your mind" (52). Then she invites Binx to move to a garçonnière in her old carriage house and, finally, she attempts to arouse Binx's sense of responsibility for Kate by saying:

> No—it is not I doing something for you. We could use you around. Kate is going through something I don't understand. Jules, my dear Jules won't even admit anything is wrong. You and Sam are the only ones she'd ever listen to. (53)

That Binx does not succumb without some struggle is attested by his *cathartic* confession, so uncharacteristic of his otherwise restrained manner:

> Now in the thirty-first year of my dark pilgrimage on this earth and knowing less than I ever knew before, having learned only to recognize merde when I see it, having inherited no more from my father than a good nose for merde, for every species of shit that flies—my only talent—smelling merde from every quarter, living in fact in the very century of merde, the great shithouse of scientific humanism where needs are satisfied, everyone becomes an anyone, a warm and creative person, and prospers like a dung beetle, and one hundred percent of people are humanists and ninety-eight percent believe in God, and men are dead, dead, dead . . .—on this my thirtieth birthday, I know nothing and there is nothing to do but fall prey to desire. (228)

This *cris de coeur*, echoing what Kierkegaard calls "demoniac despair" or "malignant" protest against the whole of existence, is followed, at the end of the chapter, by Binx's conversation with Kate. This dialogue unveils, in clear terms, what Binx's future is going to be. It will consist in his "half-hearted," so to speak, acceptance of ethical responsibilities that will enable him to live comfortably in the world without really "being of it," as suggested in this part of their conversation:

> "What do you plan to do?"
>
> I shrug. There is only one thing I can do: listen to people, see how they stick themselves into the world, hand them along a ways in their dark journey. . . . It only remains to decide whether this vocation is best pursued in a service station or—
>
> "Are you going to medical school?"
>
> "*If* [Emily] *wants me to.*" (233)

Luschei suggests that "Emily's 'ought' is Binx's annihilation" in that it compels him to assume "a role that does not suit him."[16] Though Percy has invited such an opinion, saying that "Binx jumps from the esthetic clear across the ethical to the religious. He has no ethical sphere at all,"[17] Binx's capitulation to Emily's code presents a complex problem. Percy's interviews have confused—wittingly, as Hawthorne was wont to do in his prefaces, notes, and epilogues, or unwittingly—readers on many occasions. Another apparent difficulty in reading *The Moviegoer* on the subject of Binx's development results from Percy's playful application of some of Kierkegaard's central ideas. It seems, for instance, that in his approach to Kierkegaard's "repetition" he combines both its aesthetic and its religious meaning. Percy defines repetition as the "re-enactment of past experience toward the end of isolating the time segment which has lapsed in order that it, the lapsed time, can be savored of itself and without the usual adulteration of events that clog time like peanuts in brittle" (80). Not only in this definition but also in the familiar example of repetition in *The Moviegoer*, when Binx takes Kate to see a western movie he saw at the same theater fourteen years ago, Percy seems to mock Kierkegaard. Binx makes a point of sitting in the same seat, and remembers the same smell of privet he smelled fourteen years ago. In fact, Binx himself admits that this is mockery. But not quite. If Percy alludes here to Kierkegaard's Constantine Constantius' humorous interlude (a repetition of sorts) in Berlin, which failed because, as Robert Bretall has craftily argued, it was *attempted* and because it was *pursued*,[18] he gives a much more profound insight to Binx's experience, which again intersects with Kierkegaard's ideas. Kierkegaard comments on repetition in God's plan, whereby "the world endures, and it endures for the fact that it is repetition."[19] We have an exactly parallel thought in the theater episode:

> . . . a secret sense of wonder about the *enduring*, about all the nights, the rainy summer nights at twelve and one and two o'clock when the seats endured alone in the empty theater. The enduring is something which must be accounted for. One cannot simply shrug it off. (80)

Percy's playful handling of certain Kierkegaardian ideas probably accounts for the fact that some of his critics do not take Percy seriously on the subject of Binx's progress through the stages of existence. Linda Whitney Hobson, for instance, writes that Binx at the end of *The Moviegoer* "is recovered enough to take a few steps out of the aesthetic sphere and into the religious, though he will no doubt slip back into the aesthetic from time to time."[20] One wonders what Hobson really means. Does she imply that Binx, essentially a quester after faith, will become an adept of "lunch-hour liaison"? Hobson errs in what Wyatt Prunty thinks is a common tendency among Percy's reviewers who "confuse the method of recounting details of the world's body (presented in descriptive writing) with the purposes of another mode, allegory, which is designed to bridge the gap between the physical world and a metaphysical world."[21] Percy writes primarily in Hawthorne's metonymic, or allegorical, mode, which (I note here as the subject for later exploration), as Northrop Frye has so cogently argued, lends itself particularly to existentialist writing. Binx's development, towards the end of the narrative, presents the most accurate fictional transposition of Kierkegaardian concept of the Knight of Faith. Kierkegaard contrasts this figure with the Knight of Infinite Resignation. The difference between the two rests in the ways they renounce the finite. The Knight of Resignation renounces the finite and never gets it back, whereas the Knight of Faith performs the "double movement": he renounces the finite and yet he continues to live in it. Kierkegaard humorously describes the Knight of Faith as the one who has nothing remarkable about him. He says he has "never found any such person, but . . . can well think him." And he proceeds to describe their encounter, which, for its superb ideas and humor, is worth reproducing in full:

> Acquaintance made, I am introduced to him. The moment I set eyes on him I instantly push him from me, I myself leap backwards, I clasp my hands and say half aloud, "Good Lord, is this the man? Is it really he? Why, he looks like a tax-collector!" However, it is the man after all. I draw closer to him, watching his least movements to see whether there might not be visible a little heterogeneous fractional telegraphic message from the infinite, a glance, a look, a gesture, a note of sadness, a smile, which betrayed the infinite in its heterogeneity with the finite. No! I examine his figure from tip to toe to see if there might not be a cranny through which the infinite was peeping. No! He is solid through and through. His tread? It is vigorous, belonging entirely to finiteness; no smartly dressed townsman who walks out to Fresberg on a Sunday afternoon treads the ground more firmly; he belongs entirely to the world, no Philistine more so. One can discover nothing of

> that aloof and superior nature whereby one recognizes the knight of the infinite.[22]

In the last sentence of this passage one of course recognizes the familiar figure of Hester Prynne. But even Hester, having renounced the finite, gets it back at the novel's close when she returns from England and resumes her social role. The quoted passage comes from *Fear and Trembling*, and in the subsequent paragraphs Kierkegaard, quite surprisingly in fact, describes the Knight of Faith as a married man. This is a contradiction of sorts because, we remember, his earlier work presented no satisfactory solution as to how married life could be incorporated within the religious stage of existence. The ethical, with marriage as its highest *telos*, is to be understood as a hierarchy of moral values to which man subscribes consciously or unconsciously, but for the most part automatically, in order to function comfortably in the world. The ethical choice resolves tensions inherent in the aesthetic view of life; it brings security and steadiness to existence. At the same time, however, Kierkegaard suggests incompatibility between Christian faith and the two lower stages of existence. James Collins has criticized this aspect of Kierkegaard's thought saying that "Kierkegaard's personal case impresses him so forcefully, that he is ready to conclude that marriage is the prime factor in directing personality to exclusively immanent and finite ends and in sponsoring an esthetic interpretation of religious concepts."[23] Having accepted this criticism as tenable, we still encounter a stumbling block in Kiekegaard's depiction of the Knight of Faith as a married man. The problem, strictly speaking, is how to reconcile the seemingly incompatible: the ethical choice with faith. No reconciliation is mandatory, maintains Kierkegaard, for the ethical choice equips one exclusively for life in the finite, whereas the Knight of Faith embodies "the sublime and the pedestrian." He lives in the finite without "being of it." The moral selfhood and the religious selfhood are not the same. The moral selfhood articulates itself through taking the responsibility for others, whereas the religious selfhood fulfills itself in the solitary encounter with God. If, however, Kierkegaard's Knight of Faith is a married man, he still remains in the ethical bond. The only way to account for this contradiction in Kierkegaard's terms is to apply the Kierkegaardian concept of the teleological suspension of the ethical, which Kierkegaard conveys in Abraham's sacrifice of Isaac. It thus appears that the Knight of Faith makes another double movement: he first makes the ethical choice and subsequently sacrifices the ethical for the religious.

In the interview with Dewey, conducted thirteen years after the publication of *The Moviegoer*, Percy, confessing his uneasiness with Kierkegaard's notion of subjectivity, bluntly criticizes the above aspect of Kierkegaard's thought. What he finds wanting in subjectivity is, in Percy's words, "understanding or an explanation of intersubjectivity—caring for the other person."[24] Percy approaches the subject in each of his major works and novel after novel testifies to his mounting problems with intersubjectivity. I shall venture the proposition that as long as Percy remained under the influence of existentialism, he was virtually unable to create meaningful and healthy relationships between men and women. Not only is the portrayal of womanhood distorted in his early novels, but also his male characters' inability to forge and develop meaningful relationships results from these distortions of perception. It is only after Percy had moved away from this sphere of influence that his fiction boasted a rounded depiction of womanhood and a fully meaningful relationship. Existentialism philosophically sanctioned phallocentrism. By conceiving subjectivity as essentially male, existentialism relegated woman to the position of the other. As Toril Moi has written, "patriarchal [existential, in Moi's terms] ideology presents woman as immanence, man as transcendence."[25] Even though we usually associate such views with twentieth-century European existentialism (specifically, Sartre and Camus), which in turn was indebted to American modernism, we might benefit from looking at what Kierkegaard has to say on the subject of woman's immanence:

> When woman is determined as virginity, she is thereby characterized as being for an other. Virginity is, namely, a form of being which, insofar as it is a being for itself, is really an abstraction and only reveals itself to another. The same characterization also lies in the concept of female innocence. It is therefore possible to say that woman in this condition is invisible. . . . Logically, this contradiction will be found to be *quite in order*, and he who knows how to think logically will not be disturbed by it, *but will be glad in it* [emphasis added].[26]

Whereas Percy's protagonist's subscription to this view clearly manifests itself in *Lancelot*, his first attempt at defining the focal female dates back to *The Moviegoer* and is realized in the figure of Kate Cutrer.

Kate is the fictional precursor of helpless neurotic Southern belles of Percy's later fiction. In fact, it seems a fairly standard procedure for Percy to conceive of psychotic women as marital candidates for his male figures. One possible reason of this curious mating in Percy's novels lies in the fact that most of Percy's focal males are unaccommodated men with an assortment of psychic problems. It is therefore only natural that such a man would find a suitable partner in a woman who reflects his mental condition. Moreover, all of Percy's males are embarked on unique (read: performed solitarily) quests for faith, the realization of which could be threatened by a relationship with a *single*, in Kierkegaard's understanding of the word, female individual. A woman who erases her individuality (as Kate in *The Moviegoer* does) or who is mute (as Anna in *Lancelot* is) will not threaten the male self with dispersion.

In the figure of Kate Cutrer, Percy conjures up the generations of fictive women who submit, like Catherine Barkley in *A Farewell to Arms*, "There is no me anymore," or like Marilyn Monroe in the film *Don't Bother to Knock*, "I'm anything you want me to be." Kate says to Binx, "if I marry you, will you tell me: Kate, this morning do such and such, and if we have to go to a party, will you tell me: Kate, stand right there and have three drinks and talk to so and so?" (197). Binx responds, "Sure"; nowhere, however, is it suggested what Kate may do for Binx. The intersubjectivity that the Percy critics writing in the seventies searched for in this relationship seems still a long way to come. Perhaps we could better realize it after having looked at Percy's definition of intersubjectivity, which is "that meeting of minds by which two selves take each other's meaning with reference to the same object beheld in common."[27] From what Percy allows through Binx's perspective, and of course there is no other perspective, we hardly know Kate has a mind. In the two crucial scenes towards the end of the novel, which establish Binx's position vis à vis the problem of faith, Kate proves her shallowness, lack of imagination and misapprehension of Binx's real motives. And since it seems that neither love nor sex is on the agenda (Binx proves sexually incompetent when faced with Kate's "not whorish bold but theorish bold" attempt to "seduce" him), the only way to approach this relationship is through Kierkegaard's "double movement": ethical choice and sacrifice. Where Sisyphus had the stone, Hester the scarlet letter, Binx has Kate.

It is worth noting in this context that Percy's first fictional attempt at articulating intersubjectivity surfaces in the marvellously sketched relationship between Binx and Lonnie Smith. Moreover, Binx fulfills his search through the cues he gets from Lonnie, who is the novel's sole embodiment of authenticity and faith. Lonnie incarnates the Kierkegaardian idea of the quester after the absolute *telos*, thus also exemplifying the concept of existential pathos with its inherent guilt, suffering, and repentance. But he is a figure only lightly sketched, and the novel focuses on Binx's efforts, with

Lonnie's aid, to reach the ultimate mode. Binx's only full-scale conversation with Lonnie demonstrates how the former transcends the ethical and enacts the leap of faith. Lonnie confesses to Binx his inability to "conquer an habitual disposition": the joy he derives at the death of his brother Duval. Lonnie asks Binx to face an ethical dilemma—namely, the sinfulness of rejoicing at another's death, but Binx shows his ability to transcend ethics when, in all seriousness, he says: "Why shouldn't you be [glad]? He sees God face to face and you don't" (163). In *The Moviegoer*, the only understanding between two human beings is conveyed in this scene, and the only true intersubjectivity takes place when Binx accepts Lonnie's offer of "communion":

> After I kiss him good-by, Lonnie calls me back. But he doesn't really have anything to say.
>
> "Wait."
>
> "What?"
>
> He searches the swamp, smiling.
>
> "Do you think that Eucharist—"
>
> "Yes?"
>
> He forgets and is obliged to say straight out: "I am still offering my communion for you."
>
> "I know you are."
>
> "Wait."
>
> "What?"
>
> "Do you love me?"
>
> "Yes."
>
> "How much?"
>
> "Quite a bit."
>
> "I love you too." (165)

The Epilogue reinforces the idea of communion while also reaccentuating Kate's ignorance of Binx's real motives. Like Sutter in *The Last Gentleman*, Binx demonstrates his maturity in the face of death. After he and Kate go to see Lonnie, who is dying in hospital, they discuss the fact of his death. Kate is terrified, and she reprimands Binx for what she considers his cold-bloodedness and what is, in fact, his seriousness and sincerity: what is terrifying to Binx is not Lonnie's inevitable death but what Percy has elsewhere called the "death in life." Kate also misunderstands the significance of another scene when Binx, with a frankness matching his previous conversation with Kate, attempts to explain the fact of Lonnie's death to his brothers and sisters, assuring the children that when they see Lonnie on the day of the Last Judgment, he will not be crippled:

> "He'll be like you."
> "You mean he'll be able to ski?" The children cock their heads and listen like old men.
> "Yes."
> "Hurray" cry the twins. . . (240)[28]

Kate's limited insight into the scene is revealed in her comment, "You were very sweet with them"; she entirely misses its larger import.

As the novel closes, Binx acts out his real calling of a "listener" and "counsellor" (233) as he "hands" Kate along on her journey downtown. Arguably, this final image harks back to the concluding part of *The Scarlet Letter*, specifically, to the image of Hester as a counsellor. Again, as in Hester's case, Binx's predicament is suggestive of the role Kierkegaard assigned to an "apostle," with its inherent faculty of listening to and passing of the message on to somebody who has not heard it. Both books conclude with an image of an essentially lonely figure, for both protagonists renounce the finite with hopes of gaining it back "by virtue of the absurd," as Kierkegaard says, and they live in a manner "commensurable" with this assumption. Hester's resumed intercourse with the Salem society and Binx's determination to "listen to people, . . . hand them along a ways in their dark journey," both suggest this idea.

At this stage several additional analogies between the two books become clear. Like Percy, Hawthorne was aware that the individual's actualization of spirit is to be fulfilled in the act of resignation. Immediacy, which Hawthorne's novel recasts as "daily custom" and Percy's as "everydayness," is to be renounced; immediacy as an end in itself is untenable. But both writers also emphasize that excessive resignation may lead to despair. An individual thus characterized departs from life in the sense that he becomes locked in the inwardness of self-reflection to the exclusion of all ties with actuality. Hawthorne makes this idea clear when he speaks about Hester's symbolic death, which he attributes to her departure from "passion and feeling to thought." Percy says of Binx that he has lived "solitary and in wonder, wondering day and night, never a moment without wonder" (42). Both books depict the leap of faith, the impact of which is misunderstood by the protagonists' partners: Dimmesdale and Kate. In both works, children create philosophical/theological foci: Pearl in *The Scarlet Letter* and Lonnie in *The Moviegoer*. Like Percy, Hawthorne has various fictive children fulfill this function, the most notable of them being Cyrus in "Roger Malvin's Burial" and Ilbrahim in "The Gentle Boy."

Most importantly, however, both writers—Hawthorne, with his nineteenth-century reticence and Percy, with his twentieth-century frankness—present a human predicament with its inherent dilemmas, a sense of obligations to others, and a continuous necessity for new beginnings. The last idea, it has been argued, is conveyed in *The Scarlet Letter* by Hawthorne's depiction of Hester's movement toward the absolute *telos*, which is an arduous process of becoming and, as such, involves a necessity for a "new birth" over and over again. It can be further claimed that both protagonists abandon their search: Binx, after his trip to Chicago and subsequent conversation with Emily, Hester when she leaves Salem with Pearl towards the end of the narrative. However, as Hawthorne reports,

"Hester Prynne had returned, and taken up her long-forsaken shame." "Shame" here is inseparable from the idea of guilt. Guilt, in turn, is an element of Hester's existential pathos, which has a structure of a movement with its inherent necessity for new beginnings. The Epilogue of *The Moviegoer* also clearly indicates that Binx has resumed his search.

In the final analysis, then, both books are in a sense open-ended. What each writer suggests is that resignation is not the sole gateway to the self-realization of spirit. Both books suggest that such a fulfillment can be realized in true intersubjectivity. Percy's hints at such a possibility are articulated in Binx's relationships with Lonnie and Kate, whereas Hawthorne envisages a "brighter period" in gender relations, the subject which he develops in his later novels. For both writers, such a solution will be ultimately born in "fear and trembling," to borrow Kierkegaard's phrase—that is to say, through crisis, which has its counterpart in Hawthorne's and Percy's craft of fiction.

NOTES

1. Especially illuminating in this context is Bradley R. Dewey's annotated interview, "Walker Percy Talks about Kierkegaard: An Annotated Interview," in *Conversations with Walker Percy*, ed. Lewis A. Lawson and Victor A. Kramer (Jackson: Univ. Press of Mississippi, 1985), pp. 101-29.

2. Walker Percy, *The Moviegoer* (New York: Alfred A. Knopf, 1960), p. 237. Page references are to this edition. Emphases in the quoted material are mine.

3. See John Carr, "An Interview with Walker Percy," *Conversations with Walker Percy*, pp. 64-65.

4. Lewis A. Lawson, "Walker Percy's Indirect Communication," *Texas Studies in Literature and Language* 11 (1969), p. 888, and Dewey, in *Conversations with Walker Percy*, pp. 101-129.

5. Martin Luschei, "*The Moviegoer* as Dissolve," in *The Art of Walker Percy. Stratagems for Being*, ed. Panthea Reid Broughton (Baton Rouge: Louisiana State Univ. Press, 1979), pp. 33-34.

6. Janet Hobbs, "Binx Bolling and the Stages on Life's Way," in *The Art of Walker Percy. Stratagems for Being*, p 43.

7. Tracy Kenyon Lischer, "Walker Percy's Kierkegaard," *The Cresset*, vol. XLI, no. 10 (1978), p. 10.

8. Sören Kierkegaard, *The Journals of Sören Kierkegaard*, trans. Alexander Dru (New York: Oxford Univ. Press, 1938), p. 468.

9. Dewey, in *Conversations with Walker Percy*, pp. 121-22.

10. See Blaise Pascal, *Pensées* (New York: Viking Penguin Inc., 1987), p. 245, for the discussion of the "self." See the same source (pp. 270-71) for the discussion of "être imaginaire" and "notre propre être."

11. Percy adopts Kierkegaard's concept with a twist, since in Kierkegaard's view "abstraction" is allied to the problem of guilt and repentance, i.e., existential pathos. Kierkegaard writes in *Concluding Unscientific Postscript* (trans. David F. Swenson and Walter Lowrie [Princeton: Princeton Univ. Press, 1941], p. 470):

> The more abstract the individual is, the less he is related to an eternal happiness, and the more remote he is from guilt; for abstraction assumes the indifference of existence, but guilt is the expression for the strongest self-assertion of existence.

12. Walker Percy, "Naming and Being," *Personalist* XLI (1960), pp. 153-54.

13. *Concluding Unscientific Postscript*, pp. 450-51.

14. Ibid., pp. 450-51.

15. For this insight see Wynstan Hugh Auden's introduction to *The Living Thoughts of Kierkegaard*, ed. Wynstan Hugh Auden (New York: David McKay Company, Inc., 1952), p. 18.

16. Luschei, in *The Art of Walker Percy. Stratagems for Being*, p. 29.

17. See Carr, in *Conversations with Walker Percy*, p. 66.

18. *A Kierkegaard Anthology*, ed. Robert Bretall (New York: The Modern Library, 1938), p. 136.

19. *The Living Thoughts of Kierkegaard*, p. 84.

20. Linda Whitney Hobson, *Understanding Walker Percy* (Columbia: Univ. of South Carolina Press, 1988), p. 29.

21. Wyatt Prunty, "Querns, Queries, and Quahogs: Walker Percy's Reviewers on Review," *The Georgia Review*, vol. XXXV, no. 1 (Spring 1981), p. 164.

22. *A Kierkegaard Anthology*, p. 119.

23. James Collins, *The Mind of Kierkegaard*, (Princeton: Princeton Univ. Press, 1983), p. 87.

24. Dewey, in *Conversations with Walker Percy*, p.119.

25. Toril Moi, *Sexual/Textual Politics: Feminist Literary Theory* (London and New York: Methuen & Co. Ltd, 1985), p. 92.

26. *A Kierkegaard Anthology*, p. 74.

27. Walker Percy, *The Message in the Bottle* (New York: Farrar, Straus, and Giroux, 1975), p. 265.

28. This scene is Percy's tribute to Dostoyevsky and, in particular, to a similar scene in *The Brothers Karamazov*. See Carr, in *Conversations with Walker Percy*, pp. 64-65.

PART II

CATHARSIS

Three: The Apocalyptic Vision

The House of the Seven Gables

Despite Hawthorne's acknowledged preference for his second romance, criticism has not dealt favorably with *The House of the Seven Gables*. Critics deem it the second best, after *The Scarlet Letter*, or even the third, after *The Scarlet Letter* and *The Marble Faun*. Almost invariably they criticize the book's happy ending which provides a resolution starkly at odds with the "moral" indicated in Hawthorne's Preface and voiced by several characters throughout the narrative:

> . . . the author has provided himself with a moral;—the truth, namely, that the wrong-doing of one generation lives into the successive ones, and, divesting itself of every temporary advantage, becomes a pure and uncontrollable mischief. (2: 2)

Such an unaccountable shift is, for example, Holgrave's transformation from an adherent of social reform, mid-way through the book, to a professed conservative, in the last chapter. Equally mystifying is the change of dwelling made by the focal group of characters (Clifford, Hepzibah, Phoebe, and Holgrave), who move from the cursed seat of the Pyncheon family to Jaffrey Pyncheon's comfortable countryside abode, apparently also purchased with "stained" money. Both developments seem incongruous with the book's doctrine. One should keep in mind, however, that Hawthorne, like Percy, refuses to adopt a standpoint that explicitly edifies the reader; he says that truth should be conveyed in "a far more subtile" way "than the ostensible one." The reading of *The House of the Seven Gables* proposed in this chapter will demonstrate how the book's apparent incongruities can be reconciled and how the ending reinforces the work's overall structure of apocalyptic imagery.

Northrop Frye, in his insightful *The Great Code. The Bible and Literature*, distinguishes two types of vision present in the biblical narrative: the apocalyptic (to Frye, ideal) vision and its parody, the demonic vision. Both *The House of the Seven Gables* and *Lancelot* lend themselves to a biblical exegesis *à la* Frye. Frye's schema supplies not only the philosophical and structural framework for a typological reading of the two texts, but also the conceptual terminology for pinpointing their differences: the overall vision of *The House of the Seven Gables* is primarily apocalyptic, whereas Percy, in *Lancelot*, prefers the demonic mode for the litarary incarnation of his vision. The demonic crosses the apocalyptic in Hawthorne's text when the author brings the narrative to its crisis and, like Percy in *Lancelot*, resolves tension through the application of the *cathartic* principle. Hawthorne's and Percy's "middle" texts serve as metonymies in what Peter Brooks calls the "signifying chain . . . the movement *toward* totalization under the mandate of desire."[1]

Frye's summary of the Bible begins with an analysis of the structure of its imagery, and it can be argued that this structure ideally corresponds to that in *The House of the Seven Gables*. The structure contains the images of sheep and pasture (pastoral but also paradisal, for in Frye's view the two overlap), of harvest and vintage (agricultural), of cities and temples (urban) and, finally, of what Frye perceives as "a human element." These images contribute to what Frye calls the apocalyptic world, that is, the ideal world, and he adds that this is the world which "the human creative imagination envisages, which human energy tries to bring into being, and which the Bible presents also as a form of 'revelation': the vision, the model, the blueprint that gives direction and purpose to man's energies."[2]

The very first depiction of the Pyncheon garden evokes the paradisal ideal: as Phoebe, on the morning following the day of her arrival at the seven-gabled house, looks out of the window, she first sees a rosebush which, against the background of a neglected and decaying garden, looks "as if it had been brought from Eden that very summer, together with the mold in which it grew" (2: 71). The garden, as it first appears in Phoebe's perception, can be compared to Eden, as it impressed the first dwellers, Adam and Eve. To stress the parallel, Hawthorne comments on the "species of flowers growing there in a wilderness of neglect, and obstructing one another's development . . . by their *uneducated* entanglement and confusion" (2: 73). The flowers, for all their uncultivated condition, "still sent a fresh and sweet incense up to their Creator" (2: 71). Appropriately, Hawthorne brings out the biblical analogy when he speaks of "the early sunshine—as fresh as that which peeped into Eve's bower while she and Adam sat at breakfast there." (2: 101). Much is made of this analogy throughout the narrative, with Phoebe assuming Eve's role and Holgrave playing Adam's part, though Clifford, obviously attracted to Phoebe, also likes to imagine himself as Adam.

The paradisal imagery overlaps with idealized pastoral imagery where divine order has its counterpart in an order achieved by human labor. Hawthorne evokes the idea of order in several chapters, and specifically in the chapter entitled "Maule's Well," which is devoted almost entirely to the depiction of the Pyncheon garden:

> Phoebe saw . . . that [the weeds'] growth must have been checked by a degree of careful labor, bestowed daily and systematically on the garden. The white double rose-bush had evidently been propped up anew against the house since the commencement of the season; and a pear tree and three damson trees . . . bore marks of the recent amputation of several superfluous or defective limbs. There were also a few species of antique and hereditary flowers . . . scrupulously weeded; as if some person, either out of love or curiosity, had been anxious to bring them to such perfection as they were capable of attaining. (2: 86-7)

The passage is followed by the introduction of the agricultural, or more precisely, horticultural imagery, which includes the "plebeian vegetables": squashes, cucumbers, string beans, tomatoes—so ripe and "gigantic" that they "promised an early and abundant harvest." "A pair of robins," bees, hens, chickens, even a Chanticleer, complete the pastoral picture of tranquil plenitude.

Two elements occupy a focal place in the paradisal imagery: trees and water. The description of the creation of trees in Genesis specifies fruit trees, the tree of life, and the tree of the knowledge of good and evil. Hawthorne's romance boasts not only fruit trees in the Pyncheon garden (see the above passage) but also the significantly capitalized Pyncheon Elm that grows in front of the house, "just on the edge of the unpaved sidewalk." That this tree has an important function in the overall iconography of the book is stressed through regular references to it in the narrative and particularly through its appearance at both the beginning and the end of the book. Frye argues that when Adam and Eve are expelled from paradise, they lose the tree and the water of life that are subsequently restored to redeem mankind at the end of the Bible. Thus the two images determine the beginning and the end of the biblical narrative. This structure ideally corresponds to the overall structure of *The House of the Seven Gables*. The image of water here is fairly uncomplicated, since Hawthorne tells us at the very outset that Matthew Maule built his hut by "a natural spring of soft and pleasant water," and when the Pyncheons stole his land as a site for their great house, "the spring above mentioned, entirely lost the deliciousness of its pristine quality." Consequently, Maule's Well, the name it has borne since then, is like the image of the Dead Sea, from what Frye calls the manifest demonic counterpart of the apocalyptic, or ideal, vision, for the Sea is "so full of salt that nothing can live in it or around it" (Frye, 146). In *The House of the Seven Gables*, the well is alleged to be "productive of intestinal mischief to those who quench their thirst there," and Holgrave warns Phoebe not to drink from its "bewitched" water. However, just as the Dead Sea is restored to its pristine condition in the biblical narrative, so, possibly, will be Maule's Well. Though Hawthorne establishes nothing definite in this respect the well's final appearance suggests such a possibility:

> Maule's Well, all this time, though left in solitude, was throwing up a succession of kaleidoscopic pictures, in which a gifted eye might have seen fore-shadowed the coming fortunes of Hepzibah, and Clifford, and the descendant of the legendary wizard, and the village maiden, over whom he had thrown love's web of sorcery. (2: 319)

Needless to say, "the coming fortunes" of the focal characters are foreshadowed in cheerful colors.

The tree of life and the tree of knowledge constitute, as Frye points out, the same image in the Bible, and it can be argued that both meanings cling to the Pyncheon Elm. In the biblical apocalypse, personified locusts symbolize evil spirits, an association vital for Hawthorne's novel, for towards the end of the narrative, following the storm and the corresponding crisis in the house, "singing" locusts swarm around the elm, which, upon their departure, whispers "unintelligible prophecies." The foreshadowing of the "coming fortunes" in Maule's Well and the whispering of the "unintelligible prophecies" belong to the same apocalyptic vision of the world that man lost but is eventually to regain and which, as Hawthorne implies, the book's characters will recapture.

The paradisal imagery of the Bible contains other elements which pertain to this analysis. The episode set in the kitchen of the seven-gabled house, on the morning following Phoebe's arrival in Salem, has its source in the Eucharistic rite: the sacrament's bread and wine summon up vegetable and animal worlds, the pastoral and the agricultural, which are united in the paradisal. As Frye says:

> In the Gospels harvest and vintage are frequently used as symbols of the apocalypse, and the Eucharist rite, identifying the bread and wine of the vegetable world with the body and blood of the animal world, and both with the body of Christ, is established at the beginning of the Passion. (Frye, 153)

In *The House of the Seven Gables*, Hawthorne combines the Eucharist rite with the Messianic Feast, since the breakfast Hepzibah and Phoebe concoct features Indian cake (bread) and "the finest mackerel" (fish). As Jessie Weston has underscored, the Christian Fish symbolism derived from Jewish beliefs, which, in turn, borrowed it from the Syrians. The Jewish Fish symbolism is based on the belief that, at the end of the world, Messiah will catch the sea monster Leviathan and divide its flesh to be eaten by the faithful.[3] The Messianic Feast became foreshadowed in the Jewish tradition of eating fish on Sabbath, transferred later to Friday—a custom observed to this day in Catholicism. Frye makes much of this symbolism in his analysis of the biblical narrative, and, most importantly, he associates Leviathan with chaos ("king over all the children of pride" [Job 41:34]). He thus sees it as symbolizing the evil of the subterranean world (hell), noting that medieval paintings present Christ's harrowing of hell as the descent into the throat of a large monster. Tropically, Christ's redemption of the subterranean world corresponds to his redemption of the world above, thus exemplifying the idea of *catharsis* (katados—down-going, anodos —up-coming). This mythical structure harks back to the ancient Egyptian myth, whereby a sun-god descends every night into the kingdom of darkness and, having fought his way through it, victoriously arises the next morning. It can be argued that this idea is exemplified in *The House of the Seven Gables*, and one of its representations is signalled by Phoebe's name. Hugo McPherson has argued that Holgrave represents "the young moon hero" and Phoebe "the cheerful young sun maiden."[4] Certainly, the etymology of the word "phoebe" provides illuminating details. First of all, the word signifies a small bird (also called pewit or pewee), and Hawthorne's playful handling of this meaning is evidenced in his initial depiction of Phoebe as a little twittering bird. More importantly, however, in Greek mythology, the name "Phoebe," which is the feminine of "Phoebus," derived from "phoibos" (bright) signifies a moon goddess (Artemis and Diana in Roman mythology). The masculine counterpart, "Phoebus," is Apollo, god of the sun in Greek mythology. Inherent in the name is therefore the concept of descent into darkness and ascent into the light. Thus the choice of the heroine's name points to the pivotal role of *catharsis* in Hawthorne's text and, by extension, to the apocalyptic vision it embraces.

The urban imagery of the Bible consists primarily of phenomena associated with temples, highways, and roads. Hawthorne draws on a similar fund of city imagery as Clifford watches the busy street, and registers the changes that were introduced during his imprisonment: a cab, an omnibus, and the railroad. Especially the last invention plays an important role in Hawthorne's urban imagery, since one of the most illuminating chapters ("The Flight of Two Owls") describes Clifford and Hepzibah's train ride. In the biblical narrative, however, the central image of the city is the temple, which Hawthorne's romance recasts in the form of the seven-gabled house. Hawthorne's imagery is mixed here, partaking of elements from both the apocalyptic vision and its demonic counterpart. In the apocalyptic vision, Jerusalem was founded on a hill with its temple symbolically reaching heaven; Jerusalem's demonic variant is not only the Tower of Babel but also the seven hills of Rome, the seat of the Great Whore of Babylon who is the mistress of Antichrist. The distinguishing features of height and centrality, in Hawthorne's book, are attributed to the seven gables: "On every side, the seven gables pointed sharply to the sky," and, "There it rose, a little withdrawn from the line of the street, but in pride, not modesty" (2: 11). Hawthorne proceeds to parody the religious dimension of the house:

> Maule's Lane—or Pyncheon Street, as it were now more decorous to call it—was thronged, at the appointed hour, as with a congregation on its way to *church*. All, as they approached, looked upward at the imposing edifice, which was henceforth to assume its rank among the habitations of mankind. (2: 11)

Etymologically, the word "edifice" derives from the Latin "aedes" or "aedis," which means building or temple, and "ficare" or "facere," which means "to make"; thus the two components combined suggest the making of a building or a temple, which lends a parodic cast to the seven-gabled house.

According to Frye, in urban imagery cities tend to be tropically conceived as female, as conveyed by the very word "metropolis" (mother city). Hawthorne speaks of the seven-gabled house as "a whole sisterhood of edifices, breathing through the spiracles of one great chimney" (2: 11). In the sexual imagery of the Bible, Frye reminds us, "the relation of male to female is expressed in two ways, depending on whether the two bodies or only the sexual organs are taken as the basis. In one, the male is above and the female below; in the other, the male is at the center and the female surrounds him" (Frye, 156). Thus, in Hawthorne's text, the phallic chimney is surrounded by the "sisterhood of edifices," the significance of which can be explained when we look for the meaning of the word "Hepzibah." In Isaiah (62:4) we have the following passage:

> No more shall men call you Forsaken,
> no more shall your land be called desolate
> but you shall be named Hephzi-bah (that is, My delight in her)
> and your land Beulah (that is, Wedded);
> for the Lord delights in you
> and to him your land is wedded.
> For, as a young man weds a maiden,
> so you shall wed him who rebuilds you,
> and your God shall rejoice over you
> as a bridegroom rejoices over the bride.

The imagery is that of the land married to its ruler, as Hephzibah and Beulah merge in the meaning of the land itself. The demonic counterpart of the Bride and the Bridegroom (to Frye, the human elements of the Bible) is represented by the Great Whore of Babylon, the mistress of Antichrist, who sits on the seven hills of Rome. But Frye points out that the figure of the "forgiven harlot" represents "an intermediate bridal figure between the demonic Whore and the apocalyptic Bride" (Frye, 141), signifying the forgiveness of sin through love. In that connection we should remember that Hepzibah is given a life estate in the seven-gabled house, which is often personified, and whose decay is mirrored in the description of Hepzibah's physical appearance.[5] One can argue, therefore, that Hepzibah is tropically conceived as the "sisterhood of edifices." The focus of Hepzibah's cosmos is her brother Clifford. The "great chimney" thus figures as the proximity of a male organ, in the sense Jacques Lacan uses the term "phallus": as a simulacrum. Lacan also indicates that the anxiety of castration (the discovery that the mother lacks a penis) makes the phallic function into a symbolic function, thus detaching the subject from its dependence on the mother.[6] An analysis of Hepzibah and Clifford's relationship reveals interesting details in this context, for not only does Hepzibah "mother" Clifford, but her feelings for her brother contain a strong sexual component.

In his characterization of Hepzibah, Hawthorne does not follow any of the two notorious female stereotypes; she is neither a Fair Maiden nor a Dark Lady. In their recent discussions of *The House of the Seven Gables*, Joyce W. Warren and Leland S. Person, both of whom, incidentally, reach similar conclusions on Hawthorne's feminine types, significantly exclude Hepzibah from their analyses.[7] The point importantly raised by these critics is that Hawthorne's letters written to Sophia during their courtship testify to both "spiritual" and "earthly" attraction to frail invalid Sophia. The repeated distinction between "the Dove" and "naughty Sophie" went, they further argue, into the presentation of Hawthorne's antithetical feminine types. Of course, Hepzibah is neither a woman to be sexually cherished nor the one to be worshipped unreservedly. She is thus the object of neither sexual nor marital desire, both of whom are conveyed antithetically in Hawthorne's fiction.

Furthermore, Clifford and Hepzibah form an androgynous double of sorts. In the humorous scene at the beginning of the novel, depicting Hepzibah's careful toilette, the purpose of which is to make herself becoming to Clifford, she pulls out of her bureau drawer a miniature of her brother and examines it affectionately. Revealed in it are Clifford's "full, tender lips" and "beautiful eyes, that seem to indicate . . . gentle and voluptuous emotion" (2: 32). On the other hand, Hepzibah's features are not so much masculine as overtly unattractive ("gaunt, sallow, rusty-jointed maiden"). In the scene where Hepzibah complains to Holgrave about the "indelicacy" of her profession as a shop-keeper and Holgrave attempts to comfort her, his words elicit Hepzibah's miserable reply: "But I am a woman! . . . I was going to say, a lady,—but I consider that as past" (2: 44). Though Hawthorne reserved critical comments about professional, or public, women mostly to his contemporary "scribbling" women, he here seems to summon the specter of the "lady capitalist," a woman out of her sphere.[8] Hepzibah, a true "agoraphobe" and only forced by circumstances to become *femina economica*, the role she evidently abhors, feels compelled to emphasize that she, indeed, *is* a woman.

Though Hawthorne circumscribes both focal females in *The House of the Seven Gables* in domesticity (this nineteenth-century antidote to commercialism), it cannot prevent us from seeing both women and, as I shall argue, *all* women in the novels considered here, as anything but frail and helpless. Phoebe is a good case in point.

When he first introduces Phoebe at the end of Chapter IV, Hawthorne evokes her freshness and "unconventionality," as a country girl newly arrived in the town of Salem. The second attribute is germane to the overall image of Phoebe's simplicity and innocence, rather than a comment suggesting her personal sovereignty, for Hawthorne hastily adds that she is "orderly and obedient to common rules." Clearly posited as a contrast to Hester, who is a fully developed woman, queenly in demeanor, Phoebe has a slight figure that "would hardly have suited one's idea of a countess," and a grace like that of a bird. Their backgrounds likewise differ; we have allusions to blue blood running in Hester's veins, to her powerful ancestors and careful upbringing, whereas Phoebe is a country girl, and the implication is that her family has not taken proper care of her. Where Hester excels in the art of embroidery, Phoebe's sphere of activity is the kitchen and "the scouring of pots and kettles." Hepzibah, having acknowledged her cousin's simple charm, sighs longingly, "If she could only be a lady, too!—but that's impossible! Phoebe is no Pyncheon. She takes everything from her mother!" (2: 79). Hawthorne pointedly dismisses Hepzibah's remark as irrelevant, observing that the question of whether Phoebe is a lady or not could hardly arise in "any fair and healthy mind." He concludes with the following judgment:

> Instead of discusssing her claim to rank among ladies, it would be preferable to regard Phoebe as the example of feminine grace and availability combined, in a state of society, if there were any such, where ladies did not exist. (2: 80)

Having expressed this progressive view, however, Hawthorne paradoxically dispatches Phoebe to her household tasks which, moreover, she should perform in an "atmosphere of loveliness and joy." This, and other remarks of this kind, support Louise DeSalvo's argument that Hawthorne allows Phoebe to be exploited in the book not only by men (Holgrave and Clifford) but also by Hepzibah who, as a woman of privilege, relies on Phoebe to do her work for her. Consequently, the book strikes DeSalvo as "the romance of housework," and can be read as "the forerunner of American television commercials in which women sing and smile as they scrub floors and wash their husbands' shirts." In a word, DeSalvo deems *The House of the Seven Gables* as good an example of misogyny as any one can find.[9]

Hawthorne's characterization of Phobe seems to be offensive not only to feminist readers. For instance, Agnes M. Donohue, in her commentary on Phoebe, multiplies pejorative epithets, calling her "witless but sunny," "uncomprehending," "unreal," "unbelievable," and so on.[10] Donohue uses some of the same epithets in her analysis of Hilda in *The Marble Faun*. It seems that grouping women in Hawthorne's fiction under stereotypes prevents us from viewing them as separate identities. Paradoxically, for instance, if we abstract the attributes Nina Baym uses to describe Hawthorne's allegedly dark type—the women, that is, with whom Hawthorne's males resist forming permanent relationships ("warmth, imagination, intuition, and love"[11])—from their context, they can be used as successfully to depict Hester as, indeed, Phoebe. For speaking of Phoebe we must acknowledge her skill at handling such eccentrics as Hepzibah and Clifford, her intuitive grasp of Jaffrey Pyncheon's character, and her ability to attract the interest of the individualist Holgrave. Moreover, Phoebe's decision to make her living as a housekeeper and shop assistant to Hepzibah, read by DeSalvo as merely her shrewdness ("a strategy to keep her from starving"), evidences her control over her life and, in a sense, her ambition for social promotion. Person has noted that Sophia's resistance to type surfaces in Hawthorne's characterization of several females in his fiction. Phoebe is no exception. As she matures in the novel, having inhaled the quaint atmosphere of the seven-gabled house, she becomes "less girlish" but "more womanly," and Hawthorne registers the following change in her physical appearance: "Her eyes looked larger, and darker, and deeper; so deep, at some silent moments, that they seemed like Artesian wells, down, down, into the infinite" (2: 175). She, in effect, becomes, as Person points out, "a dark lady in disguise."

The characterization of Hepzibah creates a different problem. In the scene where she muses over the miniature of Clifford, Hawthorne poses an interesting question: "Can it have been an early lover of Miss Hepzibah? No; she never had a lover—poor thing, how could she?—nor even knew, by her own experience, what love technically means" (2: 32). The question that suggests itself at this point is not only why Hepzibah never had a lover but why Hawthorne says she "could not." Not that she has always been physically unattractive; Hawthorne, in fact, attributes her physical decline to age and bitterness connected with Clifford's imprisonment. And, then, we see her face glow to near-beauty when love for Clifford is written plainly on it: "But at the indistinct murmur of his words, her whole face grew tender, and even lovely, with sorrowful affection; the harshness of her features disappeared, as it were, behind the warm and misty glow" (2: 106) Even her voice, otherwise described as "a kind of croak," had "really exquisite melody thrilling through it." Evidence that Hepzibah declined physically and acquired her notorious scowl during Clifford's absence is provided in his tactless reaction on their first encounter: "How changed! How changed! And is she angry with me? Why does she bend her brow so?" (2: 106). What the text suggests is that Hepzibah kept herself "pure" (and single) for Clifford, who has been "the only substance for her to feed upon." That Hepzibah's feelings for Clifford contain a strong sexual component surfaces in a mock-wedding scene, in which Hepzibah gives free reign to her fantasies: "She yearned to take [Clifford] by the hand, and go and kneel down, they two together" (2: 168). In an attempt to play out her fantasy, Hepzibah induces Clifford to go to church with her. They put on their Sunday best and are about to leave the house when they are stopped, not only by "mankind's great and terrible eye," but also by "the eye of the Father [which] seemed to be withdrawn, and gave them no encouragement" (2: 169).

No one can deny that, given Hawthorne's inborn reticence and the taboos of the time, *The House of the Seven Gables* reverberates with sexual overtones that claim the reader's interpretative attention. Clifford's sensual perception of Phoebe's physical appearance serves as one of several instances. Clifford, who fits the persona of Kierkegaard's aesthetic man, a "would-be" seducer ("it seemed Clifford's nature to be a Sybarite"), takes note of Phoebe's feminine charm:

> He was a man, it is true, and recognized her as a woman. She was his only representative of womankind. He took unfailing note of every charm that appertained to her sex, and saw the ripeness of her lips, and the virginal development of her bosom. All her little womanly ways, budding out of her like blossoms on a young fruit tree, had their effect on him, and sometimes caused his very heart to tingle with the keenest thrills of pleasure. (2: 141)

Clifford regrets the discrepancy of years "from his birthday to hers," and concludes that it is now "too late" for the "cup of passionate love."

Another reference to sex is provided in the implication of sexual abuse in Judge Pyncheon's abortive marriage. Hawthorne suggests this issue in the comment that the Judge's wife "got her death-blow in the honey-moon, and never smiled again," though he hastily adds that it was because "her husband compelled her to serve him with coffee, every morning at his bedside," in token of loyalty to "her liege-lord and master" (2: 123). The Judge's Puritan ancestor, Colonel Pyncheon, whose appearance and character are remarkably similar to the Judge's, "had worn out three wives," with sexual violence strongly implied in the explanation that his remorseless "weight and hardness . . . in the conjugal relations" drove all three of them to their early graves. Finally, Holgrave's interpolated narrative symbolically depicts sexual abuse in Alice Pyncheon's masochistic submission to Matthew Maule: as long as Alice lived,

> she was Maule's slave, in a bondage more humiliating . . . than that which binds its chain around the body. . . . Maule had but to wave his hand. . . . She felt herself too much abased, and longed to change natures with some worm! (2: 208-09)

The "last humiliation" of this kind sends Alice to her grave.

Likewise, in Clifford's relationship with Hepzibah as much is overtly stated as implied. At one point in the narrative, Hepzibah contrasts the phallocentric features of her ancestor—and cousin Jaffrey, who is consistently presented as a version of the powerful patriarch—with Clifford's "feminine traits, moulded inseparably with those of the other sex!" The "epicene utopia," to borrow a phrase from Jane Gallop, suggested here becomes resolved in Hepzibah's insight that Clifford resembles his mother, "and she, a lovely and lovable woman, with perhaps some beautiful infirmity of character, that made it all the pleasanter to know, and easier to love her" (2: 60). Moreover, Hawthorne suggests throughout the narrative that Clifford acts and thinks like a child. Having first introduced Clifford as "a child journeying across a floor" (2:104), Hawthorne pursues this analogy at various junctures in the narrative. He says, for instance, that Clifford "was a child,—a child for the whole term of his existence, be it long or short" (2: 148). By further commenting on Clifford's melancholic nature, Hawthorne in effect evokes the Freudian insight that melancholy (Freud's "homesickness") is a longing for a return to that lost homeland of the mother's womb[12] —something Hawthorne may have experienced after Robert Manning took him away from his mother. Gallop reads melancholy as a regret "for something elapsed or for what one has not experienced,"[13] both meanings inherent in Hawthorne's presentation of Clifford. He yearns, it seems, to return to the pre-Oedipal, or pre-phallic, stage that is prior to what Lacan, after Freud, calls "the castration complex in the masculine unconscious." In the Freudian *mythos* of a male child, the Oedipal conflict is caused by the boy's belief that his mother has been castrated by his father, who will also castrate him if he reveals his desires. As Gallop points out, both Lacan and Kristeva elaborate on this minimal clarification, indicating that the phantom of the "phallic mother" represents a threat equal to that of the Primitive Father (in fact, Kristeva suggests that the Primitive Father is "more obvious than the phallic mother and, in a sense, less dangerous").[14] Thus, Gallop concludes, "Mother must be expelled from the innocent, non-phallic paradise." Even though, or, perhaps paradoxically, for the reason that Gallop explores the feminine *mythos*, her analysis pertains to Clifford's situation, for not only is he Hawthorne's most effeminate "male" character, but also Hepzibah's attempts at mothering him, emphasized throughout the narrative, meet with steadfast rejection.

According to Freud, the energy generated in the repression of the male child's desire must be invested into other, more socially acceptable activity. In "The Arched Window," one of the most illuminating chapters of *The House of the Seven Gables,* we witness Clifford's attempt to jump out of the window. Hawthorne explains that Clifford

> needed a shock; or perhaps he required to take a deep, deep plunge into the ocean of human life, and to *sink down* and be covered by its profoundness, and then to *emerge,* sobered, invigorated, restored to the world and to himself. (2: 166)

This passage expresses, in clear terms, not only the basic meaning of *catharsis* ("sink down"—*kathados,* "emerge"—*anodos*), which is one of the book's most important themes, but also a possiblility of Clifford's attainment of adulthood. We will now follow both narrative threads in the order they are conveyed.

Cartharsis is essentially a medical metaphor or, rather, a medical term metaphorically employed by Aristotle in his definition of tragedy.[15] The concept has also been used in reference to a psychotherapeutic method (though is no longer referred to by that name) ever since Breuer and Freud first practiced it (and described in *Studies on Hysteria* [1893]) in the treatment of hysterical patients. The patient was persuaded, under hypnosis, to relive, or at very least remember, the circumstances (what Breuer and Freud call "affect") under which the hysterical symptoms originated and to verbalize or act out the repressed traumatic experience. "*Catharsis,*" says Freud "came about when the path to consciousness was opened and there was a normal discharge of affect."[16] Freud did not use the term in his subsequent works, but, as James Strachey writes in his introduction to *Studies on Hysteria,* he did employ his (and Breuer's) earlier findings in, for instance, *Beyond the Pleasure Principle* (1920). Freud's revolutionary theory in *Beyond the Pleasure Principle,* which inspired Peter Brooks' model of traditional narrative, resonates with the jargon that was first used to describe the *cathartic* method. Let us compare two passages from Breuer's part of *Studies on Hysteria* and *Beyond the Pleasure Principle*, respectively:

> Such feelings ["unpleasure"] are always generated when one of the organism's needs fails to find satisfaction. Since these feelings disappear when the surplus quantity of energy which has been liberated is employed functionally, we may conclude that the removal of such surplus excitation is a need of the organism. And here for the first time we meet the fact that there exists in the organism a '*tendency to keep intracerebral excitation constant* [Freud's insertion]'[17]

> The pleasure principle . . . is a tendency operating in the service of a function whose business it is to free the mental apparatus entirely from excitation or *to keep the amount of excitation in it constant* or to keep it as low as possible [emphasis added].[18]

Athough *catharsis* as a therapeutic method was induced by the therapist (Freud relinquished the method in the conviction that it enforced the patient's dependence on the therapist), and the pleasure mechanism is instinctual, the principle remains the same. Significantly, Freud uses the term "discharge of affect," which Brooks painstakingly employs in drawing parallels between the resolution of narratives and the climax of (masculine) sexual pleasure, in reference to both the *cathartic* method and the pleasure principle. It appears, however, that *catharsis*, with its sexually suggestive etymology, can be employed as effectively as the pleasure principle in the capacity of an intertextual link of the kind sought by Brooks to narrative fictions; indeed, it was written into literary theory twenty three centuries ago.

Nevertheless, Brooks' model seems to be invaluable where it unveils the relationship between textual "middles" and the ends of narratives. The middle, says Brooks, "the space of retard, postponement, error, and partial revelation—is the place of transformation: where the problems posed to and by initiatory desire are worked out and worked through."[19] I have already suggested that Brooks' model illuminates not so much individual texts discussed in this study as rather sequences of Hawthorne's and Percy's novels. The books discussed in the final section of this study (*The Marble Faun* and *The Second Coming*) "double back," in Brooks' words, or return to the "middle" novels (*The House of the Seven Gables* and *Lancelot*) by repeating the scenes that served there as only "partial revelation" and provide the total revelation, or what Aristotle called *anagnorisis*.

Freud discusses this phenomenon of compulsive repetition in his essay "The Uncanny" and says that "an uncanny experience occurs either when infantile complexes which have been repressed are once more revived by some impression, or when primitive beliefs which have been surmounted seem once more to be confirmed."[20] He also adds that the distinction between the two (primitive beliefs and infantile complexes) is often a "hazy one." Freud does not explain at this point what he means by "primitive beliefs" or, for that matter, by "infantile complexes," though we may surmise that the latter signify the Oedipus complex. In "Preface to Reik's *Ritual: Psycho-Analytic Studies*," however, he suggests that we might benefit from the "study of prehistory" in trying to trace the Oedipus complex. He proceeds to root the Oedipus complex, with its desire to "eliminate the father," in the archetype of archetypes—"namely, that God the Father once walked upon earth in bodily form and exercised his sovereignty as chieftain of the primal human horde until his sons united to slay him."[21]

The two Freudian concepts merge in René Girard's discussion of what he calls the "monstrous double." Girard's analysis will receive due emphasis in the discussion of the Donatello-Miriam--Model "triangle" in *The Marble Faun*. But it should be, if only summarily, outlined here, for not only does Hawthorne prepare for his powerful scene of the murder of the Model, the scene that can be read, after Girard, as ritual *catharsis*, in Jaffrey Pyncheon's mysterious death in *The House of the Seven Gables*, but *catharsis* brings about the transformation of the central male characters (Clifford and Donatello) in both texts.

According to Girard, ritual *catharsis* presupposes the existence of a single ritual victim, whose duality and monstrosity manifest themselves in both human and animal characteristics (Freud reports that the castration anxiety frequently manifests itself in a fear of the wolf). The monstrous double not only comes from outside the community, but also makes his appearance "at the height of the crisis, just before the unanimous resolution." The monstrous doubles in Hawthorne's texts (Jaffrey in *The House of the Seven Gables* and the Model in *The Marble Faun*) both come from outside the narrative community, and their respective intrusions culminate in the crisis. In order to make the ritual sacrifice palpable, it is indispensable for the artist, says Girard,

> to cultivate the future victim's supposed potential for evil, to transform him into a monster of iniquity—not for esthetic reasons, but to enable him to polarize, to literally draw to himself, all the infectious strains in the community and transform them into sources of peace and fecundity.[22]

Hawthorne's presentation of Jaffrey Pyncheon fulfills just such a function in the narrative of *The House of the Seven Gables*. The Judge makes only two appearances in the novel: the first time when he makes his acquaintance with Phoebe, who instinctively recoils from his embrace, and, the second, just before his death, when he talks to Hepzibah. In both episodes, Hawthorne surrounds him with a host of negative attributes, emphasizing "massive accumulation of animal substance about the lower region of his face," that has an "unctuous, rather than spiritual" (2: 116) look. Subsequent details reinforce his "animal" aspect: "animal substance" becomes "animal form," then "animal development." Hawthorne observes that the Judge's "Creator made him a great animal, but the dinner-hour made him a great *beast*" (2: 275), and makes explicit the import of his reiteration when he finally reveals that the remarkable affinity between the Judge and his cursed ancestor was "a kind of prophecy":

> It implied that the weaknesses and defects, the bad passions, the mean tendencies, and the moral diseases which lead to crime, are handed down from one generation to another, by a far surer process of transmission than human law has been able to establish, in respect to the riches and honors which it seeks to entail upon posterity. (2: 119)

This repeated stress on the epithet "animal" figuratively transforms the Judge into the beast (Leviathan) of the demonic parody of the apocalyptic vision. He incarnates the evil of the past, whose weight upon the present must be purged, so that the original state of innocence can be restored in the future, and everything, in Hawthorne's words, will "begin anew." Holgrave's conversation with Phoebe, in the chapter "The Daguerrotypist," addresses precisely this issue of a new beginning which can eventuate only with the *cathartic* jettisoning of the past:

> "Shall we never, never get rid of this Past?" cried he, keeping up the earnest tone of his preceding conversation.— "It lies upon the Present like a giant's dead body! In fact, the case is just as if a young giant were compelled to waste all his strength in carrying about the corpse of the old giant, his grandfather, who died a long while ago, and only needs to be decently buried." (2: 182-83)

If we try to imagine what the iconography of the latter part of this passage communicates, we, in fact, get the image of the "shapeless mass" introduced in *The Marble Faun*. In the scene when Miriam's party visits the Fountain of Trevi, Miriam bends over the basin and sees "three separate shadows, all so black and heavy that they sink into the water." Miriam recognizes the right-hand shadow as Donatello. The left-hand shadow puzzles her; it is "a *shapeless mass*, as indistinct as the premonition of calamity" (4: 145). It is, of course, the Model, who incarnates the evil of the past whose weight upon the present must be destroyed. To anticipate the discussion of the next chapter, Percy's *Lancelot* likewise offers a parallel image, the "looming shape" as "the strangest of beasts." In all three texts, the encounter with apocalypse involves the killing of the beast. The obliteration of the physical frame, characteristic of the monstrous double, is made explicit in Hawthorne's reference to the Judge's corpse in *The House of the Seven Gables*:

> . . . so heavy and lumpish that we can liken him to nothing better than a defunct nightmare, which had perished in the midst of its wickedness, and left its flabby corpse on the breast of the tormented one, to be gotten rid of as it might! (2: 252).

This passage underlies Holgrave's typography of the two bodies horizontally resting: one (the Past) on the other (the Present), and the next such image is connected with the overall imagery of chaos:

> The features are all gone; there is only the paleness of them left. And how looks it now? . . . There is no face! An infinite, inscrutable blackness has annihilated sight! Where is our universe? All crumbled away from us; and we, adrift in chaos, may hearken to the gusts of homeless wind, that go sighing and murmuring about, in quest of what was once a world! (2: 276-77)

Frye's table of demonic imagery identifies the Dragons of Chaos (Leviathan, Rahab, etc.) as the manifest demonic principle. In both *The House of the Seven Gables* and *Lancelot*, the killing of the beast in accompanied by a storm, the prototype of which is to be found in the description of chaos in Revelation.

The seven-gabled house is spared in Hawthorne's one nostalgic impulse. With the exception of one "ruinous" portal, the house remains intact, though Hawthorne mentions that the storm affects its foundations, and it shakes and "creaks." As the storm subsides, Hawthorne's fictive universe is restored to its pristine condition. Although the locusts, the only remnants of the demonic imagery, linger for a while in the Pyncheon Elm, the book closes, as does the biblical text, with the imagery of the exorcised tree and water of life, and with the agricultural and pastoral (hence paradisal) elements of the apocalyptic (ideal) vision. In Clifford's words, "And so the flower of Eden has bloomed . . . in this old, darksome house, today" (2: 308).

Even though, when viewed from this single perspective, the book appears to be little more than the major biblical narrative rewritten, the restoration of balance and harmony at its end suggests Hawthorne's coming to grips with gender roles and identities so painstakingly researched there. The *cathartic* principle Hawthorne applies to resolve the tensions inherent in the narrative is, among other things, also effective in conveying Clifford's successful achievement of manhood. In the scene already discussed when mother/wife/sister Hepzibah adoringly evokes Clifford's "feminine traits," she expresses an especially illuminating opinion by saying that "they persecuted his mother in him! He never was a Pyncheon." The "they" she refers to are the two Pyncheon patriarchs: Colonel and Judge. Clifford, it seems, is not only "threatened" with loss (Lacanian "castration complex") but virtually "deprived" (note that "deprivation," in Lacanian terms, concerns the woman). Hawthorne notes that Clifford is incapable of forming relationships with women because his "images of women had more and more lost their warmth and substance, and been frozen, like the pictures of secluded artists, into the chillest ideality" (2: 140).

I am hardly the first to suggest the incestuous relations in *The House of the Seven Gables*. Allan Lloyd-Smith, for instance, has recently argued that Hepzibah and Clifford are the "parents in the fantasy family"—parents, that is, to Phoebe and Holgrave.[23] I contend, however, that Clifford can hardly serve as a model of a paternal figure, since he is consistently presented a child. The text makes it clear, however, that we have such a model in Jaffrey.[24] During his first conversation with Hepzibah, Jaffrey proposes that the four inhabitants of the seven-gabled house move to his elegant countryside abode. He pleads with Hepzibah: "And you and I, dear Hepzibah, will consult together, and watch together, and labor together, to make our dear Clifford happy" (2: 128). What Jaffrey proposes in effect is that he and Hepzibah substitute for the natural parents of Clifford, the child. Furthermore, Hawthorne's characterization of Clifford admixes both masculine and feminine traits. It thus seems that his path to maturity involves the transcendence of the stage of paternal identification, identification which, as Girard observes, need not be determined by parentage, for "the child can select as model any man who happens to fill the role that our society normally assigns to the natural father."[25] Such identification, in Freudian terms, results in the sexual cathexis toward the mother. At this point in Girard's discussion, the theory of the monstrous double (Freud's "primitive belief") and the Oedipus complex merge, for the process of paternal identification (Girard's "mimetic rivalry") inevitably leads to violence. When Hawthorne says that Clifford "needed a shock," he implies, quite paradoxically in fact, that Clifford must subvert phallocentrism that confined him to the feminine sphere.

Whether Clifford contributes to Jaffrey's death, as Frederick Crews cannily observes,[26] or only sees Jaffrey dead, what we have here is Hawthorne's first attempt at articulating the theory of *felix culpa*, the theory that is used as a rationale for the murder of the

Model in *The Marble Faun* and that underlies Lance's quest in Percy's *Lancelot*. During the train ride with Hepzibah, Clifford says that "murderers . . . are often excusable in the motives of their deed, and deserve to be ranked among public benefactors, if we consider only the *result*" (2: 265). In the same chapter ("The Flight of Two Owls"), Hawthorne reports that Clifford's process of maturation has been accomplished:

> Thus it happened, that the relation heretofore existing between her brother and herself was changed. At home, she was his guardian; here, Clifford had become hers, and seemed to comprehend whatever belonged to their new position, with a singular rapidity of intelligence. He had been startled into manhood and intellectual vigor. (2: 258)

The achievement of this generic balance and Hawthorne's unmasking and vehement criticism of phallocentrism *en route* to it, may still leave readers of *The House of the Seven Gables* with an unsatisfied need for a woman more to the taste of the twentieth-century audience. Such readers will unanimously argue that Phoebe, as the New Eve to her New Adam (Holgrave), can hardly fulfill our hopes aroused at the end of *The Scarlet Letter*. Hawthorne seems to make matters even worse by anticipating the Hemingwayan model of marriage, in which man, in Holgrave's words, will "set out trees," "make fences" and "build a house for another generation," and woman, the line of reasoning goes, will gracefully perform traditional feminine tasks. Their relationship, conceived to fulfill a conservative ideal, bears none of the promises contained in Hawthorne's prophecy at the conclusion of *The Scarlet Letter*. Even if Hawthorne, lurking here behind Hester's thoughts, suggests a possibility of relationships between equal individuals, in *The House of the Seven Gables* he not only articulates a conventional image of the woman's role but also bitterly criticises woman's aspiration to any other (more public) role. However, Hester's thoughts suggest virtually nothing by way of gender roles *per se*. She in fact only vaguely describes the "angel and apostle of the coming revelation" as a female "lofty, pure, and beautiful," but also, as further text implies, cheerful and loving. Even if Phoebe's simplicity does not qualify her as "lofty," she nevertheless fulfills the other characteristics.

Where *The House of the Seven Gables* really demonstrates a deficiency is in Hawthorne's lack of insight into Phoebe/Holgrave relationship. Hawthorne seems to be too much preoccupied with Clifford's maturation process and, obliquely, with an attempt at getting even with his sinful ancestors through art, to provide any psychological depth to the formation of that relationship and to Phoebe and Holgrave's decision for a life together. Holgrave's marriage proposal and Phoebe's acceptance is as much of a hocus-pocus resolution as is the overall happy ending of the novel and can be read only within its entirely allegorical frame of reference. It is not until *The Marble Faun* that Hawthorne's full concentration falls on relationships between men and women.

NOTES

1. Peter Brooks, *Reading for the Plot. Design and Intention in Narrative* (New York: Alfred A. Knopf, 1984), p. 91.

2. Northrop Frye, *The Great Code. The Bible and Literature* (San Diego: Harcourt Brace Jovanovich, Publishers, 1982), pp. 139-40. Hereafter, references to this work will be placed in the text after the entry "Frye."

3. Jessie L. Weston, *From Ritual to Romance* (New York: Doubleday Anchor Books, 1957), p. 128.

4. Hugo McPherson, *Hawthorne as Mythmaker* (Toronto: Univ. of Toronto Press, 1969), p. 28.

5. "The aspect of the venerable mansion has always affected me like a human countenance, bearing the traces not merely of outward storm and sunshine, but expressive also, of the long lapse of mortal life, and accom-

panying vicissitudes, that have passed within" (2:19). Note a similar correspondence between the house and its proprietor in Poe's "The Fall of the House of Usher."

6. See Jacques Lacan, *Écrits. A Selection*, trans. Alan Sheridan (New York: W. W. Norton and Company, Inc., 1977), p. 289.

7. See Leland S. Person, Jr., *Aesthetic Headaches. Women and a Masculine Poetics in Poe, Melville, and Hawthorne* (Athens and London: Univ. of Georgia Press, 1988), pp. 94-121; and Joyce W. Warren, *The American Narcissus: Individualism and Women in Nineteenth-Century American Fiction* (New Brunswick: Rutgers Univ. Press, 1984), pp. 189-230.

8. I am indebted for this insight to Gillian Brown, "The Empire of Agoraphobia," *Representations*, no. 20 (Fall 1987), pp. 134-57.

9. See Louise DeSalvo, *Nathaniel Hawthorne* (Atlantic Highlands: Humanities Press International, Inc., 1987), pp. 77-96. DeSalvo's reading of *The House of the Seven Gables* is both biased and superficial. For example, her analysis of the interpolated story written by Holgrave and later read to Phoebe, contains a blatant error. DeSalvo writes that Holgrave's version of the Pyncheon-Maule legend describes "the vengeance undertaken by Gervayse Pyncheon, the grandson of Matthew Maule, against the Pyncheon family." Such a summary is rife with illogicalities. Why a Pyncheon would want to take revenge on his own kin remains a mystery. How Gervayse Pyncheon could possibly have descended from the Maules is equally puzzling. The rest of her analysis, based on this initial error, is equally absurd. In her interpretation, Gervayse destroys Alice Pyncheon's life; he "seeks to mesmerize Alice" and succeeds whereby she becomes "Gervayse's property" (even though DeSalvo quotes the passage from the book which explicitly states that Alice was "Maule's slave"). So obsessed is DeSalvo with the idea of incest in Hawthorne's life and fiction that, quite paradoxically, she allows it to blight her analysis of Holgrave's story, for the act of hypnotizing Alice, with its sexual overtones, is here performed by Gervayse Pyncheon, who is of course Alice's father. Admittedly, one could claim that Alice is victimized by her own father, insofar as Gervayse Pyncheon's avarice and pride put her in the situation where she is prey to Matthew Maule's vengeance. But the whole idea of the reconciliation of the two antagonistic families resulting from the union of Phoebe Pyncheon and Holgrave-Maule evaporates from DeSalvo's analysis for a reason she fails to grasp: had Gervayse Pyncheon been descended from the Maules, such a union would have been enacted prior to the narrative.

10. See Agnes McNeill Donohue, *Hawthorne. Calvin's Ironic Stepchild* (Kent: The Kent Univ. Press, 1985), pp. 68-95.

11. Nina Baym, "Hawthorne's Women: The Tyranny of Social Myths," *Centenary Review* 15 (1971), p. 258.

12. See Sigmund Freud, "The Uncanny," in *The Standard Edition of the Complete Psychological Works of Sigmund Freud*, trans. and ed. James Strachey (London: Hogarth Press, 1953-74), vol. 17, p. 245.

13. Jane Gallop, *Reading Lacan* (Ithaca and London: Cornell Univ. Press, 1985), p. 146.

14. See Jane Gallop, *The Daughter's Seduction. Feminism and Psychoanalysis* (Ithaca and London: Cornell Univ. Press, 1982), p. 118.

15. See Joseph Campbell, who basically draws on Aristotle's minimal clarification of *catharsis* in *The Hero with a Thousand Faces* (Princeton: Princeton Univ. Press, 1968), p. 28.

16. Freud, *Standard Edition*, vol 18, p. 236.

17. Josef Breuer and Sigmund Freud, *Studies on Hysteria*, trans. and ed. James Strachey (New York: Basic Books, Inc., Publishers, 1957), p. 197.

18. Freud, *Standard Edition*, vol. 18, p. 62.

19. Brooks, p. 92.

20. Freud, *Standard Edition*, vol. 17, p. 249.

21. Ibid., p. 262.

22. René Girard, *Violence and the Sacred*, trans. Patrick Gregory (Baltimore: The Johns Hopkins Univ. Press, 1977), p. 107.

23. Allan Gardner Lloyd-Smith, *Eve Tempted. Writing and Sexuality in Hawthorne's Fiction* (Totowa: Barnes and Noble Books, 1984), p. 70.

24. Frederick Crews was the first to note the presence of what he calls "ogre-father" in the figures of Jaffrey Pyncheon in *The House of the Seven Gables* and the Model in *The Marble Faun* (see *The Sins of the Fathers. Hawthorne's Psychological Themes* [New York: Oxford Univ. Press, 1966], pp. 175 and 226-27]). My conclusions, however, as I argue in "Hawthorne's Monstrous Doubles," *The Nathaniel Hawthorne Review* (in press), considerably differ from Crews'.

25. Girard, p. 170.

26. See Crews, p. 177.

Four: The Demonic Vision

Lancelot

In his essay on Herman Melville, published six years after the publication of *Lancelot*, Percy marvels at what it felt like to have written *Moby-Dick*, "an experience which Melville called being broiled in hellfire, and which was surely a triumphant taking on of hell and coming through."[1] Was it the same for Percy, one wonders, after writing his "wicked book"? Did Percy feel, as he writes of Melville, "spotless as a lamb, happy, content"? In the essay, Percy alludes to Melville's letter to Hawthorne written in response to Hawthorne's appreciative reading of *Moby-Dick*, where Melville uses the puzzling phrase "ineffable sociability [sic]," the phrase which, to Percy, is the clear expression of intertextuality that can be stated, Percy believes, "in ordinary language—without the jargon."

In this loose sense, one could argue a number of "intertexts" for Percy's *Lancelot*. Malory's version of the quest of Sir Lancelot du Lac is at once the most obvious and the most frequently applied analogy. Corinne Dale reads *Lancelot* with both this Arthurian source and *The Divine Comedy*. Robert Coles points to several affinities between *Lancelot* and Tennyson's *Idylls of the King*. Robert Brinkmeyer reads Percy's novel in the light of the twelfth--century French romance *Queste del Saint Graal.*[2]

Of a different area of associations, Lewis Lawson interestingly notes that the function of the house in *Lancelot* recalls the House of Usher, Burden's Landing, or Sutpen's Hundred.[3] To this list one could add another instructive comparison: between *Lancelot* and *The House of the Seven Gables*. Both books concern themselves with the decay of a once great house that serves as a central unifying metaphor commenting upon the decline of those who inherited it. Both writers address issues of sex: Hawthorne, in his characteristically restrained manner, Percy, more directly, as he brutally attacks the morals of his age. Both books comment upon the deterioration of marriage, in which sex plays a dominant role. The hocus-pocus endings of both books intimate a symbolic rebirth of the hero following a storm (a hurricane in *Lancelot*). The comatose states of Clifford and Lance serve as another point of comparison, and an interesting parallel arises from the function of the arched window in *The House of the Seven Gables* and the pigeonnier in *Lancelot*, both of which operate as panoptic images, whereby all experience becomes encapsulated into one wholesome vision. Finally, like *The House of the Seven Gables*, and *Moby-Dick*, *Lancelot* works on a *cathartic* principle.

The house of Lamar, Belle Isle, and the legends of the past which cling to it constitute one of the structural affinities between *The House of the Seven Gables* and *Lancelot.* In both cases, the house ages over a century and is in a dilapidated condition. Lance reports that, prior to Margot's restoration, the house reflected the impoverished condition of its inhabitants. The income of both families lags so far behind their needs that business must be conducted in the house to increase their budgets. Hepzibah inaugurates a little grocery store in the Pyncheons' house, whereas Belle Isle is displayed to tourists at a dollar a head in Lance's father's time, and at four dollars in Lance's time, thus showing the inflation that has occurred over the span of a generation. In particularly lean years, Lance tells Percival, he bought antiques elsewhere and sold them, with interest, at Belle Isle.

The ancestral legends yield another structural parallel between the two books. Lance's father's infamous involvement in bribery, which occasions his decline, corresponds to Colonel Pyncheon's notorious deed, which causes his untimely death and casts a shadow over his descendants' fortunes. Both writers allude to what Percy calls a sexual "offence" in conjugal relations: Colonel Pyncheon's "remorseless weight and hardness" dispatched three consecutive wives to their early graves, whereas Lance refers to his mother's illicit relations with his uncle Harry. Interestingly, we also find parallels in the books' interpolated narratives—Holgrave's story of Alice Pyncheon and the scenario of the movie shot at Belle Isle—both of which have some bearing on the heroes' fortunes. Although Holgrave's story mostly alludes to events in the past, the Pyncheons' greed for money and subsequent decline, it also provides a negative comment on his relationship with Phoebe, and the scenario of the movie bears some resemblance to Lance's particular situation.

Even a cursory reading of *Lancelot* reveals striking parallels also with *Moby-Dick*. The house of Lamar, Belle Isle, is as much a self-contained entity as the microcosm of Melville's *Pequod*. Lance's relationship with Elgin echoes the marriage of white and black in *Moby-Dick* (Ishmael and Queequeg, Ahab and Pip), and the merging of whiteness and blackness in the whale is re-enacted in Lance's encounter with the convulsed bodies of Margot and Jacoby as "the strangest of all beasts, two-backed and pied, light--skinned dark-skinned."[4] Like Ahab's (and Hamlet's), Lance's madness has a method in it, or, as Matthiessen says of Ahab's, is a "sanity of controlled madness."

Percy too, moreover, draws upon the biblical Ahab as a prototype, and in fact Lance exhibits even more remarkable affinities with the biblical source than Melville's does. In his portrayal of

Lance, Percy alludes to the episodes in the biblical text which present Ahab not as a popular and apt ruler but as a kind of an ill-starred buffoon who not only topples from his high place as the king of Northern Israel (by the prompting of his corrupt, licentious, wicked hussy of a wife, Jezebel) but also brings about the decline of his entire dynasty. There is a direct allusion to the biblical story when Lance asks Percival why anyone should take the matter of fidelity seriously if "even the ancients didn't seem to dwell on it too much; even the Bible is rather casual. Your [Percival's] God seemed much more jealous of false idols, golden calves, than his people messing around with each other" (16). But then, of course, he takes pains to demonstrate that what he calls "sexual offence" is the mark and religion of the new age, which, to Lance's obsessive mind, has replaced Christianity.

The story of Ahab and Jezebel belongs to what Northrop Frye calls the Bible's demonic vision.[5] Frye contrasts that vision, as pointed out earlier, with the apocalyptic (to Frye, ideal) vision. Frye's schema appears to be particularly useful when we approach what he calls the "human" element of the Bible and, specifically, when we explore biblical female figures. Maternal presentations of the Virgin Mary and Rachel, as well as marital or bridal figures, symbolically represented by Jerusalem, Christ's "spouse," belong to the ideal vision, whereas the demonic counterpart of the Mother figure is Lilith, the mother of demons, and the demonic Bride is, for instance, Jezebel, Ahab's queen, whose demonic character the narrator of I Kings conveys in both theological and sexual terms, though prevalently in the former.

The crucial episode in *Lancelot* where the maternal and bridal figures merge to create a single demonic image of womanhood is during Lance's hallucination concerning the Lady of the Camellias. Lance is drugged and finds it difficult to establish the identity of the figure he sees. He first seems to recognize her as one of the women he and Percival used to know in their adolescence. He then perceives a camellia pinned at her shoulder and, subsequently, the apparition begins to talk. She mentions Lance's mother, Lily, who was "a lovely delicate creature. Like a little dove" (note that Hawthorne used this traditional attribute of ideal womanhood in reference to Sophia). Of herself she says that she is "more a sparrow. Plain but tough" (more like Margot, in fact). She then speaks about Lily's relationship with Harry and the father Lamar's resigned acceptance of their liaison. She alludes to Lily and Harry as "Camille and Robert Taylor," which of course provides the final clue. The very heading of this part of the narrative, Our Lady of the Camellias, bluntly reveals the demonic parody of the apocalyptic, or ideal, vision. Our Lady of course refers to the Virgin Mary, whereas the Lady of the Camellias is the courtesan Marguerite Gautier (or Margot) from Dumas' *La Dame aux camélias*. The figure of the mysterious woman signifies thus a merging of the mother (Lily) and the wife (Margot) figures.

Even though the name Lily suggests purity, there is virtually nothing in Lance's recollections of his mother to support such an identification. On the contrary, the more details we get the more supportive they become of the mother's mythological function as Lilith. That name evokes the powers of the night. Early Semitic folklore believed Lilith to be a female demon, or vampire, who inhabited ruins and other desolate places. She was reputed to haunt such places during storms, and men, especially young men, were vulnerable to her playful charm. Lilith enjoyed a splendid career in European romanticism. For instance, Goethe refers to Lilith's demonic charm when he has Mephisto tell Faust:

> The first wife of Adam.
> Watch out and shun her captivating tresses:
> She likes to use her never-equaled hair
> To lure a youth into her luscious lair,
> And he won't lightly leave her lewd caresses.[6]

Percy draws on similar fund of imagery when he has Lance allude to his mother's mischievous manner, recalling "a kind of nervous joking aggressiveness about her." She used to "get" Lance in this playfully aggressive way:

> On cold mornings when everyone was solemn and depressed about getting up and going off to work or school, she would say, "I'm going to get you," and come at me with her sharp little fist boring away into my ribs. There was something past joking, an insistence, about the boring. She wouldn't stop. (215)

It is, tellingly, the Lady of the Camellias, as his mother, who hands him the bowie knife during the hurricane in the same playful-aggressive fashion:

> It was then she gave me the sword—
>
> *The sword*? Ha ha. It was a Bowie knife. Then she looked like my mother again, and when she gave me the Bowie knife, she picked it up from the desk and thrust it at me point first in the same insistent joking way my mother would bore her sharp fist into my ribs. (226)

The bowie knife is an important "requisite" in the novel. Primarily, Lance alludes in the passage to the Arthurian source because Lance's namesake, Sir Lancelot, received his sword from his foster--mother, the Lady of the Lake, who kidnapped him when he was an infant. More importantly, however, the knife functions as one of several phallic attributes in the novel. When Lance first meets Margot on the occasion of The Azalea Festival held at Belle Isle, she invites herself to the pigeonnier; then, again taking initiative, she requests that Lance bolt the door and when he obliges she wants to see the key he has just turned in the lock, "I lay down and gave her the iron key. She held it in one hand and me in the other and was equally fond of both" (80). In Lance's recollection of another erotic scene, Margot grabs the bedpost, not as "a point of anchorage or leverage in the storm-tossed sea of love," but to explore "the delicate fluting of the heavy columns" (119). As pointed out earlier in reference to *The House of the Seven Gables*, this iconography may remind one of the new ambiguity that, as John Muller and William Richardson write in their reader's guide to Lacan's *Écrits*, oscillates between "[the phallus'] role as signifier and its role as real or imagined organ."[7] Clifford's castration anxiety is transferred from the mother to the sister, Lance's from the mother to the wife (Margot). In Lacanian dialectic of desire, generic relationships revolve around the "to be" or "not to be" and the "to have" or "not to have" of the phallus. We well remember the cryptic sign from the beginning of the book which reads:

Free &
Ma
B

Notwithstanding what the complete sign says, which Lance plans to find out upon leaving the asylum, it possibly communicates a vital message: Free of mother in order to be. Thus Lance's anxiety of castration becomes resolved in Oedipal violence, but not in the Freudian sense reserved for the father of a male child, but rather directed at the "phallic" mother-wife. Here ensues one further analogy with Lacan's argument. In one of his earliest articles, "Aggressivity in Psychoanalysis," Lacan notes that "the structural effect of identification with the rival is not self-evident, except at the level of fable."[8] We can indeed leave the fable aside, for what we have in *Lancelot* is rather a post-Freudian identification of the father as a disgraced rival; there is no question of his being a venerated model, a distinction that Freudian psychoanalysis maintained. The figure of the father becomes compromised by two discoveries Lance makes. One, when still a child, he incidentally came upon a cache of ten thousand dollars hidden in his father's bureau—evidence of his father's corruption. The second discovery Lance also made as a child, but he did not realize its full import until much later: his father's resigned or, as Lance believes, cowardly acceptance of Lily's liaison with the jovial uncle Harry. The irony of Lance's situation is that even though he knows the reasons for the old Lamar's gradual decline, he ultimately falls into his cuckolded father's footsteps, impotent, drinking and apathetically watching life go by. And one day, in the pigeonnier, he makes another chance discovery, this time of Margot's infidelity, with which disclosure comes the disconcerting realization that he cannot possibly be the father of his second daughter. He now becomes a Raymond Chandler character, a Marlowe (his own analogy), or a Chillingworth, and proves not only that Margot was unfaithful to him but that she still is, whereupon he systematically plans his bloody vengeance.

The fallacy of Lance's quest (a monstrously twisted quest for love) is that he does not understand any of the women he loves or, as he obsessively repeats, "loves." Lance wants Percival to believe that his first wife Lucy was part and parcel of his romantic dream ("a slim brown dancer in a bell jar spinning round and round in the 'Limelight' music of old Carolina long ago" [119]). However, this portrayal of womanhood ultimately becomes ambivalent when Lance speaks of Lucy's legs that "scissored and flashed under her white skirt" (82). We need only recall Fay Greener's "scissoring" legs to realize the full import of Lance's description. He dismisses all of his second marriage with a single sentence ("We were married, moved to Belle Isle, had two children" [84]), and he reports that when Lucy had died he felt neither sad nor bereft but

> simply curious. How curious that she should grow pale, thin, weak, and die in a few months! Her blood turned to milk—the white cells replaced the red cells. How curious

> to wake up one morning alone again in Belle Isle, just as I had been alone in my youth! (84)

Not even female children are spared in Lance's paranoid vision of womanhood. The "scissoring" legs and "boring" fists are tokens of his "daughter" Siobhan's demonic, Lance believes, nature.

It should be apparent by now that in Lance's account of any woman in his life we cannot see the "real" woman but only his own story or metaphor for this woman. Margot is the case most in point. When Lance first meets Margot, she is one of the belles in hoop skirts, who show Belle Isle to rich tourists, and Lance intimates his first impression of Margot—namely, that Margot was not "like Scarlett." A casual remark, true, but it becomes meaningful as we pursue the analogy a little further. What Lance apparently has in mind is that Margot is not pretty. She is nevertheless remarkably like Scarlet in her practicality, her lust for life, her lack of moral scruples, her "male" ways, her self-confidence, wilfulness, even her healthy appetite. Lance reports that Margot eats "like a horse," drinks from the bottle, drives a car "like a man . . . not push-pulling with two hands but palming the wheel around with one hand" (33). She knows what she wants, and she pursues it determinedly. She first wants Lance and Belle Isle, and even though Lance likes to think that at their first meeting he took the lead, it is entirely on her own initiative that Margot secures both. Moreover, Lance, needless to say, is no Rhett Butler.[9] The fact is that Margot and Lance are as androgynous a couple as any one could find. She is strong, possessed of iron will, demanding, loud, resourceful, brimming with energy and initiative. He is weak, quiet, and passive. In an odd way, they resemble the marriage of "énergie femelle et . . . faiblesse masculine" of the Bette and Steinbock couple of Balzac's *La Cousine Bette*. Consider, for instance, this litany of explicitly masculine features of Margot's physical portrait:

> Her face was shiny and foreshortened . . . her mouth too wide . . . her coarse stiff hair invited the hand to squeeze it to test its spring . . . her back was strong and runneled. . . . she . . . had voluptuousness, the boyishness being just a joke after all when it came to her looking straight at me. (74)

A difference between the couples is that Balzac's Bette, who is described in very much the same fashion (large feet, strong arms, warts), never marries Steinbock, and so the androgynous couple never really forms.[10]

With Margot, Lance makes another puzzling discovery: a "lustful woman." Their relationship appears to be successful for a number of years, but when she completes the restoration of Belle Isle and Lance "takes to the bottle" and becomes an incompetent lover, she turns to other men and other jobs. Lance's impotence typically originates in his fear of the castrating mother of pre-Oedipal fantasy, which becomes reactivated by what Christopher Lasch perceives as "apparently aggressive overtures of sexually liberated women."[11] To Lance, Margot epitomizes the characteristics of the "she-man," a female type emerging from the ruins of the chivalric code. But this discovery comes too late: had he really known Margot he would either have not married her or have not lost her. Margot pertinently sums up Lance's divided conscience regarding womanhood in her last utterance in the novel, "With you I had to be either—or—but never a—uh—woman" (245).

Lucy, who was a virgin when he married her, had incarnated Lance's dream of the Southern past, and Lance imagines that he can recapture this dream with Anna, his neighbor in the asylum, since "the violation she suffered [she was gang raped] has in some sense restored her virginity, much as a person recovering from the plague is immune to the plague" (86). Interestingly, the creation of Anna resembles Hélène Cixous' metaphor for a woman's life. Cixous says: "She [a sleeping beauty] sleeps, she is *intact*, eternal, absolutely powerless. He has no doubt that he has been waiting for him forever [emphasis added]."[12] Lance dreams not of a relationship with Anna, but of her virginity and her domestication. What he covertly tries to sell to Percival is the notion that the very fabric of civilization depends upon there being a sweet helpless woman, like Anna, in the house to minister to the physical as well as psychical wellbeing of her husband. Her very presence maintains the generic equilibrium. This generic tension in Lance is nowhere more evident than in the passage where he relates to Percival his dream of domestication in which Anna played the "New Woman":

> There was perfect quiet. Yet I was not alone in the house. There was someone else in the next room. A woman. There was the unmistakable sense of her presence. How did I know it was a woman? I cannot tell you except that I knew. Perhaps it was the way she moved around the room. Do you know the way a woman moves around a room whether she is cleaning it or just passing time? It is different from the way a man moves. She is at home in a room. The room is an extension of her. (36)

As suggested earlier in this study, Percy's fiction presents a considerable group of psychotic helpless women who are almost invariably marital candidates for his males. There is Kate in *The Moviegoer* whom Binx has to "hand along," and tell what to do and say. There is a mute girl in *The Last Gentleman* with whom Will Barrett recalls playing Chinese checkers in the hospital, when he was treated for amnesia. There is psychotic mute Anna in *Lancelot*, schizophrenic Allison in *The Second Coming*, who can hoist an iron stove but cannot make herself comprehensible, and any number of psychotic women with speech disorders in Percy's last novel, *The Thanatos Syndrome*. The idea of a mute girl may be traced biographically to Percy's own traumatic discovery that his first daughter was born deaf and mute. But the curious mating in Percy's novels has yet another significance. When we look at his focal male figures, what we invariably find is an unaccomodated man with all sorts of psychic problems. It is therefore only natural that he would find a suitable partner in a woman who reflects his mental condition, and though certainly nothing guarantees that such an accord will last, most of Percy's novels end with a promise of a lasting relationship.

Inevitably, however, *Lancelot* is an exception. Annoyingly judgmental, confused, raging with hatred and sanguinely convinced of his own salvation, Lance propounds his theory of *felix culpa* to Anna, whose repudiation is outright and complete:

> "Are you suggesting," she said to me, "that I, myself, me, my person, can be violated by a *man*? You goddamn men, Don't you know that there are more important things in this world? Next you'll be telling me that despite myself I liked it." (251)

Interestingly, this passage is the only direct report of Anna's contribution to conversations with Lance. Again we might benefit from Cixous' insight: "once awake [Anna's silence parallels Cixous' 'sleep'], it would be an entirely different story. Then there would be two people, perhaps. You never know with women. And the voluptuous simplicity of preliminaries would no longer take place."[13] Lance's misogyny reaches its peak when he reflects upon Anna's words and remembers St. Augustine's account of the Visigoths' rape of the nuns who "enjoyed it despite themselves." "No doubt howled with delight," he adds. In Lance's recollection of his hallucination, the figure who hands him the bowie knife is fantasized into Joan of Arc, a militant virgin. Is then Anna another version of the archetypal feminist, Ann Lee, a victimized woman, founder of the Shakers? Lance's vision gains momentum when, just before the explosion of the house, he looks at Margot, lying on her side, and imagines this time not his mother, but Anna. Thus, in remembering this scene, he kills them all.

Women, to borrow a phrase from Cixous, "function within" Lance's discourse; he either patronizes or demonizes them. Hence, we are back at Frye's schema, where the differences between the apocalyptic, or ideal, vision and its demonic counterpart are conveyed primarily through the presentation of female figures. Frye notes, however, that the term "whoredom," as used in the biblical narrative, denotes not so much sexual irregularities, as theological ones. This connotation derives from the practice of maintaining cult prostitutes in Canaanite temples, both female and male, the latter known as "sodomites" (I Kings 14:24). Jezebel, Ahab's wife, incarnates both sexual and theological evil, for not only did she cuckold Ahab, which appears to be of slight importance to the narrator of Kings, but also, and primarily, because she introduced the worship of Baal, the "false god," into Northern Israel. The reality of a "false god" is a devil, Frye maintains, the word "Baal" appearing in several concatenations suggestive of this meaning as, for example, in "Beelzebub" (Hebrew "ba'alzevuv," god of insects) who is the chief devil or Satan. Baal functioned among ancient semitic people as a god of fertility, or a sun-god, the meaning associated also with Lucifer (light-bringing). It remains to be said that Lance's ascent from the inferno of Belle Isle is conveyed as the upward movement of Lucifer:

> Without a sound the room flowered. All was light and air and color and movement but not a sound. I was moved. That is to say, for the first time in thirty years I was moved off the dead center of my life. Ah then, I was thinking as I moved, there are still great moments. I was wheeling slowly up into the night like Lucifer blown out of hell, great wings spread against the starlight. (246)

One of the rites that the worshippers of the god Baal introduced was the fertility rite whereby they "gashed themselves with swords and spears until the blood ran" (I Kings 18:28). The significance of the rite is not only to express the desire for fertility but also to identify the worshipper's body with that of the fertility god. Frye cites a similar rite, known as the "gardens of Adonis," where plants in pots, which were symbolically associated with female sexual organs, were dipped in water by a group of females as a rain charm. A female counterpart of Baal was a fertility goddess, Asherah, whose emblems were carved wooden poles and a star (*stella maris*). And the Bible makes reference to the prophets of Baal and Asherah as Jezebel's "pensioners."

It is impossible to ignore the structural and symbolic parallels between *Lancelot* and the biblical text. The god of fertility becomes the god of sexual evil, who is worshipped by Margot and the Hollywood moviemakers (Margot's "pensioners"). Margot does not "carry" a star but is one, and her special dedication in restoring wooden surfaces of antiques at Belle Isle are both suggestive of Percy's source. Sex, or what Lance obsessively calls the sexual sin (the unholy grail he seeks), is time and again conveyed in religious terms.

"The first feature" of the video recordings of the sexual antics of his wife and daughter ends with this passage:

> Still there is no conversation but presently a voice says, . . .: *Oh oh oh ah ah aaah, oh my Jesus oh ah ah sh—sh —sh—*
>
> ???
>
> But the voice is not immediately recognizable as either Margot's or Jacoby's, being hoarser than Margot's and higher than Jacoby's.
>
> A prayer? (190)

Similarly, "the second feature," recorded from the actress Raine's room, which reveals the triple sex of Raine, Lance's daughter Lucy, and the actor Dana ("a six-arm Shiva"), concludes with a similar association:

> No words are audible except near the end an unrecognizable voice which is neither clearly male nor female seems to come from nowhere and everywhere—and only fragments at that: *Oh Christ dear sweet Jesus oh oh—*
>
> Another prayer? (192)

Percy evokes this image once again in the scene during the hurricane, just before the explosion of the house, when Lance conceives of the two bodies, Margot's and Jacoby's, on the Calhoun bed, as his encounter with the "beast" which "held discourse with itself in prayers and curses" (239). The iconography of this last scene is perhaps most interesting as it partakes of two mythical sources: biblical and Arthurian.

In the episode of Queen Guinevere's abduction to the kingdom of death, Sir Gawain and an anonymous knight, who turns out to be Sir Lancelot, undergo a series of trials to rescue the Queen. In their second trial, a dwarf leads them into a tower where they stay for the night. Two beds are prepared for them, but there is also a third bed, which "possessed all the excellence that one could think of in a bed." The hostess of the tower cautions them against sleeping in this bed, but Sir Lancelot disregards the warning. At midnight, a lance with a blazing pennon descends from the rafters, and the bed catches fire. Sir Lancelot narrowly escapes the lance and puts out the fire. This "marvel bed" has it counterpart in Percy's book, in an episode which marks Lance's transit to the world beyond. Having left Raine's room, Lance goes to Margot's bedroom, where a flash of a lightning reveals the bed:

> It was the great Calhoun bed, built by my ancestor for his friend John C. Calhoun to sleep in in the White House in 1844. But Calhoun never slept in the White House so Royal Moultrie Lamar kept the bed. It was like a *cathedral*, a Gothic bed, posts as thick as trees, carved and fluted and tapering to spires and gargoyles above the canopy. The headboard was as massive and complex as an *altar* screen. Panels of openwork braced posts and rails like flying buttresses. (emphasis added—237)

In what follows, Percy transposes, in fact, two myths. As Lance approaches the bed, he perceives two convulsed bodies, of Margot and her lover Jacoby. The scene impresses him as the descent of the beast (Leviathan). However, as Heinrich Zimmer has argued, the divine bed of Sir Lancelot and the queen (yet another archetypal bed) is conceived in divine terms (note the italics in the passage above), which suggests the mythical union of two lovers. Thus, their love play corresponds, as Zimmer observes, to the dance of Hermaphrodite or the dance of the god Shiva, who unites in himself the female and the male. Such a bisexual symbol, Zimmer argues, represents "the embodiment in a single form of all the pairs of opposites, a transcendence of the contraries of phenomenality; and this incarnate Form of forms is then conceived of as One whose dance is the created world."[14] Let us now look at Percy's iconography:

> My eyes began to make things out. No darkness is absolute. The candle glow from the foyer made the faintest glimmer on the white walls. It was possible to make out the *looming shape* of the bed. I was standing. There was a shape on the bed. Its skin was darker than the white sheets. Now I could see it, the strangest of all *beasts, two-backed and pied*, light-skinned dark-skinned, striving against itself, holding

> discourse with itself in prayers and curses. (emphasis added—238-39)

Percy, of course, parodies the mythical iconography, for the "great Calhoun bed" that Lance and Margot once shared is now the seat of adultery. The lovers' "dance" is the world they have created, which, to Lance, is the world as Sodom. Like the archetypal bed, the Calhoun bed catches fire as Lance ignites the fume, and the house, pumped with gas, explodes. The sodomites, Margot, Jacoby, Raine, and Dana are relegated to the world beyond, where they properly belong, according to Lance. After Lance survives the explosion, he risks his life a second time, to rescue not Margot, as the newspaper headings imply, but the bowie knife. These three scenes are characterized by the distortion of audience's view, owing to the defective video-recording in the first two, and in the third, to the absence of light, except for the candleglow from the hall. In all three cases Lance guesses at whom and what he sees rather than actually seeing them. As noted in the previous chapter, such distortions are also conveyed in Hawthorne's texts, in the depiction of "three shadows" in *The Marble Faun*, the third of which is qualified as a "shapeless mass,"and in *The House of the Seven Gables* in the presentation of two giants horizontally placed one on the other (signifying the past and the present), with the same effect, the loss of distinction. A direct parallel to the latter idea manifests itself in *Lancelot* when Lance speaks about three worlds, "the old dead past world, the hopeless screwed-up now world, and the unknown world of the future" (63). Margot, in our iconography, represents the past, since she is both an extension of Lance's mother (the Lady of the Camellias) and of the house itself, whereas the film crew is synonymous with the middle world, the "now world." The iconography is thus familiar, even though the order of the bodies is somewhat reversed here.

What role, in the above scheme, can we then assign to the silent addressee of Lance's confession? Percival's "religious" name, the name he adopted after ordination, is John, and, at one point, Lance wonders: "Is it John the Evangelist who loved so much or John the Baptist, a loner in the wilderness?" (10). He himself suggests the answer when he says that Percival *was* a "loner." In the Gospel, the prophecy of Elijah's return fulfills itself in the figure of John the Baptist (Matthew: 11:14). According to the biblical account, when Elijah flees from the priests of Baal, he hears the noise of earthquakes, thunder, and fire, after which "a still small voice" speaks. It tells Elijah that he need not worry because the followers of the god Baal will be slaughtered in due time. The weaving of this context together with its wonderful phrase into the ending of Percy's text undoubtedly constitutes a masterstroke. Percival, like Elijah in the biblical account, has envisaged the thunder and fire of Lance's apocalyptic story, and his tacit "Yes," with which the book ends, parallels the biblical "still small voice." What his inner voice, the voice of God, tells him he is ready to pass onto his raging patient. Whether Lance is ready to hear this message remains a question. Having just given Percival his mad rant, Lance paradoxically claims that there is no confession "forthcoming." What he surely means, and what the priest awaits, is an act of penance. The reader, and Percival too, may hope in vain that the message will disclose the "secret" Lance has taken so much pain to search for elsewhere. Though, arguably, at the end of *Lancelot*, there resonates a note of reintegration of human and divine love, the reader must wait until Percy's next novel for its realization.

It is thus apparent that *Lancelot*, like *The House of the Seven Gables* and *Moby-Dick*, works on a *cathartic* principle. The analogy with *Moby-Dick* seems all the more pertinent as in both books the meaning of *catharsis* is experienced not by respective protagonists (Ahab, Lance), that is, unlike *The House of the Seven Gables*, where *catharsis* transforms Clifford, but rather by the books' authors. Perhaps also by Ishmael and Percival.

Admittedly, the final chapter of *Lancelot* begins with a Wordsworthian "tranquil restoration." Similar resolution concludes *The*

House of the Seven Gables, as a comparison of the two passages, from Percy's and Hawthorne's texts, respectively, indicates:

> What a beautiful day! Don't you think so? The last day of the hurricane season. All danger of hurricanes past. The morning sun bright and high and refracted through the clear crystal prism of northern air with that special moderation, the promise of warmth, of fine November days in New Orleans. Everything is mild and unexceptional here, isn't it? even the weather. By eleven o'clock the winos on Camp Street will be creeping out of their holes and stretching out or curling up like cats in sunny doorways to take a little nap. Not a bad life. (249)

> Nature made sweet amends, that morning, for the five unkindly days which had preceded it. It would have been enough to live for, merely to look up at the wide benediction of the sky, or as much of it as was visible between the houses, genial once more with sunshine. Every object was agreeable, whether to be gazed at in the breadth, or examined more minutely. Such, for example, were the well-washed pebbles and gravel of the sidewalk; even the sky-reflecting pools in the centre of the street; and the grass, now freshly verdant, that crept along the base of the fences, on the other side of which, if one peeped over, was seen the multifarious growth of gardens. Vegetable productions, of whatever kind, seemed more than negatively happy, in the juicy warmth and abundance of their life. (2: 284)

The famous Pyncheon Elm remains intact after the storm, "except a single branch, that . . . had been transmuted to bright gold," and Lance intimates that the rain trees in the cemetery that he can see from the window are "bright as new copper pennies." One has only to compare both passages with the description contained in Revelation 21-22 to understand the scope of the two writers' shared vision.

Thus, here, as in *The House of the Seven Gables,* we must deal with this lingering dream for prelapsarian, primal innocence presented anew which has been such a temptation for generations of American writers. Lance resembles both Clifford and Holgrave, who entertain a dream of innocence in which Phoebe plays the role of Eve to both Adams. Lance is a former hedonist whereas Clifford is a hedonist *manqué*. For both Clifford and Lance the new life begins after prison and is induced by shock. Both need a crisis to restore them to some kind of sanity. In the train episode Clifford for the first time demonstrates that he is capable of analysis. This episode features the famous passage where Clifford speaks about "real-estate" as "the broad foundation on which nearly all the guilt of this world rests," and he condones violence, if its aim is "purging away the grossness out of human life." He bluntly says that even "murderers . . . are often excusable in the motives of their deed, and deserve to be ranked among public benefactors, if we consider only its *result*" (2: 265). Thus, Hawthorne for the first time voices the hopeful possibility of good emerging from evil, and this is, of course, the rationale of Lance's quest:

> Can good come from evil? Have you ever considered the possibility that one might undertake a search not for God but for evil? . . . In times when nobody is interested in God, what would happen if you could prove the existence of sin, pure and simple? Wouldn't that be a windfall for you? A new proof of God's existence! If there is such a thing as sin, evil, a living malignant force, there must be a God! (51-52)

However, there can be no doubt that purgation does not transform Lance. At least, not in the text. He complains to Percival of the numbness and chill he feels, and once again with cold logic he outlines his plan ("We know what we want. And we'll have it. If it takes a sword, we'll use the sword" [256]).

To say that the ending of the novel poses a binary choice (either Percival's way of divine love or Lance's way of secular wrath), and that Percival's unspoken words after the novel ends will lead Lance to faith would surely hackney what no doubt still remains Percy's most complex novel. Some readers assign to Percival the role of a final resolver of the book's contextual tensions. They see Percival as their friend, rather than Lance's. They acknowledge the irreconcilable polarities of the book, but they claim that its system is sustained by some final assertion that gives *Lancelot* its aesthetic wholeness.

But Percival is more than a moral nucleus of the novel; he is a literary device. His presence, like Ishmael's in *Moby-Dick*, not only organizes *Lancelot* but, in so doing, purges it of Lance's demonism. He patiently bears Lance's vision, yet without, as Murray Krieger says of Ishmael, "denying an affirmative power to the universe and its Author."[15] Like Ishmael, he understands the moral integrity of Lance's quest, but he does not accept its immoral perpetration. Lewis Lawson seems to hit the mark in claiming that both Lance and Percival are parts of Walker Percy. Hence the polarities they embody are irreconcilable; no synthesis can be reached without what Krieger calls a "newly disruptive synthesis." What Krieger says of Gide, which in his scheme applies also to Conrad and Melville, we may say of Percy—namely, that he

> does not exhaust himself even in his most intensely created character but creates such a character as but one extreme of the dialogue the self conducts with the soul, an extreme that the very act of dialogue—so long as it is a disciplined act—manages partly to tame. The author is more than his creature . . . and proves it by the mere fact that he has

> created him, and has created him within a larger aesthetic whole that contains him as but a part of it.[16]

In his essay on Melville, Percy says that a writer's satisfaction comes from the "ineffable sociability [sic]," and that is when "the writing works and somebody knows it." Conceivably, every professional writer creates with this belief. Melville's joy at getting his vision across to reticent Hawthorne, whom he ranked with Shakespeare, was ecstatic. Like Melville's and Hawthorne's, Percy's vision in *Lancelot* passes through the hellfire of its antithesis but there always remains a chance that the reader will go with this vision and become chastened by its extremity. And many have confessed this. How meaningful is the fact that many a Melville reader finds the neat moral solutions in *Billy Budd* disturbing, just as we have criticism to similar effect of Percy's *The Second Coming*.

And thus, rather than seek for a principle of cohesion in *Lancelot*, we may concede with Harold Bloom that confusion is beautiful because it cannot be resolved or, as Gabriel Marcel says, because it remains a mystery. Percy's vision in *Lancelot*, like Hawthorne's in *The House of the Seven Gables*, moving heaven and earth and descending into hell, terrifies us but it returns us, purged by its extremes, to our midearth existence.

NOTES

1. Walker Percy, "Herman Melville," *The New Criterion* 213 (November 1983), p. 41.

2. Respectively, Corinne Dale, "*Lancelot* and the Medieval Quests of Sir Lancelot and Dante," in *Walker Percy: Art and Ethics*, ed. Jac Tharpe (Jackson: Univ. Press of Mississippi, 1980), pp. 99-106; Robert Coles, *Walker Percy: An American Search* (Boston: Atlantic-Little, Brown, 1979), pp. 213-16; and Robert Brinkmeyer, Jr., *Three Catholic Writers*

of the Modern South: Allen Tate, Caroline Gordon, Walker Percy (Jackson: Univ. Press of Mississippi, 1985), pp. 160-61.

3. Lewis A. Lawson, "The Fall of the House of Lamar," in *The Art of Walker Percy. Stratagems for Being*, ed. Panthea Reid Broughton (Baton Rouge: Louisiana State Univ. Press, 1979), pp. 219-45.

4. Walker Percy, *Lancelot* (New York: Farrar, Straus and Giroux, 1977), p. 239. All further references to this novel are from this edition and will be cited parenthetically in the text.

5. Northrop Frye, *The Great Code. The Bible and Literature* (San Diego: Harcourt Brace Jovanovich, Publishers, 1982), pp. 140-42.

6. J.W. Goethe, *Faust*, trans. Walter Kaufmann (Garden City: Anchor Books/Doubleday and Co., 1961/63), p. 381.

7. John P. Muller and J. William Richardson, *Lacan and Language. A Reader's Guide to Écrits* (New York: International Universities Press, Inc., 1982), p. 337.

8. Jacques Lacan, *Écrits. A Selection*, trans. Alan Sheridan (New York: W. W. Norton and Company, Inc., 1977), p. 22.

9. This, in fact, is Percy's second allusion to the generic tensions as viewed by Margaret Mitchell in *Gone with the Wind*. During the Chicago trip in *The Moviegoer*, Binx fantasizes the sexual episode with Kate, which turns out to be a failure, as his "dispatching" Kate "into as sweet a sleep as ever Scarlett enjoyed the morning of Rhett's return."

10. See Dorothy Kelly, *Fictional Genders. Role and Representation in Nineteenth-Century French Narrative* (Lincoln and London: Univ. of Nebraska Press, 1979), pp. 1-2.

11. Christopher Lasch, *The Culture of Narcissism. American Life in an Age of Diminishing Expectations* (New York: W. W. Norton and Company, Inc., 1979), p. 346.

12. Hélène Cixous, "Sorties: Out and Out: Attacks/Ways Out/Forays," in Hélène Cixous and Catherine Clement, *The Newly Born Woman*, trans. Betsy Wing (Minneapolis: Univ. of Minnesota Press, 1986), p. 66.

13. Ibid., p. 66.

14. Heinrich Zimmer, *The King and the Corpse. Tales of the Soul's Conquest of Evil*, ed. Joseph Campbell (Princeton: Princeton Univ. Press, 1956), p. 178.

15. Murray Krieger, *Visions of Extremity in Modern Literature*, vol. I: *The Tragic Vision* (Baltimore: The Johns Hopkins Univ. Press, 1973), p. 250.

16. Ibid., p. 253.

PART III

INTERSUBJECTIVITY

Five: The Broken—Un-Broken World

The Marble Faun

The Marble Faun, published four years before Hawthorne's death, was his last completed romance. He had difficulty deciding the title. Possibilities he considered, only to reject them, included: *Monte Beni; or, The Faun. A Romance*, *The Romance of a Faun*, *The Faun of Monte Beni: a Romance*, *Miriam: a Romance*, *Hilda: a Romance*, *Marble and Man: a Romance*.[1] These titles bluntly testify to Hawthorne's indecisiveness as to which of the four main characters occupies the focal place in the narrative. Significantly also, the book begins and ends with the four characters grouped together, as even suggested by the titles of the first and the last chapter, while the bulk of the novel explores their viewpoints separately, thus observing the division of the gender lines. This fictional strategy, together with the vision the book embraces, testifies to Hawthorne's indebtedness to Shakerism, an analogy, as I will further argue, used also by Percy in *The Second Coming*.

The English version of the book came out on February 28, 1860, with yet another title, apparently also suggested by Hawthorne: *Transformation: The Romance of Monte Beni*. This first edition concluded with the chapter where Hawthorne features the four focal characters: Miriam, Hilda, Donatello, and Kenyon. But both the readers and the reviewers demanded "further elucidations respecting the mysteries of the story" (4: 463), and Hawthorne, not without misgivings ("it's good for nothing. The story isn't meant to be explained; it's cloudland"),[2] was forced to write a Postscript, which appeared in the second English edition of March 14, 1860, and in the American edition of March 7, 1860, entitled *The Marble Faun. The Romance of Monte Beni.* However, the mystery remained unclarified.

The insights of a French philosopher, Gabriel Marcel, throw considerable light on Hawthorne's understanding of "mystery." Marcel draws a distinction between "problem" and "mystery." A problem he defines as "something met with which bars my passage. It is before me in its entirety."[3] On the other hand, a mystery is "something in which I find myself caught up, and whose essence is therefore not to be before me in its entirety" (*HD*, 80). In his specific example, the title of the detective story *The Mystery of a Yellow Room*, the word "mystery" implies that the author will eventually present the key towards the unveiling of a certain problem, which is made enigmatic and impenetrable at the beginning of the story. The skill of the author consists precisely in rendering the beginning as obscure as possible. The mystery thus understood puzzles us as long as the key whereby the enigma can be solved is not revealed. The reader is certain from the very outset of the story that the solution will become available as the story progresses. Conversely, mystery, as conceived by Marcel, applies to what cannot be approached as a problem, to what is "repugnant to problematizing." He adds that

> the mysterious evoked here must be looked for in the direction of light rather than in the direction of obscurity. Whatever is obscure is, in effect, for the mind the initial phase of a certain elucidation; and, inversely, no elucidation is

> possible except in regard to a datum which is relatively obscure. (*HD*, 82)

Similarly, Marcel claims, when we discuss the problem of evil, we should rather employ the word "mystery." For evil, in its very essence, does not yield itself to explanations for the reason that it should not be there in the first place. Here, one of the major affinities between Hawthorne's and Marcel's ideas can be traced, and we will presently see that the way Hawthorne uses the term "mystery" is akin to Marcel's concept. Towards the end of the narrative, Miriam voices the idea of the Fortunate Fall, which Kenyon later repeats in his conversation with Hilda. The word "mystery" is used to introduce the very idea. Miriam says:

> I delight to brood on the verge of this great *mystery*. . . . The story of the Fall of Man! Is it not repeated in our Romance of Monte Beni? And may we follow the analogy yet farther? Was that very sin—into which Adam precipitated himself and all his race—was it the destined means by which, over a long pathway of toil and sorrow, we are to attain a higher, brighter, and profounder happiness, than our lost birthright gave? (4: 434)

Whether the mystery here implied lends itself to such reasoning is an issue I shall address later. In the last chapter, Hawthorne propounds an explanation, which is to account for the complexities of his novel, saying that "the actual experience of even the most ordinary life is full of events that never explain themselves, either as regards their origin or their tendency" (4: 455). The term "mystery" gains further emphasis by being placed at the very end of the last chapter (4:462)—traditionally a position of weight. Hawthorne was inevitably irritated by his readers' demand to explain the "mysteries" of the plot because he was fully aware of the fact that the mystery of life, what Marcel calls the "ontological mystery," is inexplicable.

Another important distinction Marcel addresses is the distinction between communication and communion. Communication without communion Marcel dismisses as "unreal communication," citing as an example: I am in the same room with another person, who is visible and audible to me, yet his presence does not make itself felt, something important is lacking. To Marcel, this missing factor is the rapport between persons, which would enable them to experience each other *qua* persons. This absence of mutual rapport between persons, together with a lack of personal integrity, which is replaced by inauthenticity and what he calls "infidelity," contributes to Marcel's vision of a "broken world," that is, a "world which seems to have lost its inner unity, its living center—a broken world where each person is concerned only with himself" (*HD*, 90-91). He hastily adds, however, that this is not an only world.

We can now undertake to read Marcel personalist philosophy in intertextual relation to Hawthorne's presentation of the focal characters in *The Marble Faun*, since in no other text does Hawthorne evince as much interest in communication between characters, in this mutual rapport between individuals, as in *The Marble Faun*. My analysis focuses on the presentation of three people: Hilda, Miriam, and Donatello. Kenyon is not dealt with individually in this analysis because his role in the narrative boils down to that of a voyeur and mediator, faintly reminiscent of Nick Carraway's function in *The Great Gatsby*. But unlike Nick, Kenyon is basically conceived as a marginal figure, mostly as a mouthpiece for others, seldom expressing his own views. Moreover, he neither participates in the act of murder, which constitutes the crucial event of the narrative, as Miriam and Donatello do, nor witnesses it, as Hilda does. Thus his knowledge of the situation, and for the most part of the narrative, is limited.

The climactic event functions as an ordeal whereby the three characters undergo the transformation suggested by the title of the first English edition. One of Marcel's concepts again proves illuminating here. Marcel introduces the notion of "ordeal" in the context of love. Intersubjectivity, which culminates in love, or which is love, transcends all explanation and all reduction. In this sense, it is true to say that love addresses itself to what is eternal. Miriam voices this idea when she translates Donatello's exclamation "Why should [love] have any end? How long! Forever!—forever!—forever!" into a round thought, "Here, in those few, natural words, he has expressed that deep sense, that profound conviction of its own immortality, which genuine love never fails to bring" (4: 81-82). To Marcel, the "proof" of such an assertion is revealed when love exposes itself to a challenge, an ordeal, which calls into question the significance and the value of love. In Marcel's words: "love, far from merely requiring the acceptance of risk, demands it in a certain manner; love seems to be calling for a challenge to be tested because it is sure to emerge a conqueror" (*HD*, 74). We shall now see how the three Hawthornian characters in question "emerge" from the ordeal.

HILDA

Taking a lead from Marcel, it can be argued that Hilda's development in the narrative follows from unavailability to availability, from infidelity to fidelity, in its most accomplished form, that of "creative fidelity." Marcel roots unavailability ("indisponibilité") in alienation. Alienation thus understood stems from the inability to react to the other's presence. In Kenyons's apt summary of Hilda's character, these features come to the fore:

> It is strange, with all her delicacy and fragility, the impression she makes of being utterly sufficient to herself! . . .

> She is abundantly capable of sympathy, and delights to receive it, but she has no need of love! (4: 121)

Hawthorne's irony is skillfully hidden under all this "delicacy and fragility." The person lurking behind this passage is singularly self-centered, delighting in receiving, rather than in giving, loving no one except herself. Marcel pertinently relates unavailability to what he calls "egocentric topography." Accordingly, he defines an egoist as the one who "becomes the centre of a sort of mental space arranged in concentric zones of decreasing interest and participation," the one who surrounds himself with "a kind of shell which gradually harden[s] and imprison[s] him; and this sclerosis is bound up with the hardening of the categories in accordance with which [he] conceive[s] and evaluate[s] the world."[4] Hilda's moral absolutism constitutes this kind of "shell," behind which resides her utter egocentricity. Significantly, prior to the act of murder, she instinctively condones the stabbing of Virginia by her father, who thereby saved his daughter from disgrace, and is about to retract her words when Miriam says, "Is there such blessed potency in bloodshed? . . . Nay, Hilda, do not protest! I take your meaning rightly" (4: 163). But shortly after the murder, she severely shuns her tormented friend when Miriam pleads for understanding. Again, we might benefit by looking at Marcel's explanation. He introduces the notion of the "moi" (myself), which is not "my entire experience, but that portion or aspect of my experience I mean particularly to protect from a certain attack or infraction which may jeopardize it" (*HD*, 102). This "moi," he further argues, cannot be separated from the situation *here* and *now*, and only such a situation can elicit an egotistic response. Consequently, the filicide from ancient history has no bearing whatsoever upon Hilda's life, so she expresses an unguarded sentiment. Whereas the murder she has witnessed wrecks the foundations of her pleasant and sheltered existence, so she automatically condemns those who got her involved in it. The shell she has built around her ego is so "hardened" that virtually every emotion from outside shatters against it. All of Kenyon's attempts to penetrate it end in a fiasco. In the chapter featuring the two women as they discuss the murder, Hilda complains that she has no friend to whom she could confide her secret. She implores Miriam, who "was" her "dearest friend," to tell her what to do. Miriam suggests that Hilda confide her secret to Kenyon, which brings Hilda's instantaneous reply: "He cannot be my friend, . . . because . . . I have fancied that he sought to be something more!" (4: 211). Nowhere in the entire book does Hilda's self-love and egocentricity receive as much emphasis as in this conversation. She repudiates her friend on the ground that Miriam's "powerful magnetism" would be "too much" for her, and she adds, "The pure, white atmosphere, in which I try to discern what things are good and true, would be discoloured. And therefore, Miriam, before it is too late, I mean to put faith in this awful heart-quake, which warns me henceforth to avoid you!" (4: 208). Hilda's "I," which surfaces in the entire conversation ("It is not I, Miriam . . . not I that have done this," "I am a poor, lonely girl," "I am alone—alone"), allows no room for anybody but herself.

Hilda has been traditionally included in the group of Hawthorne's females stereotyped as Fair Maiden. The attributes almost invariably given to this group include: "frail," "pale," "sunny," "gentle," etc. But Hilda is neither pale nor frail. Both attributes imply a kind of withering, physically unfit female, which Hilda simply is not. In his initial characterization of Hilda, Hawthorne speaks of her "physical organization, which was at once *healthful* and exquisitely delicate" (4: 57), and of her "delicately tinged but *healthful* cheek" (4: 63). Mounting the "three hundred steps, at least" leading to the tower Hilda inhabits leaves Miriam breathless. But Hilda untiringly climbs them several times a day, back from her incessant rounds of galleries and museums, and to Miriam's complaint she responds, "but it will do you good." She is healthy, possessed of a strong will and independence, and singularly egocentric. Hilda is the only female character in Hawthorne's fiction, regardless of type, whose portrayal partakes of what Hawthorne considered to be a purely male characteristic: "masculine egotism." Her characterization evokes such staunch male egoists as Elliston, Dimmesdale, Chillingworth, and Clifford, to mention just a few.

Part of the confusion in interpreting Hilda's character derives from Hawthorne's own hesitations and ambivalences as regards her presentation. For instance, at one point he evokes her "sensitivity" and "intelligence," at another says that "she would probably have been puzzled by the technical terms of her own art" (4: 62). He is even indecisive about the color of Hilda's hair, first introducing her as "brown-haired" but forty pages later as "fair-haired." Another ten pages, and Hawthorne marries the two colors and speaks of Hilda's "light-brown ringlets." In Hawthorne's incessant use of art works as symbols, he likens both Miriam *and* Hilda (a very misleading analogy if we accept the thesis that the two women identify the standard polarities of the Gothic romance) to Guido's *Beatrice Cenci*, and speaks of the "hidden luxuriance of [Beatrice's] *auburn* hair." In popular usage, "auburn" of course signifies reddish-brown, but etymologically, the meaning of "auburnus," derived from "albus" (white), is influenced by an association with Middle English "brun" (brown)—hence, light-brown. In Hilda's copy of Guido's masterpiece, Beatrice's suffering is conveyed by "a little redness about the eyelids, very slightly indicated, so that you would question whether or no the girl had been weeping" (4: 64), which may indicate post-lapsarian Hilda of the latter part of the book. Subsequently, however, Hawthorne says that "it was a sorrow that removed this beautiful girl out of the sphere of humanity, and set her in a far-off region, the remoteness of which . . . makes us shiver at as at a spectre," which echoes a passage from *The Scarlet Letter*, where Hawthorne discusses the psychological transformation wrought in Hester as a consequence of her sin.

Similarly with flower symbols: Critics usually associate Hilda with a rose (the attribute, which also clings to Phoebe), alluding to the scene at the end of *The Marble Faun*, where Hilda pelts Kenyon with a rose-bud. But earlier in the narrative, Hawthorne makes it quite clear, speaking of Hilda, that the time for a "crimson rose" has not yet come:

> . . . it is very beautiful (though the lover's heart may grow chill at the perception) to see how the snow will sometimes linger in a virgin's breast, even after the Spring is well-advanced. In such alpine soils, the summer will not be anticipated; we seek vainly for passionate flowers, and blossoms of fervid hue and spicy fragrance, finding only *snow-drops* and *sunless violets*, when it is almost the full season for the crimson rose. (4: 373-74)

Although this description belongs to the narrative stance, Kenyon acutely senses the remnants of the winter chill in Hilda, and he even designs a "little statue of maidenhood gathering a snow-drop." But even as he hopes for better things from Hilda, he never puts his design into marble because he "soon recognized it as one of those fragile creations which are true only to the moment that produces them" (4: 375).

Hilda takes time to change, but she changes nonetheless. Hers is one of the transformations Hawthorne alluded to in the title of the first English edition. The change in Hilda is conveyed on three levels: in reference to her art, her religion, and, most importantly, her attitude to her fellow beings. Hilda is a skillful copyist, which Agnes Donohue finds a "fitting occupation for the one who never has an original idea."[5] Even Hawthorne's apologia for her copy-work, when he, for instance, says that "she chose the better and loftier and more unselfish part, laying her individual hopes, her fame, her prospects of enduring remembrance, at the feet of those great departed ones" (4: 60), cannot conceal the fact that her main reason for choosing this form of art is that she lacks "the reality which comes only from a close acquaintance with life" (4: 55). Here, Marcel's notion of "fidelity" will be especially helpful in establishing Hilda's attitude to art before and after her traumatic experience. Speaking about aesthetic creativity, Marcel juxtaposes two notions: "presence" and "effigy":

> A presence to which we are faithful is not at all the same thing as the carefully preserved effigy of an object which has vanished; an effigy is . . . nothing but a likeness; metaphysically it is *less* than the object, it is a diminution of the object. Whereas presence, on the contrary, is *more* than the object, it exceeds the object on every side. (*PE*, 23)

A presence that Marcel evokes in this passage is the presence of the world to the artist, "to his heart and to his mind, . . . to his very being." This idea expresses the essential meaning of "fidelity," which is "the active perpetuation of presence, the renewal of its benefits—of its virtue which consists in a mysterious incitement to create" (*PE*, 22).

We gather that Hilda relinquished copying after her traumatic experience. But we also see that, after returning Hilda to the fictive universe after several chapters from which she was absent, Hawthorne endows her with a new perception of art works. Where she once searched for beauty in her "venerated" masters, she now "saw beauty less vividly, but felt truth, or the lack of it, more profoundly" (4: 338). What she now finds lacking in some of the paintings that she revered in the past is "an inevitable hollowness . . . [which] essayed to express to the world what [the artist] had not in [his] own soul" (4: 338). But she also senses that "there is something beyond almost all which pictorial genius has produced" (4: 375). She recognizes, perhaps even more acutely than any other character in the book, that what Hawthorne calls "spiritual revelation," and Marcel "mystery," cannot be reduced to describable qualities. The act of creation, like the act of participation (intersubjectivity), must ultimately remain a mystery, beyond all reasoning and beyond all verbal expression. Here, the Greek word Marcel uses, *syneidesis*, which he translates as "a flash of insight," most aptly conveys Hilda's new perception of art. It is revealed to her, in a flash of insight, a *syneidesis,* that "a work of genius" involves "deeper *mysteries* of Revelation," and brings them closer to "man's heart," and makes him "tenderer to be impressed by [mysteries], than the most eloquent words of preacher or prophet" (4: 340).

Thus, one remarkable transformation wrought in Hilda, on the level of art, is the kind of transcendence conveyed by *syneidesis.* Another concerns Hilda's capability of what Marcel calls "secondary reflection," or "recollection." "It is within recollection," Marcel says, "that I take up my position—or, rather, I become capable of taking up my position—in regard to my life; I withdraw from it in a certain way, but not as the pure subject of cognition; *in this withdrawal I carry with me that which I am and which perhaps my life is not*" (*PE*, 12-13). "Withdrawal" is evidently the key term here, but Marcel also cautions us that "to withdraw into oneself is not to be for oneself." The latter defines an egocentric attitude, whereas the former manifests itself in what Marcel calls "secondary reflection" whereby self-consciousness is awakened. Hilda's utter loneliness and suffering make her sensitive to the suffering of others, and she searches the museums and galleries for some point of reference between her own condition and a similar predicament expressed in an art form. She at last identifies with an image of lonely, suffering humanity epitomized in Perugino's Christ bound to a pillar. The impact of Hilda's new perception, faintly resembling the voice of Whitman's persona in *Song of Myself*, is that Hilda no longer celebrates her spotlessness, and where she once shied from Miriam's "powerful magnetism," she now humbly identifies with suffering sinful humanity.

Hawthorne's incessantly repeated opinion that Hilda is "a daughter of the Puritans" makes us anticipate that this assertion will be challenged at some point in the narrative. Her attraction to Catholicism, evidently shared by Hawthorne, only enhances this anticipation. Hilda needs a challenge whereby her faith will be tested. Here, as with the issue of "creative fidelity," Marcel's insights prove especially illuminating. To begin with, Marcel disagrees with Henri Bergson on the relationship between fidelity and creativity. To Bergson, creativity lies in inventiveness, in spontaneous innovation, whereas fidelity tends to be interpreted as a routine, or an "observance" in the sense of its being "an arbitrary safeguard against the power of renewal which is the spirit itself" (*PE*, 21). Marcel argues, however, that the disparity between the two ideas disappears if fidelity, or faithfulness, is "the active recognition of something permanent, not formally, after the manner of a law, but ontologically." In this sense, fidelity is the exact opposite of inert conformism, and refers to what Marcel once again conceives as a "presence" in the broadest sense, as "something which can be maintained within us and before us as a presence." But he also indicates that it is in the "active and continuous struggle against the forces of interior dissipation, as also against the sclerosis of habit," that fidelity emerges a conqueror over the inertia of conformism. No doubt, this argument harks back to Kierkegaard's idea of existential pathos that involves, we recall, inwardness, struggle, despair, fear and trembling, and, ultimately, faith. The complexity of Hilda's case vis à vis religion reflects Hawthorne's own religious dilemma. He records meticulously, if somewhat grudgingly, Hilda's response to Catholicism permeating the eternal city: Grudgingly, because every allusion to a possibility of her conversion elicits Hilda's passionate rejection. Yet she explicitly states that her dedication to trimming the lamp and supplying fresh flowers at the shrine of the Virgin Mary in the tower above her "dove-cote" has a "religious significance" for her. Whether this devotion indicates mere girlish exaltation or suggests something more profound in Hilda's character is ultimately revealed in two great chapters, "Altars and Incense" and "The World's Cathedral."

Desperately looking for some way to alleviate her agonizing suffering and loneliness, Hilda wanders into St. Peter's. The first chapter opens with Hilda's meditations on the advantages of

Catholicism over Protestantism. As the chapter progresses, the pros are augmented with the cons and, as the chapter draws to its close, Hilda's mind regarding the primacy of one over the other seems firmly set.

Although Hawthorne deems the sacrament of confession a "mere convenience," there can be no doubt that the essential promise of absolution inherent in the Catholic sacrament was to him, and to Hilda, very tempting. How far back in his life and literary career this fascination can be traced is hard to determine. We of course remember Dimmesdale's agonizing experience resulting from his inability to reveal his sin. But perhaps we should also consider another possible influence in Hawthorne's brief and ill-fated acquaintance with the Shakers, to whom the ritual of confession was an important dogmatic element.[6]

It would be far-fetched, no doubt, to argue that the vicissitudes of Hawthorne's fascination with the Shakers' dogma and ritual resemble his attraction to Catholicism. However, in both cases Hawthorne could not accept the disparity between the ideas professed by the adherents of these respective denominations and the imperfection of the individuals who represented them. In his criticism of Catholicism he echoes his previous disillusionment with the Shakers, especially when he speaks of his disgust with "the pretense of Holiness and the reality of Nastiness, each equally omnipresent" (4: 326). In "Altars and Incense" Hawthorne's ambivalent feelings accompany Hilda as she takes notice of a young man "writhing" before a shrine, who then kneels down to "weep and pray." Hawthorne records Hilda's thoughts, "If this youth had been a Protestant, he would have kept all that torture pent up in his heart, and let it burn there till it seared him into indifference" (4: 347). We need only recall Hester Prynne's transformation from "passion and feeling" to "thought," the words "indifference" and "frozen calmness" used alternatively, to realize the full impact of the last words of this passage.

The next paragraph brings the change of emphasis, since Hawthorne indicates that Hilda's "delicate appreciation of art stood her in good stead and lost Catholicism a convert." Hilda finds it blasphemous to kneel at the shrine of a saint who "was merely the flattered portrait of an earthly beauty; the wife, at best, of the artist." Hawthorne superbly anticipates here the "non-representational" art of the following century, the surrealists' departure from the external model and discovery of the internal model, which reveals the sphere of subjective experience. Accordingly, Hilda, surveying the figures on the shrines, looks for "something more":

> . . . a face of celestial beauty, but human as well as heavenly, and with the shadow of past grief upon it; bright with immortal youth, yet matronly and motherly, and endowed with a queenly dignity, but infinitely tender, as the highest and deepest attribute of her divinity. (4: 348)

The chapter ends with two brief scenes where Hilda's religion is ultimately tested. One is when she dips her fingers into the holy water, and is about to make a sign of cross, when what she feels is the spirit of her mother "looking down upon her child, *the daughter of Puritan forefathers*," stops her in mid-motion. The second scene starkly reveals that Hilda's religious dilemma has been solved, if not yet for Hilda herself, then surely for Hawthorne. The passage deserves to be quoted at length:

> Suddenly, and as if it were done in a dream, Hilda found herself kneeling before the shrine, under the ever-burning lamp that throws its rays upon the Archangel's face. She laid her forehead on the marble steps before the altar, and sobbed out a prayer; *she hardly knew to whom*, whether Michael, the Virgin, or the Father; *she hardly knew for what*, save only a vague longing, that thus the burthen of her spirit might be lightened a little.

> In an instant she snatched herself up, as it were, from her knees, all a-throb with the emotions which were struggling to force their way out of her heart by the avenue, that had so nearly been opened for them. Yet there was a strange sense of relief won by that momentary, passionate prayer; a strange joy, moreover, whether for what she had done, or *for what she had escaped doing*, Hilda could not tell. But she felt as one half stifled, who had stolen a breath of air. (4: 352)

Even though Hilda is still too confused to quite sort out her thoughts, Hawthorne's emphasis rests, no doubt, upon the latter alternative, on what she has escaped doing.

What follows in the next chapter has a tremendous psychological significance, though not in the religious sense. Hilda goes to confession, and the change in her that Hawthorne communicates to his reader clearly betrays the idea of purification as the ultimate stage of *catharsis*. The word "relief" is used here again, but in a quite different sense from what it signified in the previous passage:

> And, ah, what a relief! When the hysteric gasp, the strife between words and sobs, had subsided, what a torture had passed away from her soul! It was all gone; her bosom was as pure now as in her childhood. She was a girl again: she was Hilda, of the dove-cote; not that doubtful creature whom her own doves had hardly recognized as their mistress and playmate, by reason of the *death-scent that clung to her garments!* (4: 358)

The relief experienced by Hilda following the confession and terminating her agony of suffering clearly indicates that to gain self--knowledge, which ultimately leads to self-transformation, one must die and be born again. As one of Marcel's characters in the play *Un Homme de Dieu* tells his wife who, after some traumatic experience for both of them, invites him to participate in an inter-subjective communion, "it is as if you have been given back to me from the dead."[7] To borrow this phrase from Marcel, Hilda, who enthusiastically greets Kenyon in the next chapter, is given back to him from the dead. Kenyon thinks that she has never been "so delightful as now; so softened out of the chillness of her virgin pride; so full of fresh thoughts, at which he was often moved to smile" (4: 370).

Hawthorne focuses the chapter "Reminiscences of Miriam" on yet another self-transformation in Hilda, which occurs on a personal level. Kenyon, now with the knowledge of Miriam and Donatello's part in the murder of the Model, brings up the subject of Miriam's guilt, and Hilda first presents her former self-righteous self, saying that she believes in "only one right and one wrong"; but Kenyon's pertinent remark that she needs no mercy and is, therefore, incapable of showing any, forces Hilda into "second reflection" on the subject of her relationship with Miriam. She thinks that there are, perhaps, "other questions to be considered, aside from that single one of Miriam's guilt or innocence; as, for example, whether a close bond of friendship . . . ought to be severed on account of any unworthiness, which we subsequently detect in our friend" (4: 385). These thoughts directly anticipate Marcel's insight on the subject of love. Love, he maintains, rests on the unconditional assumption *I shall love you no matter what happens*, which is but another way of saying what Hawthorne has expressed via Hilda's considerations: "For, in these unions of hearts, (call them marriage, or whatever else,) we take each other for better, for worse" (4: 385). Marcel contrasts this unconditional commitment with what he calls "the conditional commitment," which presupposes "a *de facto* if not a *de jure*" relationship which works only "under the limited circumstances in which it is made" (*HD*, 74). Moreover, we might recall, love not only requires risk but consciously exposes itself to a challenge because "it is sure to emerge a conqueror." Such is, in fact, the result of Hilda's meditations, "the tie between Miriam and herself had been real, the affection true, and . . . therefore the implied compact was not to be shaken off" (4: 386).

MIRIAM

The typology of Miriam's development in the narrative resembles Hilda's in the sense that the murder of the Model furnishes a caesura beyond which Miriam undergoes transformation. What distinguishes their developments, however, is that Miriam takes less time to change and that the areas of personal encounter affected by the ordeal are different in her case. In speaking of personal encounter, we must first of all investigate Miriam's attitude to Donatello before and after the murder. Quite strikingly, whenever the two of them are accompanied by Hilda and Kenyon, Miriam more frequently speaks *of* Donatello than *to* him. Such a situation indicates, to Marcel, the absence of mutual rapport between persons. He says that "a person spoken of in this way feels that he is being treated as an object and so is being relegated to the level of things—or, at best, to the animal level. He is being deprived of his status as a subject" (*HD*, 40). Accordingly, Donatello is conveyed as a "bulldog" or a "hound," following in Miriam's footstep, or, at best, a faun, whose innocence gets as much emphasis as does his animal nature:

> So full of *animal life* as he was, so joyous in his deportment, so handsome, so physically well-developed, he made no impression of incompleteness, of maimed or stinted nature. And yet in social intercourse, these familiar friends of his habitually and instinctively allowed for him, *as for a child* or some other lawless thing, exacting no strict obedience to conventional rules, and hardly noticing his eccentricities enough to pardon them. (4: 14)

The issue, which this passage underlies, looks ahead to Marcel's distinction between "protective" love and reciprocal love between fully mature people. Protective love, Marcel tells us, is oriented toward the development of the weak, the defenceless. But this kind of love, as John B. O'Malley in his analysis of Marcelian thought aptly notes, is dependent on love in the fuller sense, "in its *trust* to that point where it is capable of mature love, which only then will be fully free."[8] What the reader may take as Miriam's patronizing attitude towards Donatello, prior to the murder, in fact stems from her urgency to protect her vulnerable, innocent friend from the harsh world, and from herself. But this urgency is not the same as the "exigency" Marcel has spoken of. The exigency of being is a yearning for fullness, which can be realized solely in intersubjectivity, in the *I-Thou* relationship, where the mystery of being is open to us.[9] Kenyon's opinion quoted below, on the nature of Miriam and Donatello's relationship, sounds almost like a line from Marcel: "The mysterious process, by which our earthly life instructs us for another state of being, was begun for you by her" (4: 321). This synopsis comes midway through the book, and Donatello perceives the "truth" of it in a flash of insight. However, Miriam knows it all along. Immediately following the murder, she tells Donatello: "The deed knots us together, for time and eternity. . . . One wretched and worthless life has been sacrificed, to cement two other lives forevermore" (4: 175). While these words superbly communicate the idea of intersubjective communion, the reader may at the same time question the psychological credibility of a union, which, as Donatello reflects upon Miriam's assertion of love, "consists in guilt. Cemented with blood, which would corrupt and grow more noisome forever and forever" (4: 175). Henry James has demonstrated that even less traumatic experiences produce irreparable damage in the people involved. But Hawthorne has insisted on convincing his reader that humanity is always gained at a high cost, and that self-knowledge can either be attained through the arduous process of inwardization (as in Hester's case) or else can be induced by shock. Hester alludes to this idea when she says that her ethereal child needs "a grief that should deeply touch her, and thus humanize and make her capable of sympathy" (1: 184). Clifford in *The House of the Seven Gables* is literally awakened from his torpor following Jaffrey Pyncheon's death, and, of course, shock jars loose the three focal characters in *The Marble Faun*.

Miriam is apparently puzzled when Donatello tells her that she encouraged him to murder the Model. "Could it be so?" she thinks, "Had her eyes provoked, or assented to this deed? She had not known it" (4: 172). Little as she remembers of the actual scene, she recalls two emotions: ecstasy and then horror. The scene is as much of a "dim show" for Miriam as it is for the reader.

The scene bears close scrutiny, for Hawthorne depicts here with minimum detail a very complex situation. Miriam and Donatello walk away from the rest of the company, and approach "the ominous precipice." Looking around, Miriam perceives that they are being followed by the Model. The sensation she now experiences is definitely indicative of some threat, possibly gestured by the Model, which is thus conveyed:

> She must have had cause to dread some unspeakable evil from this strange persecutor, and to know that this was the very crisis of her calamity; for, as he drew near, such a cold, sick despair crept over her, that it impeded her breath, and benumbed her natural promptitude of thought. (4: 171)

Presently, Miriam falls on her knees, and the rest of the scene is a "dim show" for her to the extent that ultimately she cannot "distinguish what was done and suffered; no, not even whether she were really an actor and sufferer in the scene" (4: 171). The fact that Miriam kneels down is significant and suggests three possibilities.

First, she kneels down to avoid the Model's lunge. Second, she kneels down before her persecutor to beg his mercy. Finally, the whole episode faintly resembles the scene in *Hamlet*, in which the prince, now determined to kill Claudius, stops short on finding his stepfather kneeling and praying. Whatever actually has passed among the three people, Hawthorne, quite unexpectedly, presents us here with a legal case—namely, that the murder was performed in Miriam's defence. He drops this clue in what follows, for his concentration falls on a much broader issue. He says that "an individual wrong-doing melts into the great mass of human crime, and makes us—who dreamed only of our own little separate sin —makes us guilty of the whole" (4: 177). We cannot help recall Dostoyevsky's moral dilemma, especially exemplified in *The Brothers Karamazov*, where he has Father Zossima echo Hawthorne's thought in claiming the responsibility of each of us for the sins of all.[10]

However, at the opposite pole of the vision shared by Hawthorne and Dostoyevsky is a conviction that to deprive man of guilt is to deprive him of the chance for moral growth. Conversely, Albert Camus, in an analogous context to Hawthorne's,[11] asserts that there is no guilt, or moral evil, conceivable in man. As Murray Krieger notes, for Camus there is only "the primary evil," which "arises out of the absurd universe and not out of man."[12]

Unexpectedly, Jac Tharpe argues this point for Hawthorne, saying that action, for him, is meaningless, and that he "proposes inaction in the face of utter bewilderment. There is nothing he knows to do. He is therefore completely agnostic, except in disapproving action."[13] These words deftly characterize the fictive universe of John Barth (the writer Tharpe discusses in another book). Yet they seriously limit Hawthorne's vision. If we accept Tharpe's reasoning, the inevitable conclusion is that a Hawthorne character must adopt an attitude of indifference matching his bewilderment and his disapproval of action. We are then caught in a ruse because Hawthorne has time and again demonstrated that indifference hampers the individual's actualization of spirit. Moreover, the crux of Tharpe's argument, consistent with the above thesis, is that a character's transformation, in Hawthorne's terms, is inconceivable. He quotes Miriam's words uttered on the morning following the murder, "Am I not the same as yesterday?", to which Tharpe answers that "she is simply what she always was." Tharpe's considerations appear to take no account of the essential ambiguity with which Hawthorne depicts Miriam's character. Hawthorne argues this point consistently throughout the narrative, beginning with this statement:

> There was an ambiguity about this young lady . . . She resembled one of those images of light, which conjurors evoke and cause to shine before us, in apparent tangibility, only an arm's length beyond our grasp; we make a step in advance, expecting to seize the illusion, but find it still precisely so far out of our reach. (4: 21)

Hawthorne uses the "mask" image to convey this special quality of Miriam's character. The "mask" image, we remember, that Hawthorne attributed to Hester Prynne signified the departure from life, as it were, stemming from the attitude of total resignation. Here its meaning is far more complex. In the only extensive conversation between Miriam and the Model, the latter says: "You must throw off your present mask, and assume another" (4: 97). While these words have their direct context in the Model's knowledge of Miriam's past, they also effectively summarize Miriam's character. She time and again communicates, specifically through her art, her wish to be another. When Donatello visits Miriam at her studio, his attention is drawn to a strange figure of a woman represented on one of her paintings. She explains that:

> It is a lady of exceedingly pliable disposition; now a heroine of romance, and now a rustic maid; yet all for show, being created, indeed, on purpose to wear rich shawls and other garments in a becoming fashion. This is the true end of her being, although she pretends to assume the most varied duties and perform many parts in life, while really

> the poor puppet has nothing on earth to do. . . . I . . . seem to be describing nine women out of ten in the person of my lay-figure! For most purposes, she has the advantage of the sisterhood. *Would I were like her!* (4: 41-42)

Subsequently Miriam gives Donatello a portfolio of sketches "which indicated a happier mood" of the artist. They depict the scenes from "common life": two lovers sitting between the branches of a shrub, a young couple at the fireplace, and a rustic scene "of humble enjoyment by a cottage door." In all these drawings, "a figure was pourtrayed apart," whose "face and form had the traits of Miriam's own" (4: 46). The impact of what Hawthorne attempts to articulate here can be inferred from the passage in the same chapter where Hawthorne's mind strays from Miriam and Donatello to extol the wonders of needlework as "distinguishing women from men." "There is something extremely pleasant," he says, "in this peculiarity of needlework. . . . A vast deal of human sympathy runs along this electric line [the thread], stretching from the throne to the wicker-chair of the humblest seamstress, and keeping high and low in a species of communion with their kindred beings" (4: 39-40). He then adds that when "the needle involuntarily ceases to fly, it is a sign of trouble." Donatello, who sees an unmended glove in Miriam's lap, thinks that "something was amiss." Hawthorne has evidently symbolized what Roy R. Male calls "the humane qualities of investment" in the feminine devotion to sewing. Male argues that this devotion reflects the function of the heart, "the feminine role of conserving and clothing in time."[14] It is at once obvious, however, that this role does not go to Miriam, even though she seems to envy "this advantage of the sisterhood." It is equally evident that Hawthorne perceives Hilda in this role, especially Hilda of the last pages of the book, who relinquishes her art to become a "household saint," "enshrined" and "worshipped" at her husband's fireside. Miriam so acutely covets Hilda her femininity and dreams of living up to her image that she feels that she has lost her identity. After the murder and Hilda's rejection, she bluntly tells Kenyon that Hilda has set her free:

> Well, my dear friend, when you go back to Rome, tell Hilda what her severity has done! She was all Womanhood to me; and when she cast me off, I had no longer any terms to keep with the reserves and decorums of my sex. Hilda has set me free! Pray tell her so, from Miriam, and thank her! (4: 287)

Kenyon, no doubt, recalls this confession later on, when he concludes that the "mask" Miriam once assumed was only an "interlude," as she now "resumed her proper character" (4: 397).

Whether Hawthorne has idealized Hilda, at times to absurdity, with a genuine intention to please his wife, or, as Donohue suggests, to get back at Sophia, "whose negative aggression made him her slave in the early days of their marriage,"[15] he consistently brings his vision, as he announced in *The Scarlet Letter*, of "the angel and apostle of the coming revelation" to its close. Viewed through Hawthorne's sympathetic understanding of Miriam's inner drama, her great zeal for life, her courage in the face of adversities, her fidelity to friends, and her mature love for Donatello, the reader tends to find in Miriam the characteristics of the New Woman. But Hawthorne, needless to say, draws a decisive line here.

Despite inconsistencies in Hawthorne's presentation of his American heroine in *The Marble Faun*, we should not doubt that he ultimately intended Hilda, and not Miriam, as some critics have argued, in the role of a new Eve. As the novel closes, Hilda is the sovereign incarnation of his apocalyptic (ideal) vision, whereas Miriam, despite the formerly confusing iconography, is relegated to its opposite, the demonic vision. Repeated allusions in the text to the biblical account of the fall have given several critics an incentive to assign scriptural roles to Hawthorne's characters. Thus, for example, Donohue identifies Donatello with Adam, Miriam with

Eve-Lilith, and the Model with the serpent, whose murder inevitably occasions Donatello-Adam's initiation into evil. Male argues that Miriam's rebellion against her father makes her a candidate for the role of Eve "after her first depravity," the name "Miriam" originally signifying "rebellion." But Miriam, in Male's scheme, is also "potentially" a second Eve because, as he reminds us, the name "Mary" derives from Greek "Mariam" and Hebrew "Miryam." Various allusions to Paradise and to Miriam and Donatello's expulsion from it make both interpretations tenable. But the iconography gets complicated as the narrative unfolds, and even initially is obscured by parallels between Miriam and Rachel, whom Jacob deemed worth "wooing seven years, and seven more." This last analogy is of special importance, if only because the number "seven" had a considerable significance for Hawthorne, but in order to grasp the meaning Hawthorne has reserved for Miriam, we must sort out all these images. First of all, as Frye reminds us, Eve and Lilith do not embody the same kind of vision. They are both maternal figures, but Lilith (mother of demons) belongs to the demonic vision, whereas Eve (also Rachel, the symbolic mother of Israel) represents what Frye calls an "intermediate" type of mother figure, which means that she occupies a place between the demonic and the apocalyptic vision, since she goes through the cycle of sin and redemption.[16] A question suggests itself at this point: Can we really identify Miriam with the biblical mother figure? That Hawthorne seemed to have doubts about it can be deduced from yet another parallel in the text: between Miriam and the "virgin-widow" Judith. Miriam gets "widowed" twice in the narrative: the first time, when Donatello, tormented with guilt despite Miriam's endless efforts to comfort him, goes for his "penitential pilgrimage"; the second time, which is apparently terminal, when he confesses the crime and goes to prison. But even this parallel cannot be taken as Hawthorne's last word concerning Miriam. As the narrative moves to its close, we get a "cumulative" image of Miriam associated with colors: red and gold, but also with *seven* Etruscan gems and the *seven* hills of Rome. During the second Carnival scene, Kenyon perceives two figures in the crowd of merry dancers, male and female: a peasant and a contadina. The peasant turns out to be Donatello, accompanied by Miriam, who is wearing "one of those brilliant costumes, largely kindled up with scarlet, and decorated with gold embroidery" (4: 426). Incidentally, when Miriam greets Kenyon earlier from a splendid carriage, she is wearing a red stone. In most paintings of the crucifixion scene, the Virgin Mary is represented in a blue garb and Mary Magdalene in red. Whether Hawthorne has intended this affinity, that is, Miriam as Mary Magdalene (Male's second interpretation of her name would apply here as well), is hard to determine. Supportive of this analogy would be the fact that Mary Magdalene, as an "intermediate" bridal figure between the demonic Whore and the apocalyptic Bride, represents the idea of man's redemption from sin through love. This interpretation stands only if we accept the thesis that Miriam *is* redeemed through her love for Donatello. But, then, the image of red and gold combined indicates yet another possible source—namely, the woman who appears in Revelation 17 "clothed in purple and scarlet and bedizened with gold and jewels and pearls." The woman, who is, of course, the Great Whore of Babylon and Rome, rides on a beast with seven heads matching the seven hills on which the Whore resides.

Before Hilda and Kenyon leave Rome, the American girl receives a wedding gift from Miriam, a priceless bracelet "composed of seven Etruscan gems, dug out of seven sepulchres, and each of them the signet of some princely personage, who had lived an immemorial time ago" (4: 462). Hilda remembers that in the past she "amused herself with telling a mythical and magic legend for each gem, comprising the imaginary adventures and catastrophe of its former wearer" (4: 462). As the passage unfolds, we get "seven" repeated three times in one sentence: "seven wondrous tales," "seven sepulchres," and "seven-fold sepulchral gloom." The reader cannot go wrong: The message incorporated in this image alludes to the biblical account of the meanings of the beast's seven heads. The seven hills of Rome represent the first meaning the guiding angel intimates to the narrator of Revelation, but they also stand for "seven kings, of whom five have already fallen, one is now reigning, and the other one is yet to come." Such is the final image of Miriam, except for the ironic remark in the Postscript that "her crime lay merely in a glance," and this image is as much condemnatory as generating hope inherent in the vision of the end of the world. Hence, Hilda, who "had a hopeful soul," even as she sadly contemplates Miriam's fortunes, still "saw sunlight on the mountain--tops."

DONATELLO

Speaking of Donatello, we must first of all acknowledge a theme, which is expertly interwoven into the overall subject matter of the encounter between people—namely, the theme of the double. Practically every character has her or his double, even several doubles, the scenes, or fragments of narrative, are doubled, and so are fragments of conversations. Donatello as the Faun of Praxiteles is the most persistent double image in the narrative. Like *The House of the Seven Gables*, *The Marble Faun* makes the case for the presence of the monstrous double. What distinguishes Hawthorne's vision in this novel from that in *The House of the Seven Gables*, and at the same time makes it more harmonious with René Girard's theory, is that both Donatello and the Model are conveyed in such terms as inhere in Girard's definition of the monstrous double. The image, according to Girard, combines animal, human, and divine elements. His first example is taken from *The Bacchae*, where Pentheus identifies the double vision with the vision of the monster incarnated in Dionysus, who is man, god, and bull in one person. Much is made in *The Marble Faun* of the faun's goat-like ears, which

Kenyon and Miriam playfully attribute to Donatello. Girard maintains that the duality of the monster is conveyed in such a manner that ultimately all distinctions blur, "all differences are abolished," and he becomes a real flesh and blood double. In this context, let us consider the paragraph depicting Donatello's gamboling on the grounds of Villa Borghese:

> He ran races with himself along the gleam and shadow of the wood-paths. He leapt up to catch the overhanging bough of an ilex, and swinging himself by it, alighted far onward, as if he had flown thither through the air. In a sudden rapture, he embraced the trunk of a sturdy tree, and seemed to imagine it a creature worthy of affection and capable of a tender response; he clasped it closely in his arms, as a Faun might have clasped the warm feminine grace of the Nymph, whom antiquity supposed to dwell within that rough, encircling rind. Then, in order to bring himself closer to the genial earth, with which his kindred instincts linked him so strongly, he threw himself at full length on the turf, and pressed down his lips, kissing the violets and daisies, which kissed him back again, though shyly, in their maiden fashion. (4: 74)

The blurring of features is even more pointedly depicted in the figure of the Model. The gradual unveiling of the Model's monstrous characteristics reveals the subtleties of Hawthorne's art. He suggests the area of connotations, divinity and monstrosity combined, when he first introduces the Model:

> He looked as if he might just have stepped out of a picture . . . being no other than one of those living models, dark, bushy-bearded, wild of aspect and attire, whom artists convert into *Saints or assassins*, according as their pictorial purposes demand. (4: 19)

Thereafter, chapter after chapter, leading to the climax, Hawthorne accumulates the Model's evil characteristics, a strategy similar to his characterization of Jaffrey Pyncheon in *The House of the Seven Gables*. In both books the tactic is meant to prepare the ground for the sacrifice of the victim.

The typology of the monstrous double in *The Marble Faun* is a remarkable achievement on Hawthorne's part that combines psychology with myth. The two carnival scenes form a framework of the cyclical structure of the book connected with two fundamental impulses, hate and love. Hate is the culminating point of the first scene, love of the second carnival. The first carnival scene, prolonged into the following chapters and culminating in the murder, exhibits striking analogies with a sacrificial rite. Such a rite, maintains Girard, takes the form of "hysterical mimesis," whereby the excitement aroused by chants, dances, and mock combats reaches a pitch of intensity, and first "young men, then adult men and women are overcome. They stagger about among their companions, then fall to the ground in convulsions, moaning and emitting piercing cries."[17] These rites generate an aggression in the participants that finds its outlet in an act of sacrificial murder, from which new order is to emerge. During the first carnival, Donatello is overcome and "frisks" around Miriam "bubbling over with joy," gesticulating extravagantly, and in no time he infects Miriam with his exuberance. Now, they run "races with each other, side by side, with shouts and laughter," pelt each other with flowers (mock-combat), and Miriam playfully teases Donatello: "When your curls shook just now, methought I had a peep at the pointed ears!" (4: 86). Then other people become infected and are "drawn to the spot, and struck into the dance, singly, or in pairs, as if they were all gone mad with jollity" (4: 87). But the scene does not last long, and just before it ends Hawthorne introduces another double image, which transparently indicates the source of the overall iconography. He compares the described proceedings to "the sculptured scene on the front and sides of a sarcophagus," in which "some tragic incident is shadowed forth" (4: 89). Hawthorne accentuates the analogy between the sculptured scene and the sylvan dance in bringing the latter to its close as Miriam is suddenly confronted by "a strange figure that shook its fantastic garments in the air, and pranced before her on its tiptoes almost vying with the agility of Donatello himself. It was the Model" (4: 89). The twofold function of the last passage is to bring out the Model's imitation of Donatello's behavior, which indicates the same mythical source: the monstrous double; and to stress the Model's re-enactment of the hysterical trance that leads to the collective expulsion, which also inheres in the description of the sacrificial rite. Following the appearance of the Model, "the music ceased, and the dancers came abruptly to a pause. All that motley throng of rioters was dissolved as suddenly as it had been drawn together" (4: 89-90).

The dialogue between Miriam and Donatello that immediately follows this scene clearly alludes to the impulse of hatred culminating the sacrificial rite. On another level of perception, Hawthorne refers here to a psychological mechanism generating hatred. We might resort once again to Marcel's thought, and specifically to his analysis of hatred. Contrary to love, which presupposes subjective participation, hatred stems from the objective attitude because in hating someone we do not approach her or him as a person *qua* person but as a kind of "disperson" who is reduced to a mere object of our hatred. A genuine manifestation of hatred is the act of focusing our emotions not on a hated person, but on some defect which this "disperson" incarnates. Marcel's analysis of hatred presents an extreme attitude characterized by the absence of genuine participation, whereby a person is relegated to the level of things, or to the animal level. This idea finds expression in Miriam and Donatello's perception of the Model, just before their assertion of hatred:

> His lips were drawn apart so as to disclose his set teeth, thus giving him a look of animal rage, which we seldom

> see except in persons of the simplest and rudest natures. A shudder seemed to pass through his very bones.
>
> "I hate him!" muttered [Donatello].
>
> "Be satisfied; I hate him too!" said Miriam. (4: 91)

In *The Marble Faun*, the violence culminating the sacrificial rite gets postponed until a later chapter, presumably because Hawthorne needs time to amalgamate the monstrous characteristics of the Model to make the awesome vision of evil palpable. The murder is significantly preceded by a scene, reminiscent of the carnival proceedings (another double), in which Miriam, unaware of being observed, "began to gesticulate extravagantly, gnashing her teeth, flinging her arms wildly abroad, stamping with her foot."[18] Here again Hawthorne kills two birds with one stroke. Miriam's "fit" can, on the one hand, be read in conjunction with the sacrificial rite. However, immediately after the scene Hawthorne resorts to the realm of psychology to explain Miriam's extravagant behavior with the generalization that "persons in acute trouble, or labouring under strong excitement, with a necessity for concealing it, are prone to relieve the nerves in this wild way" (4: 157). The next chapter culminates in the murder of the Model. Girard draws our attention to yet another fact—namely, that the sacrificial rite is "directed toward order and tranquillity, not violence. It strives to achieve violence solely in order to eliminate it."[19] Hawthorne must have had something of this kind in mind because, as has been already noted, in the murder scene Miriam is a "potential" victim before she condemns the Model with her glance.

The postponement of sacrificial violence in *The Marble Faun* has yet another function: it prepares the ground for our understanding of what Girard calls "the role of violence in awakening desire." It is of considerable import that Miriam's mysterious follower is referred to not by his real name but by the name of the Model, significantly capitalized. Furthermore, the Model's mysterious claim on Miriam has a strong implication of past sexual union, though never fully explored, and Miriam's tutelary affection for Donatello, before the murder of the Model, is constantly underscored.

Returning to Freud's theory of "primitive beliefs" and "infantile complexes," we recall that the distinction between them is often a "hazy one." Girard emphasizes the underlying principle of the sacrificial rite, and the Oedipal conflict, as that of rivalry. The triangle Girard draws is between the subject, the object, and the rival; in my scheme, Donatello, Miriam, and the Model, respectively. "The rival," says Girard, "desires the same object as the subject, and to assert the primacy of the rival can lead to only one conclusion." And, we might add, to only one solution: the elimination of the rival. Preceding this solution is what Girard calls "mimetic rivalry" or reciprocity, the latter especially pertinent to Hawthorne's text. Girard observes that "to make the reciprocity complete, . . . the disciple [the subject] can also serve as a model, even to his own model. As for the model, no matter how self-sufficient he may appear, he invariably assumes the role of disciple."[20] In the sylvan dance described above, we remember, the Model's appearance is depicted as "vying with the agility of Donatello himself." The Model thus represents the monstrous patriarch or, in other words, the merged embodiment of Freud's "primitive beliefs" and "infantile complexes."

The detente that follows the crime has vast psychological significance and fully demonstrates Hawthorne's tremendous skill in relating carnal and spiritual love. The tutelary love Miriam cherished for Donatello, before the crime, in recognition of his weakness and defencelessness, transforms itself into mature love, even as Donatello's boyish infatuation turns out to be genuine feeling which calls for a challenge to be tested, and from which, indeed, it emerges the conqueror. That flesh and spirit become one is expressed in the scene of their rapturous embrace:

> She pressed him close, close to her bosom, with a clinging embrace that brought their two hearts together, till the

> horrour and agony of each was combined into one emotion, and that, a kind of rapture. (4: 173-74)

Following this passionate scene of reunion, however, Donatello's love is exposed to yet another test, the test of conscience. Guilt-ridden Donatello cannot find solace in Miriam's reciprocal love. He bids her farewell, and goes to his native home, Monte Beni, to come to grips with his remorse. Here the real process of transformation unfolds.

During the process of Donatello's education through sin, two problems come to the fore. One is hinted at prior to his departure, when Hawthorne comments upon the disappearance of the resemblance between Donatello and the Faun of Praxiteles. The other concerns the theme earlier investigated by Hawthorne, specifically in *The House of the Seven Gables*—namely, the heredity of features within family, what Marcel calls "the mystery of the family." Both themes are characteristically conveyed on two levels: those of myth and psychology. As Donohue aptly suggests, one of Hawthorne's most challenging tasks in *The Marble Faun* is to make a palpable figure of faun-like Donatello, whose ancestors of the Arcadian period not only lived in close relationship with nature but also, as is time and again emphasized, possessed some animal features. She perceives Hawthorne's chief task in convincing his reader that Donatello is "some kind of throw-back to this age of unsophistication—an unaccommodated man who grows into manhood through the reality of sin."[21]

During his solitary meditations in the tower and his subsequent talks with Kenyon, Donatello becomes increasingly aware of the ties between his progenitors and himself. Marcel investigates this idea of kinship under the notion of "the mystery of the family" with its analogue in the "divine" family:

> . . . contrary to the persistent humanistic illusion, we have good reason to assert that family relationships, like human

> matters in general, afford no consistency, no guarantee of solidity. It is only when they are referred back to a superhuman order, which here below we cannot grasp apart from its signs and indications, that their truly sacred character becomes apparent.[22]

There cannot be any doubt that Hawthorne thought along the same lines. The only kind of love that is "consecrated" to Hawthorne is marital love and, accordingly, the "heavenly bliss" emanates from Phoebe-Holgrave and Hilda-Kenyon relationships. Significantly also, Donatello bids farewell to his pre-mordial and pre-moral ancestors and looks up to the image of "divine motherhood" for consolation, "because the mild face of the Madonna promised him to intercede, as a tender mother, betwixt the poor culprit and the awfulness of judgment" (4: 297).

The episode in the Apennines serves the double purpose in the narrative. Peter Brooks' application of Freud's Masterplot to textual analysis calls attention to repetition in the text (in my scheme, we remember, to sequences of texts), which creates "return" or what he calls a "doubling back." This return, argues Brooks, may be of a double-bind: "a return *to* or a return *of*: for instance, a return to origins or a return of the repressed."[23] In Donatello's retreat we find both concepts interlaced. In Hawthorne's survey of the ancestral legends of the Monte Benis, one seems especially tantamount to Donatello's situation. He tells Kenyon that one of his progenitors fell in love with a nymph, who taught him her language so as to enable him to call her from the depth of the fountain to spend "many a happy hour together." The lovely pastoral episode ended when "one fatal noontide" the young man came to call his beloved but she did not appear to greet him. The youth dipped his fingers in the fountain as if to catch the nymph, but the water shrank away from his hands. Apparently the story ends here but Kenyon demands an explanation, so Donatello tells him that the nymph did not return the young man's call and the water shrank away from his hands because he "tried to wash off a blood stain." We have thus another nameless crime and one which has precise bearing on Donatello's predicament.[24]

Moreover, Donatello's return to the origins functions as a repetition of an earlier motif—namely, of Clifford's trauma in *The House of the Seven Gables*, for Miriam's tutelary love for Donatello may remind one of Hepzibah's attempts at "mothering" Clifford. Both men are obliged, in Freud's words, to "*repeat* the repressed material as a contemporary experience instead of . . . *remembering* it as something belonging to the past."[25] The chapter focusing on ancestral legends is brought to its climax at the point when Donatello boasts to Kenyon of having once possessed the skill of animal language. Kenyon, naturally skeptical, bids Donatello to demonstrate this unique talent, and Donatello attempts to do so—in vain, of course. But prior to his attempt, he tells Kenyon: "I doubt . . . whether they will remember my voice now. It changes, you know, as the boy grows towards manhood" (4: 247). The breaking of the voice in puberty, to which Hawthorne alludes here, gives the whole scene its psychological credibility, and we hardly need Kenyon's Jamesian remark, "It is the price we pay for experience," to grasp Hawthorne's meaning.

To paraphrase what Isaac Balshevis Singer once remarked, a writer has a place of reference (a city, a street, a house, or a place in a house) to which his thoughts obsessively return and which has the function of a kind of panoptic image, whereby all experience becomes encapsulated into one wholesome vision. According to Singer, this returning image has invariably its source in the writer's own past, denoting his roots, as Krochmalna street in Warsaw does for Singer. For Hawthorne, this function is taken by a secluded spot, having its prototype in Hawthorne's lonesome chamber in Salem, where his characters come to grips with their life. Hester's solitary cottage, Clifford's arched window, and Donatello's tower in his Monte Beni home carry precisely this meaning. In fact, the pigeonnier in *Lancelot*, where Lance spends many an hour contemplating, discovering his wife's infidelity, and detailing his Machiavellian plot—especially the pigeonnier prior to Margot's restoration, inhabited mostly by pigeons that accompanied Lance in his solitary browsings—resembles Donatello's tower in which only "a pair of owls" keep him company. It is in this tower that Donatello "recollects himself," proving, in Marcel's words, that "he is not a living creature pure and simple, a creature, that is to say, which is at the mercy of its life and without a hold upon it" (*PE*, 12). Donatello, who emerges from the confinement of his tower, is, as Hawthorne wants us to believe and as we do believe, an intelligent man "revolving grave and deep thoughts in his breast," who can now face Miriam as an equal partner.

SYNEIDESIS

No other word than *syneidesis* depicts this unique quality of double communion which takes place towards the end of *The Marble Faun*: between Miriam and Donatello and between Hilda and Kenyon. The closest Marcel ever comes to explaining his understanding of *syneidesis* is in the following passage:

> Person-commitment-community-reality: here we have a chain of notions, not strictly deducible from each other . . . but capable of being grasped in their unity by an act of mind which is fittingly described not by the sullied term of intuition but by the too little used one of *syneidesis*, the act by which an *ensemble* is maintained under the mind's regard.[26]

The passage comes from the first English edition of *Homo Viator*, where the italicized words are the ones Marcel uses in the French original. The second edition in English, published in America, translates "syneidesis" to "synopsis," and "ensemble" to "group," which distorts Marcel's meaning. First of all, "syneidesis" and "synopsis" are not synonyms. Second, "group" indicates an "ensemble" of more than two persons, and while Hawthorne's first illustration of *syneidesis* comes fairly close to this sense because the experience is shared by three people, the world "ensemble" in the above context is closer to the French notion "entre nous" ("between you and me"), or English "togetherness," which implies an experience or reflection shared by two people which, all things considered, is more probable. O'Malley's interpretation of the concept will give us a fuller grasp of these nuances. Thus *syneidesis* is

> a withdrawal from experience only in the sense of being a withdrawal in total concentration from the fragmented experience of the world of problematic reflection or from the unreflected experience of routine consciousness into the deeper, reflected experience of ontological communion in which self and other are contemplated in the fellowship of their common participation in Being.[27]

The parallels between the fragments of Hawthorne's text given below and *syneidesis* thus defined are most arresting.

At a time appointed by Miriam, Kenyon brings Donatello to Perugia, and the three meet under the bronze statue of Pope Julius. Miriam attributes special significance to this statue because she is impressed by its "paternal aspect" and, as she tells Kenyon, she once "fancied" that a blessing was passed on to her from the Pope's outstretched hand. She evidently hopes for the recurrence of this symbolic approval of her union with Donatello. The two of them hand in hand, with Kenyon nearby, glance upward at the statue, and the idea of *syneidesis* starkly surfaces in this passage:

> There is a singular effect, oftentimes, when out of the midst of engrossing thought and deep absorption, we sud-

> denly look up, and catch a glimpse of external objects. We seem at such moments, to look farther and deeper into them, than by any premeditated observation; it is as if they met our eyes alive, and with all their hidden meaning on the surface, but grew again inanimate and inscrutable, the instant that they become aware of our glances. So, now, at that unexpected glimpse, Miriam, Donatello, and the sculptor, all three imagined that they beheld the bronze Pontiff endowed with spiritual life. A blessing was felt descending upon them from his outstretched hand; he approved, by look and gesture, the pledge of a deep union that had passed under his auspices. (4: 323-24)

The passage requires no comment, for Hawthorne's skill reveals everything necessary here.

The second communion takes place during the carnival that winds up the whole narrative. The resemblances to the first carnival are arresting: masked individuals, mock battles, etc. Even the famous balcony scene, where Hilda throws a rose-bud at Kenyon, is a flash-back to the previous carnival. Hawthorne critics seem curiously silent on the subject of this repetition. Even Rita K. Gollin, who scrutinizes the text in her excellent analysis of the role of dream in Hawthorne's fiction, seems to have missed this point. But Kenyon distinctly remembers that, during the previous carnival, "Hilda, sitting demurely in a balcony, had hit the sculptor with a single rosebud—so sweet and fresh a bud that he knew at once whose hand had flung it" (4: 438). It is true that this scene is evoked through Kenyon's memory, and that Hawthorne has never intimated it before. A possible answer to this omission might be that the former carnival scene would have lost its emphasis, had he introduced it then. We may recall that the former carnival scene concluded with the appearance of the Model, a dissonance which occasioned the outburst of hatred that eventually led to the crime.

The second carnival culminates in an act of communion shared by Hilda and Kenyon.

It is worth pointing out that this scene is not only doubled but, in fact, tripled. We first get Kenyon's retrospective recreation, then its almost exact repetition from Kenyon's viewpoint and, finally, from Hilda's. In the first scene from the first carnival Kenyon is hit with a single rose, whereas in the other scenes two "missiles" pelt him, "a single rose-bud, so fresh that it seemed that moment gathered," and a cauliflower from a passing carriage. As Gollin aptly notes, "the cauliflower suggests Kenyon's summons to mundane reality, and the rosebud his opportunity for love."[28] Thus, the cycle "person-commitment-community-reality" finds its accomplishment in Kenyon's experience, as it does in Hilda's, "in whose gentle *presence* his own secret sorrow and the obtrusive uproar of the Carnival alike died away from [Kenyon's] perception" (4: 454).[29] Therefore, "the act by which an *ensemble* is maintained under the mind's regard" finds here its most intimate realization.

Marcel interestingly remarks that "togetherness," having no equivalent in French, is, as it were, a substantive of the French notion "entre nous" (between you and me). Being together is the being *with* another person *qua* person that can be fulfilled only in love. This is the essence of Marcel's "exigency of being," and to attain to such being is equivalent to coming home. Thus, Kenyon's plea, "O Hilda, guide me home," acquires two meanings at once: literal—home, to America, and symbolic—home to your presence, i.e, your love. Love is the presence that is at once granted and gained. Being together, or being *with* "can only be granted to us as a gift," which we accept with wonder and return with generosity. In the exchange between Hilda and Kenyon immediately following Kenyon's synopsis of the Fortunate Fall, no words of love are directly communicated. The communion between the two persons occurs in a flash of insight, as they both express their loneliness and realize that it can be shared. Thus, the predicament contained in the French phrase "solitude à deux," having its precedent in Hawthorne's marriage with Sophia, is re-enacted in Hilda and Kenyon's union.

The last chapter, in which Kenyon propounds two morals to Hilda that are to account for the ambiguities of the story and that Hilda refuses to accept, has constituted a point of intense disagreement between critics. Hyatt Waggoner maintains that Kenyon's synopsis, voiced previously by Miriam, is nothing other than what he calls a "line of reasoning."[30] It is rejected both by Hilda and, as most critics have agreed, by Hawthorne in the precise measure of its being a line of reasoning. Donohue, on the other hand, offers an interpretation that succinctly summarizes the views of another group of critics. In her view, the apparent incongruity between Hilda's reaction to Kenyon's synopsis of the Fortunate Fall and the final image of Hilda looking with hope towards Miriam and Donatello's future testifies to Hawthorne's failure to "perceive" the meaning his last words imply. The disparity between Hilda's condemnation of the sinners, Miriam and Donatello, and her hope concerning their future proves, to Donohue, that Hilda is a "moral imbecile."

Criticism has been traditionally harsher with Hilda than with any other heroine of the alleged "fair" type. Even such an early critic of *The Marble Faun* as William Dean Howells comments on Hilda's "cold spirit" and "ruthless self-pity."[31] Almost unanimously, condescension of Hilda rests not so much on the portrait Hawthorne paints of her in the early chapters of the book as on her moral absolutism voiced in response to Kenyon's synopsis of the Fortunate Fall. Hilda's response is all the more striking, though germane to her views expressed earlier in the narrative, if we remember that Hawthorne indeed shows her transformed through suffering in the chapter preceding her disappearance. Of her disappearance we know nothing, and speculation on this subject adds nothing to our understanding of her. But we should keep in mind that Hilda is not a phantom of her own making as some critics, engrossed in condemnation, make her out to be. We would also do well by remembering that she is the only woman of the "fair" type whose development in the narrative involves suffering.

If we apply the logic of descriptive writing to *The Marble Faun* (a risky procedure with Hawthorne's texts), we may find it inconsistent that Hawthorne, having staked out Hilda's independence, at the end confines her to a traditional feminine role. We may also wonder with Mary Schriber why Hawthorne makes Kenyon, who knows how "severe" and "heartless" Hilda is, wish nevertheless to marry her.[32] Schriber suggests that the conventional ending of the novel and Hilda's rectitude both testify to Hawthorne's attempt to conform to the "culture's horizon of expectations." Admittedly, never before was Hawthorne as concerned with acting in "accordance with [the views] of the Public" (he states in the Preface), as in this novel. We must remember that the book culminated a seven--year period of absence from America. Hawthorne voices his own dilemma when, just after Hilda accepts a marriage proposal from Kenyon, he speaks of "deferring" the reality of life when absent from home. Schriber argues that Hilda is not condemned by the authorial voice for her "heartless character" because, if she is to accept her role, her purity, "a woman's pearl beyond price," must be asserted beyond the shadow of a doubt.

I want to suggest a new way of accounting for these complexities. In his creation of Hilda, Hawthorne adhered to the source, which any student of Hawthorne's fiction is familiar with, though none have applied to the discussion of gender relations in his fiction. Before proceeding to identify the source, however, it is necessary to rehearse, if only summarily, some of the characteristics in Hawthorne's portrayal of Hilda. She is independent, has a spine of steel, matures through suffering, and in this identifies with the figure of Christ. She heroically defends her faith. Her relationship with Kenyon is purely spiritual. And finally, she emerges as a Savior in the concluding pages of the novel. Where else but in Shakerism could Hawthorne have found such a woman? In Calvin

Green's synopsis of the Shaker dogma published in 1823, we find this illuminating passage:

> As the true church of Christ, which is his body, is composed of male and female, as its members; and as there must be a correspondent spiritual union between the male and female, to render the church complete, as a spiritual body; so it is essentially necessary that such a spiritual union should exist in the head of that body, which is Christ. . . . It must be admitted by every reasonable person, that the order of man cannot be complete without the woman . . . for, "neither is the man without the woman, nor the woman without the man, in the Lord." (1 Cor. xi. 11.) . . . Since then, Christ must appear in every female, as well as in every male, before they can be saved; and since that Divine Spirit has appeared in one man, whom God has chosen as the Captain of our salvation, and an example of righteousness to all men; is it not reasonable and consistent that the same anointing power (which is Christ) should also appear in a woman, and distinguish her as a leader, and an example of righteousness to all women?[33]

We learn from another source that Ann Lee, the founder of the Shakers, was imprisoned because of her "preaching of repentance and righteousness," that she was the woman "on whose perfect purity, through perfect freedom, the very life of the race depends."[34] The author reports on her "literal mind," maintains that she never knew "real love," and that "it was essential to the success of her great mission to humanity that she should not see all." The import of the last opinion to this analysis will become clear when we compare it with what Hawthorne intimates of Hilda—namely, that "with respect to whatever was evil, foul, and ugly, . . . she had trodden as if invisible, and not only so, but blind" (4: 387). There can be no doubt that Shakerism influenced Hawthorne's portrayal of the couples on the run. Neither can we doubt that he modelled Hilda after Mother Ann. In Shakerism Hawthorne found the expression of gender equality. If he could not bring his belief quite into the open, it was due as much to what Schriber calls the "culture's horizon of expectations" as to his fear of criticism from Sophia, who, of the two, had a more conservative mind. Hence, he disguised his real intention and cast it in the robes of myth. From the perspective of a modern reader, he could not do a better job, for Shakerism, as evaluated today, was not only the religion led by a woman, but also the only religion that promoted an expression of equal empowerment of women.

In conclusion: Hilda's joy at the end of the novel is evidently all-embracing. Now Miriam, and not Hilda, a mute witness of the scene between the two lovers, passes on to them a gesture of blessing, but at the same time defies them to approach her. But, as Hawthorne's final words testify, Hilda's generosity is a vast sphere which has room for saints and sinners alike. With this realization the book ends, though certainly nothing guarantees that Miriam and Donatello will be together in this life. In the final analysis, it matters little which couple attracts our sympathy and understanding. We can of course guess on which side Hawthorne wanted to be, but his irrefutable achievement lies in convincing his reader that both couples have achieved true unity in freeing themselves from what Marcel has called "the broken world." The title of this chapter has been borrowed from Marcel's *Le Monde cassé* which, like *The Marble Faun*, ends with an instantaneous realization of intersubjectivity, whereby "two human beings feel as one." As in Hawthorne's, nothing in Marcel's work guarantees that this accord will last, and in both texts the final emphasis is put rather on the interrogative note. But as Marcel says, this interrogative note

> is tied to an *ambiguity* the principle of which resides in the very structure of our being. But there is the further danger in this domain of making oneself a prisoner of a formula.

> My persistent effort has, perhaps more than anything else, consisted in struggling against the temptation of any formula whatsoever, and this in the name of human experience which we must confront in all its complexity, aware of the incessant interplay of *light* and *shadow* suffusing the whole of our existence. (*HD*, 93—emphasis added)

In view of all that has been said, there can be no doubt that Hawthorne would readily subscribe to these words.

NOTES

1. See *First Editions of the Works of Nathaniel Hawthorne together with Some Manuscripts, Letters and Portraits* (New York: The Gollier Club, 1904), pp. 46-47.

2. Ibid., p. 47.

3. Gabriel Marcel, *The Existential Background of Human Dignity* (Cambridge: Harvard Univ. Press, 1963), p. 80. Hereafter, references to this work will be identified in the text by the abbreviation "*HD*," followed by the pertinent page number.

4. Gabriel Marcel, *The Philosophy of Existence*, trans. Manya Harari (New York: Philosophical Library, 1949), p. 27. Hereafter, references to this work will be identified in the text by the abbreviation "*PE*," followed by the pertinent page number.

5. Agnes McNeill Donohue, *Hawthorne. Calvin's Ironic Stepchild* (Kent: The Kent State Univ. Press, 1985), p. 305.

6. Hawthorne visited the Shaker settlements three times in his life. His first visit to the community near Canterbury, New Hampshire, in 1831, was probably most influential, and found its literary representation in two tales, "The Shaker Bridal" and "The Canterbury Pilgrims." Following this first visit, Hawthorne wrote his sister Louisa that the Shakers had a "good and comfortable life and if it were not for their ridiculous ceremonies, a man might not do a wiser thing than join them. . . . I spoke to them about becoming a member of the Society, but have come to no decision on that point" (Nathaniel Hawthorne to Louisa Hawthorne,

August 17, 1831; Essex Institute). It is not at all clear whether Hawthorne spoke of genuine intention or merely teased his sisters with a possibility of adopting the Shakers' celibate way of life. What Hawthorne must have found alluring in Shakerism was their reclusiveness. After the third visit, with Melville in 1851, to the settlement near Hancock, Hawthorne utterly condemned the Shakers for their lack of personal hygiene. Nevertheless, I perceive Shakerism as one of the major influences in Hawthorne's fiction. The recurring motif of retreat enacted by the couples in his works, both tales and novels, the idea of female messiahship surfacing in *The House of the Seven Gables* and *The Marble Faun*, and heralded in the concluding paragraphs of *The Scarlet Letter*, even the traditional division of labor (viewed by some critics as an argument *against* identifying Shakerism with feminism) surfacing in the Phoebe/Holgrave relationship in *The House of the Seven Gables*, all indicate Hawthorne's indebtedness to this source.

7. Cited in E. L. Allen, *Existentialism from Within* (London: Routledge and Kegan Paul, Ltd., 1953), p. 168.

8. John B.O'Malley, *The Fellowship of Being. An Essay on the Concept of Person in the Philosophy of Gabriel Marcel* (The Hague: Martinus Nijhoff, 1966), p. 125.

9. See Gabriel Marcel, *The Mystery of Being*, trans. G. S. Fraser and R. Hague (Chicago: Henry Regnery Company, 1960), pp. 31-32.

10. See Fyodor Dostoyevsky, *The Brothers Karamazov*, trans. Constance Garnett (New York: The New American Library, 1957), pp. 296-97.

11. I refer here to Camus' *L'Etranger*, where, legally speaking, Meursault kills the Arab in self-defence.

12. Murray Krieger, *Visions of Extremity in Modern Literature*, vol. I: *The Tragic Vision* (Baltimore and London: The Johns Hopkins Univ. Press, 1973), p. 152.

13. Jac Tharpe, *Nathaniel Hawthorne. Identity and Knowledge* (Carbondale and Edwardsville: Southern Illinois Univ. Press, 1967), p. 149.

14. Roy R. Male, *Hawthorne's Tragic Vision* (New York: The Norton Library, 1957), p. 8.

15. Donohue, p. 298.

16. See Northrop Frye, *The Great Code. The Bible and Literature* (San Diego: Harcourt Brace Jovanovich, Publishers, 1982), p. 140.

17. René Girard, *Violence and the Sacred*, trans. Patrick Gregory (Baltimore and London: The Johns Hopkins Univ. Press, 1977), p. 166.

18. There is a parallel scene in *The Scarlet Letter*, where Dimmesdale's mental torment culminates in a "brief fit of madness," again significantly preceding the procession scene.

19. Girard, p. 132.

20. Ibid., p. 147.

21. Donohue, p. 303.

22. Gabriel Marcel, *Homo Viator. Introduction to a Metaphysic of Hope*, trans. Emma Craufurd (New York: Harper and Brothers/Harper Torchbooks, 1962), p. 71.

23. Peter Brooks, *Reading for the Plot. Design and Intention in Narrative* (New York: Alfred A. Knopf, 1984), p. 100.

24. I refer here to the fact that, earlier in the narrative, Miriam is also implicated in a nameless crime.

25. Cited after Brooks, p. 98.

26. Gabriel Marcel, *Homo Viator. Introduction to a Metaphysic of Hope*, trans. Emma Craufurd (London: Victor Gollancz, Ltd., 1951), p. 27.

27. O'Malley, p. 95.

28. Rita K. Gollin, *Nathaniel Hawthorne and the Truth of Dreams* (Baton Rouge and London: Louisiana State Univ. Press, 1979), p. 184.

29. Note the italicized "presence" in the quoted passage, which directly corresponds with Marcel's insight on the same subject. See *The Existential Background of Human Dignity*, pp. 66-68.

30. Hyatt H. Waggoner, *Hawthorne: A Critical Study* (Cambridge: Harvard Univ. Press, 1955), p. 219. Male uses initially the same argument as Waggoner's but he then disagrees with Waggoner's distinction between Hawthorne's "intended" and "achieved" meanings in *The Marble Faun*. See Male, pp. 175-77.

31. William Dean Howells, *Heroines of Fiction* (New York and London: Harper and Brothers Publishers, 1901), pp. 183-89.

32. Mary Suzanne Schriber, *Gender and the Writer's Imagination from Cooper to Wharton* (Lexington: Univ. Press of Kentucky, 1987), pp. 60-63.

33. Calvin Green, *A Summary View of the Millennial Church, or United Society of Believers, Commonly Called Shakers* (Albany: C. van Benthuysen, 1848 [reissue of the original 1823 edition]), pp. 215-17.

34. Paul Tyner, "The Christ Ideal in Shakerism," in *The Manifesto* I. XXVi, 6 (1896), pp. 95-97.

Six: Gambling on Faith?

The Second Coming

In his interview with Jan Nordby Gretlund, Percy said that after he had finished *The Second Coming* he felt "as if [he] had been a woman who had been pregnant four years."[1] He compared his condition to a postpartum depression. "I went into a terrible depression," he said, "and all I knew was that I would never write another novel again as long as I lived."

Not only does Percy, like Pushkin having written *Eugene Onegin*, significantly identify here with feminine experience, but also the latter part of the quotation underlies the point I wish to argue in this chapter—namely, that *The Second Coming* terminates a period in Percy's literary career.

Already in 1961, Gabriel Marcel disavowed any indebtedness to what he called the "extreme existentialism" of J.-P. Sartre. Marcel then said that all he wished to do was "to assert the rights of phenomenology in the light of which the primacy of experience over what could be called pure thought must be rigorously preserved."[2] Likewise, Percy, in a number of interviews he gave in the eighties, expresses his unease at the intellectual promiscuity with which the term "existentialism" is used. In an interview with Jo Gulledge, for instance, he goes so far as claiming that, unlike Norman Mailer, to whom existentialism signifies, Percy observes, "acting on impulse," he does not even know what the term "means."[3] Despite the disingenuousness of this remark, and in spite of Percy's own ambition of old to "Americanize the movement,"[4] what he pertinently implies is that existentialism has been so eclipsed that we "forget" its importance and we "forget" its faults.

As I have argued, Percy's indebtedness to existentialism has hindered his presentation of women characters. As long as he remained under this influence he was virtually unable to create meaningful relationships between men and women. Not only is his portrayal of womanhood distorted in the novels written before *The Second Coming*, but also his male characters' inability to forge and develop meaningful relationships results from these distortions. It is only after Percy moved away from this sphere of influence that his fiction boasted a rounded depiction of womanhood and a fully meaningful relationship. Percy himself admits that *The Second Coming* is his first "unalienated" novel, and he also confesses his satisfaction with the portrayal of the central female character there, Allison Huger.[5] Many a critic has found fault with the book's enforced solutions, with its sentimental ending. Notwithstanding the validity of such criticism, I totally share Percy's opinion: *The Second Coming* is his first unalienated novel and, I am convinced, Allie Huger is the character any feminist would want to shake hands with.

The allegory in *The Second Coming*, as was the case in *The Marble Faun*, concerns Percy's playful handling of his historical source—the story of Mother Ann as a female messiah. Whereas in *Lancelot* the identification of Anna as Ann Lee, this much neglected symbol of liberated womanhood, was only an understatement, *The Second Coming* offers an eloquent context for the analysis of this influence. A reader who will harbor misgivings about seeing Percy's vision in *The Second Coming* in the light of Shakerism and will argue for the consistent Catholicism of Percy's viewpoint, might consider the fact that Percy was wont to convey religious meaning through quite unorthodox means. Lance's inverted quest for the devil as a quasi-quest for God in *Lancelot* or what Percy called Will's "nutty" experiment in the cave in *The Second Coming* come to mind as just two examples. Moreover, Percy makes two explicit references to the Shakers, one in *Lancelot* where he mentions the "simplicity and beauty of the Shaker furniture" and the other in *The Second Coming* when he speaks of "backwood churches where people speak in tongues."[6]

Similarly to *The Marble Faun*, Percy's book is structured along independent gender lines. Percy's strategy, like Hawthorne's, is to identify closely his two focal characters with each other. In fact, we get two narratives alternately focusing on Allison Huger and Will Barrett until they merge at the end of the novel. Will makes several intrusions into the parts of the narrative depicting Allie's survival in the greenhouse, the third of which is the most crucial as regards the book's message. Percy explicitly echoes Marcel's conviction that the self is defined through ordeal, which, Percy contends, "the psychologists don't tell people," and, he adds, it is through ordeal ("Will has to almost shoot himself and Allie has to go crazy")[7] that they come to "a sense of self."

The Second Coming, representing Percy's final literary confrontation with existentialism, weaves together all the threads of Percy's earlier novels. The text alludes to Pascal by name on several occasions. Will's understanding of Father Weatherbee's message in the penultimate scene in *The Second Coming*, which is a replica of the episode pivoting *The Last Gentleman*, hinges on Kierkegaard's notion of the "apostle." And the nuances contained in the depiction of Will and Allie's relationship testify to Percy's coming to grips with intersubjectivity.

Both *The Last Gentleman* and its sequel, *The Second Coming*, allude to Pascal on several occasions, thereby inviting a comparison with Pascal's thought. In one of the sections of the *Pensées* critical of diversion, Pascal maintains that men's habit of diverting themselves distracts them from thought on the subject of "what they are, where they come from and where they are going."[8] Another "pensée" brings this reflection:

> When I consider the brief span of my absorbed into the eternity which comes before and after . . . the small space I occupy and which I see swallowed up in the infinite immensities of spaces of which I know nothing and which know nothing of me, I take fright and am amazed to see myself here rather than there: there is no reason for me to be here rather than there, now rather than then.[9]

Several characters in *The Last Gentleman* and *The Second Coming* echo these thoughts. Val, in the former book, tells Will Barrett that she does not want Jamie to die an "unprovided death," and she further explains, "I don't want him to die without knowing why he came here, what he is doing here, and why he is leaving."[10] The two focal characters in *The Second Coming* express very much the same idea: Allison, when she says, "Only because I have to know enough of where I've been to know which way I'm going" (93), and Will, as he states, "I do not cast forward and backward from myself, am here in the here-and-now, and know what I am going to do" (179-80).

Percy is a trained scientist who discovered the inadequacy of objective-empirical thinking in dealing with the human condition, yet still a scientist who has striven to describe man's predicament and suggest the therapy. Though it may seem a rather far-fetched analogy, this division in Percy does remind one of a division in Pascal's scientific and rational thinking, on the one hand, and his theological thinking, on the other: "a gap crossed only by a dramatic conversion, understood in terms of a mystical or pathological experience."[11] Authoritative interpreters of Pascal's work argue the therapeutic goals of the "pari" (wager). Percy has Will dismiss

Pascalian wager on the ground of its frivolity. We will see, however, that in the nuances of Will's quest after faith, Percy echoes Pascal's "arguments" expressed in the section of the *Pensées* devoted to the wager.

WILL

The idea for what was to become Will Barrett's central dilemma in *The Second Coming* occurred to Percy when he heard the story his old friend came to tell him:

> After graduation, I married and went up North. Soon my wife and I were doing well and we joined all kinds of organizations where we made lots of friends. My business was doing more than thriving when I began to get restless—I felt there was more out there than either of us knew about. So I retired early. We pulled up stakes and moved to the mountains of North Carolina. We found the perfect lot with a great view and decided to build on it. When the house was finished, we moved into it, found just the right place for everything, including the piano and the art we had collected, and sat back to relax after all our hard work. Things were fine—for a while. And then it slowly came to me that something was wrong; I had missed it. I didn't know how to explain this strange restlessness to my wife, especially after she had to leave all our friends to move to North Carolina.
>
> One Sunday, I told her I was going out for some cigarettes. I found myself instead at the bus station and hopped on the bus that was going the farthest—the one to New Orleans. On my way down here, I remembered, Walker, that you lived not far from here—and here I am. I don't

> know where else to go now, or really what to do. Do you have any idea about this boredom and restlessness?[12]

A truly Hawthornian context. Not only because Percy's friend has most obviously suffered from the Wakefield syndrome, but also because Hawthorne's inspiration for "Wakefield" likewise came from a hearsay source.

The Second Coming, which is situated approximately twenty years after *The Last Gentleman*, narrates the events of Will's life after he has already had his share of diversion. From Santa Fe he returned to New York, married a rich woman, and became a Wall Street lawyer. By any bourgeois standards, Will has made it. When the novel opens, he is living in a small town in North Carolina; "after a fairly normal life, a fairly happy marriage, a successful career, and a triumphant early retirement to enjoy the good things of life" (180), Will is a widower with a handsome inheritance and an acute sense of malaise. Sutter, Will's mentor from *The Last Gentleman*, came to nothing; he still lives in Albuquerque and kills time watching soap-operas, talking only during commercials, and waiting for his pension checks. Sutter, who, Will believed, "knew what was what," is as immersed in diversion as anybody else.

The organic symptoms from *The Last Gentleman* intensify in *The Second Coming*. Will is probably the most physically, mentally and spiritually handicapped of all Percy's protagonists. He is aware of the anomaly of the world and of the "suck of self." This phrase, with its full impact, is akin to Pascal's notion of "amour-propre." At the beginning of the novel, Will experiments with a Luger and eventually holds its muzzle against his temple:

> Yes, that is possible, he thought smiling, that is the one way to cure the great suck of self, but then I wouldn't find out . . . why things have come to such a pass and a man so sucked down into himself that it takes a gunshot to knock him out of the suck. (14)

The parallel will be even more meaningful when we consider its full context. Prior to his experiments with the Luger, Will gets out of the Mercedes and, glancing at the side mirror, sees a reflection of a stranger. Another look at the rearview mirror reveals the same person, Will himself. Pleasant recognition follows: the two dimensions establish for Will the social context; instead of being "a self sucking everything into himself," he becomes "a man among men." He then looks down at his wrist and the same revelation ensues. What he sees is The Wrist, "part of the whole into which everything was sucked and drained out" (14). The *Pensées* provide a corresponding passage:

> The separated member, no longer seeing the body to which it belongs, has only a wasting and moribund being left. However, it believes itself to be a whole, and, seeing no body on which it depends, believes itself to be dependent only on itself and tries to make itself its own centre and body . . . Eventually, when it comes to know itself, it has returned home, as it were, and only loves itself for the body's sake.[13]

Two problems emerge upon comparing Percy's illustration with the ideas this passage underlies. First, the "suck of self," which succinctly comments on the self's narcissism, can be cured by bending, in Percy's words, "far enough out of everyday lifeline," that is, by relinquishing diversion. Second, the episode with the Luger functions as a prelude, as it were, to Percy's theory of the communal living. This issue is too briefly addressed in Pascal's thought to allow any definite conclusions at this point. However, contrary to some popular views, conversion, as Pascal conceived of it, involves not withdrawal but rather, as Jan Miel argues, "reentry into human society with purified motives."[14] It is truly Christian conversion because it involves a change of heart; man is no longer motivated by the demands of self-love, but rather by charity for the sake of others and, consequently, of God. Thus, even though the analogy should not be carried too far, the idea of reaching God through the other (especially reminiscent of Buber's *I and Thou* concept or Marcel's idea of "communion") harks back again to Pascal. And this problem constitutes the focal point of *The Second Coming.*

Will's spiritual malady derives from his supposition that the Jews leave North Carolina and the United States which "fact," according to the prophecy, is the anticipation of the Second Coming of Christ and the end of the world. It is Will's conviction that the center does not hold any longer, that the end is inevitable. On a personal level, Will, like Lancelot in Percy's previous novel, speaks of love in quotation marks, admitting that he is not sure what the word means. Moreover, his malaise has organic symptoms. As these accumulate, Will contemplates suicide and, ultimately, acts on his convictions. He insures his life for one million dollars, appoints Sutter a beneficiary, and devises a scheme that eliminates suicide. He subsequently goes to a mountain cave to await a sign from God which, should it materialize, will confirm his belief. If he receives no sign, the end will be his and not the world's.

In his letter to Sutter, Will mentions Pascal, describing the wager at length and ultimately dismissing it on the ground of its frivolity. His views express one of the commonest arguments against the wager which, simply stated, is that it proposes that we believe without any concern for the proofs of that belief. The point in Pascal, as in so much Catholic thought, is that faith *by definition* defies reason. If reasoned, faith stops being faith, but becomes the recognition of a rationally explicable phenomenon.

At this point two problems must be, if only very summarily, pointed out. First, Pascal's thoughts which precede the wager demonstrate the transience, the futility—in a word, the paltriness of diversions. The wager, then, functions as something therapeutic, and it appeals to the need for liberation and healing. Second, in the wager part of Pascal's *Pensées*, which is conceived in the form of a dialogue between Pascal and his interlocutor, there is an exchange in which the latter says: "I confess, I admit it, but is there really no way of seeing what the cards are?" to which Pascal answers: "Yes. Scripture and the rest, etc."[15] In other words, the proofs, if one insists on them, are to be found in the Scripture and specifically, for instance, in the prophecies. These are the only proofs which, to Pascal, have any validity; he precisely disregards rational proofs as irrelevant. Percy, by contrast, rather perversely, in fact, uses a quasi-scientific method in *The Second Coming,* "the first scientific experiment in history to settle once and for all the questions of God's existence" (192). But then, of course, it must be remembered that Will considers what he imagines as the exodus of the Jews as the sign of God's plan which, again, corresponds to Pascal's conviction that the essential role of the Jews was to prophesy. Their prophecies were the necessary preparation for the coming of Christ.

Various references to the end of the world in the text achieve a special edge when confronted with Will's initial identification of Linville, North Carolina, with Rome before its fall ("Most Romans worked and played as usual while Rome fell about their ears" [4]). Not only does this casual allusion evoke Hawthorne's vision in *The Marble Faun*, but also several other affinities between the two books merit close attention. First of all, both texts explicitly address a religious dilemma. Despite contrary resolutions, Hilda's wavering between Puritanism and Catholicism may recall Will's poise between two religious influences embodied in the priests Curl and Weatherbee. Moreover, both texts can serve as commentaries on the writers' biographies. In *The Marble Faun* two such motifs are Hilda's religious dilemma, which reflects Hawthorne's own; and Donatello's attempt to come to grips with his life through the recounting of ancestral legends, which reflects Hawthorne's guilt--stricken conscience for the sins of his Puritan ancestors. Donatello, in his conversations with Kenyon, brings his progenitors back to life precisely in order to forget them and, parentless, hails to the Virgin Mary as the Divine Mother.

In *The Second Coming*, Will evokes the memories of his father, who committed suicide when Will was still a child. One memory seems particularly painful and bewildering: "Only one event had ever happened to him in his life. Everything else that had happened afterwards was a non-event" (52). A latter-day Cyrus Bourne, who however survived the hunting expedition, Will dwells on the quail--hunt, during which his father attempted to shoot both himself and his son. Will obsessively returns to this event through memory, trying to find reasons for his father's attempt to kill him and for his subsequent suicide. His initial recollection finds a key in his father's assertion that he and Will "are the same," and that Will "already know[s] too much," which "is too bad in a way." But it takes Will considerable time to grasp the knowledge he and his father share. He ultimately realizes that his father was a remnant of things past, of Southern Stoicism, who could not tolerate the modern age. Will's realization entails the discovery of the name of their common enemy, "the living death":

> The name of this century is the Century of the Love of Death. Death in this century is not the death people die but the death people live. Men love death because real death is better than the living death. That's why men like wars, of course. Bad as wars are and maybe because they are so bad, thinking of peace during war is better than peace. War is what makes peace desirable. But peace without war is intolerable. Why do men settle so easily for lives which are living deaths? Men either kill each other in war, or in peace walk as docilely into living death as sheep into a slaughter-house. (271)

This realization harks back to what Percy has voiced in his earlier novels, for instance in Kate Cutrer's intimation that the only time she felt alive was when she had an accident in which her boy-friend was killed, or in Lance's confession that "the only time members of my family have ever been happy, brave, successful was in time of war."[16] Such statements proliferate in Percy's fiction and can be, in fact, read in a much broader context than the one supplied by the above passage. It is Percy's profound conviction, moreover, one that he shares with Hawthorne, that crisis, or what Marcel has called "ordeal," is indispensable for the spiritual awakening of an individual. Clifford Pyncheon's condition in *The House of the Seven Gables* appears to be characterized precisely by what Percy calls "the living death," and it is crisis that affects the symbolic rebirth of Clifford, just as crisis transforms Hilda, Miriam, and Donatello in *The Marble Faun*. Percy sets a precedent with *Lancelot*, where he posits his protagonist's symbolic rebirth following *catharsis*. He further elaborates on this idea in *The Second Coming*.

Lewis Lawson remarks that Will would have killed himself had his life remained "perfect."[17] The point, however, is that had Will considered his life "perfect," the idea of suicide probably would never have entered his mind. For a considerable part of the narrative, he resembles Binx Bolling and the younger Will of *The Last Gentleman* in that he simply does not care for the pleasures of "ordinary life." His is the condition depicted by Albert Camus in *The Stranger*, whereby nothing matters, every choice is arbitrary and, and thus to choose means exactly the same as not to choose. Very characteristic is Will's meditation on the motives of his marriage with Marion. He apparently married her neither for love nor for money. Unable to establish one positive reason, he muses, "Why not?" His reaction to Marion's death resembles Lance's after Lucy's death, "What struck him was not sadness or remorse or pity but the wonder of it" (124).

Various people in the book attempt to pinpoint Will's condition. Thus, Lewis Peckham, a voracious reader and a failed poet, finds the reasons for what he sees as Will's "depression" in "the death of a spouse" and early retirement. He assures Will, "After all, . . . you got it all. You got everything a man needs." Will wants to know what Peckham would do if he "had it all," and Peckham unwaveringly responds: "I'd raise beef cattle, listen to Beethoven and Wagner, read and write" (152). He asks: "You don't enjoy such things, Will?", to which Will replies, "Sure." This reply, which may mean the positive as well as, ironically, the negative, seems to sum up Will's detached and indifferent manner. One of the two priests in the book, the Episcopalian Jack Curl, ascribes Will's problem to his lack of religion, and he urges Will to join his church. However, when Will asks Curl if he believes in God, the priest first answers, "Well, if I didn't, I'd say I needed some vocational counseling, wouldn't you?" Will repeats the question:

> "Do you believe God exists?"
>
> "Yes," said the chaplain gravely. The chaplain's face, he imagined, went keen and fine-eyed in the failing light. Could it be? the lively expression asked. A God-seeker? A man wrestling with Doubt? (He, the chaplain, had never made a convert.)
>
> "Why?"
>
> "Perhaps he is trying to tell you something at this moment," said the chaplain solemnly. (God, don't let me blow this, I've got a live on hooked.)
>
> "What?"
>
> "Grace is a mysterious thing," said the chaplain.
>
> "What does that mean?"
>
> "Perhaps the answer lies under our noses, so to speak, in fact within ourselves. If only we would take the trouble to ask the question."
>
> . . .
>
> "I said only that the question can be put in such a way that an answer is required. It will be stipulated, moreover, that a non-answer, silence, shall be construed to mean no."
>
> "There you go," said the chaplain uneasily. It made him uneasy to talk about religion . . . There is a time to talk religion, . . . to be God's plumber, to have solemn yet

> joyous bull sessions with men during a weekend with God, to horse around at a party. He was at home doing any of these but not when they were mixed up. (138)

This conversation transparently testifies to Percy's often expressed conviction that a person's inauthenticity betrays itself on a linguistic level. We might recall Binx's remark in respect to the language his half-brother uses, which "gives [Lonnie] an advantage foreigners have: his words are not worn out."[18] Lance thinks that he and Anna may invent a new language that will counterbalance "the old worn-out language," and tells Percival that they would talk "simply." Percy reflects here what one philosopher of language has called "a philosopher's paradise," whereby participants "converse in a maximally efficient, rational, co-operative way: they . . . speak sincerely, relevantly and clearly, while providing sufficient information."[19] Percy articulates his dream towards this end through Allison Huger's peculiar idiom.

Will, we recall, will neither bet on God's existence nor go with the flux of insignificant events that characterize what he calls "the living death." When he goes to a mountain cave equipped with a thirty-two-day supply of sleeping pills, he challenges God to manifest Himself. What issues in the course of events may be interpreted as an apogee of Percy's cynicism or as an expression of his unique sense of humor. Will develops a severe toothache which, together with the sleeping pills taken for seven consecutive days on empty stomach, produces a cosmic nausea that drives Will out of the cave. Robert H. Brinkmeyer claims that "the possibility that the toothache could be God's sign . . . never crosses [Will's] mind."[20] In the cave, Will is too drugged and in pain to give anything a single thought except searching for the way out. Afterwards, convinced of its frivolity, Will never considers a possibility that his toothache was a sign from God. Nevertheless, a remarkable thing does transpire as Will searches for the way out of the cave. Following the light he sees, Will comes to the tract connecting Allie's greenhouse to the mountain chimney for ventilation and constant temperature, and he falls into this tract:

> Resting elbows on the sill, he meant to poke his head through for a look, but both vines and sill were rotten and he fell, thinking even as he fell that it couldn't be much of a fall, what with the vines and the ridge itself not being much higher than a man. But this was a fall through air not vines or bushes, through air and color, brilliant greens and violet and vermillion and a blue unlike any sky, a free-fall headfirst with time enough to wonder if he might be dead after all, what with this tacky heaven and the great black beast of the apocalypse roaring down at him, eyes red, jaws open and ravening, when, wood splintering first then exploding into kindling, he hit the table, then concrete, but not too hard, with one shoulder mostly but the back of his head some. He shut down, turned off like a light. (226)

Here the text of *The Second Coming* "doubles back," in Brooks' words, for of course we have a precedent of this scene in *Lancelot*, though Lance's movement, after his encounter with the apocalyptic beast is conceived as Lucifer's ascent from hell, whereas here Percy comes closest to exemplifying the notion of *catharsis*, since Will's movement is literally downward. Will "shuts down" the memories of the first days in the cave: of his "old mole" of a father, dead wife, and unloving (though possibly also unloved) daughter. All these memories become exorcized as Will lands on the floor of Allie's greenhouse. Tended affectionately by her, he recovers from the fall, even as he terminates his search for the reason to live: He will marry Allie.

ALLISON

Whether or not Percy intended it, the gang-raped mute Anna (also, the mute girl in *The Last Gentleman*, whom Will Barrett recalls playing Chinese checkers with in the hospital where he was treated for amnesia), and Allison Huger in *The Second Coming*, who loses her language and then reinvents it, bring to mind what recent feminist criticism has to say on the subject of the repression of femininity. According to Mary Jacobus, femininity is "the repressed term by which discourse is made possible. The feminine takes its place with the absence, silence, or incoherence that discourse represses."[21]

Of course, it is always possible to trace the motif of a mute girl in his fiction to Percy's traumatic discovery that his first daughter was born deaf and mute. However, a look at what transpires in recent Southern women's writing bluntly reveals how very symptomatic of the transformation of Southern womanhood Percy's mute and insane females are. One might resort for additional insight to the classic Derridean ambivalence as regards women's writing: both to remain silent and to speak (write) is to conform to the structure of the phallocentric logos, one through repression, the other through contradiction. Hence, to write, for a woman, means to either stay sane accepting, or conforming to, the phallocentric logos (as some Southern women authors, for instance, Anne Tyler and Shirley Ann Grau, indeed do), or to work "ceaselessly and simultaneously," says Elizabeth Meese, to deconstruct it. These nonconforming violators of the logos, feminist writers, Meese argues, are "mad (angry) about the specific oppressions that have written women's historic condition."[22] Though the complexities of recent Southern writing created by women need not be rehearsed here in detail, Meese's argument appears to be extremely pertinent to the works of such authors as Jill McCorkle, Ellen Gilchrist, Gail Godwin, or Lisa Alther.[23] To remain sane and at the same time defy the logos is to subvert it through language as, for instance, Alice Walker does in *The Color Purple* (a book Percy greatly admired). In *Lancelot*, when Anna recovers her language, it is precisely to defy Lance and through defiance to challenge the language and culture of patriarchy.

It is, however, Allison Huger in *The Second Coming* who effectively subverts phallocentrism with her unique argot and her consciousness. She is one of the most seductive female characters in contemporary American male discourse. Percy surely intended Will, and not Allison, to be the protagonist of *The Second Coming*. But Allie somehow got out of hand and took over the narrative.

Allison is a recent escapee from a psychiatric institution where she was treated for schizophrenia. It rather goes without saying that her failure at living is as obvious a story of privation as that of Esther Greenwood from Sylvia Plath *The Bell Jar*. Before she gathers strength and courage to flee from the asylum, the phallocentric logos is defined for her by her father, her first lover and the Pakistani doctor who "looks after" her in the hospital. The names of the latter two ("Sarge" and "Dukhipoor," the latter of which, as John Hardy notes, meaning "legion"[24]) and the mannerisms of her father (reminiscent of General Patton, Allie reports—an echo of Plath's "panzer man") evoke military associations. Moreover, Allison, reminiscing the moments of intimacy with Sarge, thinks that pleasing him was like "doing well" for her father ("look at my report card, Daddy, straight A's. A Plus in music"). She asks herself: "But what do you do after you get straight A's for Daddy and Sarge?" The answer, for Allison, was to seek compensation and forgetfullness in drugs and, after her mother discovered her lying in the closet "with the shakes," in silence.

Allison, who after her flight from the asylum, is reborn into the world like Rip Van Winkle (her own analogy), finds her voice to utter her name aloud:

> At first it sounded strange. Then she recognized it as her name. Then it sounded strange again but strange in a differ-

> ent way, the way an ordinary word repeated aloud sounds strange. Her voice sounded rusty and unused. She wasn't sure she could talk. (24)

Percy, echoing Freud's question "What do women want?" in two interviews, one before, one after the publication of *The Second Coming,* ostensibly seems to be much more aware of the feminist issue than he wishes to acknowledge. The saga of Allison's survival in the greenhouse meticulously records her tasks, which require tremendous physical strength and competence and which she accepts with surprising matter-of-factness. In Percy's words, "she was a hoister, a mistress of mechanical advantage. And here was something to hoist. If she could hoist this monster of a Grand Crown stove, she could do anything in life" (199). Her real problem is with words and, specifically, with naming. She says that "naming is knowing," and in these words she expresses one of the most central feminist concerns. As Dorothy Smith puts it, "We are confronted virtually with the problem of reinventing the world of knowledge, of symbols and images."[25]

Allison speaks with disarming directness. At times, her words are full of wisdom. At other times, and especially when she confesses her emotional turmoil, her language verges on adolescent ingenuousness. Whereas Will's chapters are marked by (characteristic to the Percy hero) irony, often verging on cynicism, Allison's passages are permeated by an intelligence whose strength and warmth color the entire narrative and are unchecked or unguarded by irony.

Like Will, Allie makes the discovery that "the secret of talking is to have something to say," and, also like him, she senses that inauthenticity manifests itself in language. She notes, for instance, "If a person says to you: *I hate to tell you this but*—she doesn't hate to tell you. She likes to tell you" (92), which curiously resembles a number of Pascal's "pensées" on language as, for example, "I have been embarrassed by such compliments as: I have given you a lot of trouble, I am afraid of boring you, I am afraid it may take too long. One is either persuasive or irritating," or "Eloquence is a depiction of thought, and thus those who add still more once they have done the painting are producing a picture instead of a portrait."[26] The language Allie invents, even if a symptom of her illness, is peculiar but effective.

As Allison and Will's relationship develops, they both agree that it will be founded on a unique difference. They both concede that Will needs Allison for "hoisting" (he tends to fall), and she wants him to "interpret" her language to others (one really wonders why; her idiom seems to be as effective as any one can find). Even if these reciprocal tasks might suggest androgyny, in the sense that the masculine here implies logic and the feminine "masculine" physical strength, they in fact triumphantly transcend androgyny since the female and male selves are more than opposite; they are complementary gender identities which must be united in order to make true selfhood possible for each. They are intimately combined selves, sharing the same human consciousness, and their relationship is defined more by similarities than by differences. As Allison tells Will, "why is it I seem to have known you before I knew you. We are different but also the same."

The book not only presents the second coming of Will Barrett, Kitty Vaught, and Sutter (a hearsay figure), the focal characters of Percy's second book, *The Last Gentleman*, but it also "reincarnates" Anna from *Lancelot* as Allison Huger. Percy has Kitty, Allie's mother, interpret what an old black cook has once said of Allie, "That chile don't belong in this world," as an acknowledgement of Allie's incomplete reincarnation. Kitty says that "Allie had come from another life but had not quite made it all the way," which may indicate that Allie belongs to both narratives, *Lancelot* and *The Second Coming*, which in turn implies her second coming as a fictional character, though it can also carry a number of other meanings, several of which are suggested by Kitty.[27]

Towards the end of the book Kitty tells Will that before Allie's confinement in the asylum, she discovered her daughter lying in a closet with the "shakes," obsessively repeating, "I'm no good, I'm a liar, I'm the original hooker" (286). Kitty apparently consulted a certain Ray ("a true mystic") and learned that Allie's previous incarnation was "a courtesan spy for the North in Richmond." "Don't you see?" Kitty tells Will, "Then she was too much of this world, she knew too many men, talked too much, lied too much, and abused her body. So now she is not of this world, knows nobody, can't talk enough to lie, doesn't use her body at all" (286). The whole passage is playfully tricky and suggests a number of possibilities. Most obviously, a "hooker" is a prostitute. But the word "hooker," which derives from a "hook," in nautical slang signifies an "anchor," whereas the verb may signify "to pull," for instance in golf jargon. Admittedly, in reference to Will, Allie fulfills the functions suggested by both meanings. When Will complains to Allie of his black-outs, she tells him that she can "hoist" him. But we may derive even further meanings working on the assumption that, as Percy says in his essay on Melville:

> The freedom and happiness of the artist is attested by his playfulness, his tricks, his malice, his underhandedness, his naughtiness, his hoodwinking the reader. So happy is the metaphorical distance between the novelist and his narrative that he's free to cover his tracks at will.[28]

Percy's hoax reminds one of John Fowles' in *A Maggot,* where a fictitious courtesan, Rebecca Lee, is an eighteenth-century Joan of Arc and Mother Lee, the founder of the Shakers. Her intelligent individual Dissent overcomes the forces of the past and paves the way for the women's liberation movement. The clues Percy supplies in the book point to his playful handling of the Shakers' dogma and ritual, yet the conclusion we can reach upon scrutinizing these clues is most crucial for our understanding of the book's theological issue.

Allison, we recall, was, before her confinement in the asylum, discovered lying in the closet with "the shakes." Her confinement and the story of her mistreatment in the hospital bring to mind Mother Ann's imprisonment in a "house of correction," which period, in particular, marked her ascendancy as the leader of the sect. The Shakers fully credited the story of her martyrdom in prison, where she claimed to have been treated with utmost cruelty. Edward Deming Andrews debunks this myth, pointing to various inconsistencies in Ann Lee's account, but perceives its significance in exemplifying "the persecutory complex" commonly demonstrated by the early adherents of the sect.[29] Likewise, Allie evokes through memory her treatment in the hospital, which consisted primarily of ECT, which she calls "buzzing" or "frying." She says, "Fried is crucified," which not only qualifies Allie for a literary transfiguration of Christ (or, rather, we might say, the second embodiment of Christ in the figure of Mother Ann), but also harks back to Hawthorne's similar vision as regards Hilda's suffering in *The Marble Faun*. The spells of amnesia afflicting Allie result from ECT. She makes as much clear in the notes she writes down (Instructions from Myself to Myself) in preparation for her escape from the hospital:

> You may not remember this when you come to (about 9 a.m.). Your jaw will hurt and your teeth will be sore from the mouthpiece. You will be conscious but still paralyzed from the Anectine (curare), lying there bright-eyed and still, like a parrot shot by the poisoned arrow of a pygmy's blowgun (which you have been). You'll be drowsy from the Brewital and your mouth will be dry from the atropine. . . . Nobody is going to bother you—they're too busy buzzing the others. (27)[30]

In view of the symbolically loaded details Allie depicts here, Dr. Dukhipoor's ("poor in spirit") interpretation of her experience as "a kind of expiation for guilt. Having expiated, one naturally feels better" (104), sounds outright cynical, even if suggestive of Percy's source.[31]

The sect's separation from the world is realized in Allison's flight from the asylum and in her solitary dwelling in the greenhouse. Her peculiar idiom harbors the notion of "speaking in tongues." Fowles pertinently refers to the word of his fictitious Ann Lee as "Logos," for the historical Ann Lee proclaimed upon receiving her calling, "I am Ann the Word." Needless to say, the theological importance of this statement intersects with the focal feminist concern. Allison's instinctual and competent handling of Will after his "nutty," in Percy's words, experiment parallels the Shakers' ability to heal the sick. The Shakers' ideology of equality and partnership between men and women is realized in Allison and Will's relationship. In one of the sources as regards Shakerism we learn of their "hugging gift."[32] Allison's last name may suggest Percy's playful adaptation of this source. Even the division of the narrative into Allison's and Will's alternate chapters evokes the sect's insistence that "the sexes be separated and organized along independent yet parallel lines."

After his third intrusion into Allison's retreat, Will says, simply and without his habitual quotes, "I love you now and until the day I die." The novel does not end here, though it closes on a note which only emphasizes the personal encounter that takes place in the greenhouse. In between we have all sorts of complications that befit a romantic story: family interventions, the disappearance of a lover, etc. But the novel inevitably moves towards its happy ending, with two highly symbolic scenes. In the first, Will, just about to consummate his union with Allie, is visited for the last time by the ghost of his father. The latter, like the Lady of the Camellias in *Lancelot*, hands him the "sword," commanding: "Go like a man, . . . a Roman, here's your sword" (337). Go and settle accounts not with the world but with yourself, the ghost seems to advise Will. Will takes the two guns, the Greener, with which his father shot himself, and the Luger, which has always reminded him that he might follow in his father's footsteps, goes to the edge of the gorge, and hurls both over it. The scene has a ritual tinge, reminiscent of the hurling of the Model over the Tarpeian Rock in *The Marble Faun*. Will exorcizes the past for the last time, and in the following scene the victory of Eros over Thanatos in complete.[33]

This scene, which embraces the idea of partnership, prepared for by Will and Allie's assertion of their reciprocative tasks ("I need you for hoisting and you need me for interpretation" [329]), constitutes one of Percy's masterstrokes:

> They stayed in bed all day and all night except for meals, loving and laughing, frolicking, exchanging many a kiss and smacks on the ass while carts creaked outside and maids tapped on doors with keys. Frowning, she peered closely at his cheek and squeezed a blackhead. He straddled her thighs and rubbed her back, sore from hoisting, pressed his thumbs in the two dips at the bottom of her spine, marveling at how she was made. Each tended to each other, kneading and poking sore places. She examined him like a mother examining a child, close, stretching skin, her mouth open, grabbing hair to pull his head over to see his neck, her eyes slightly abulge with concentration, checking his cave wound, picking at scabs. When her eyes happened to meet his, they softened and went deep. . . . Then she smiled and flew against him again. Her supple bent-back strength and coverage astounded him. (341-42)

Not only does the Percy hero for the first time give of himself to a woman, but also the rituals of caretaking in *The Second Coming* remake the rigidly fixed gender roles. We might benefit from comparing this passage with a remarkably similar scene of intimacy in Toni Morrison's *Song of Solomon*:

> She put salve on his face. He washed her hair. She sprinkled talcum on his feet. He straddled her behind and massaged her back. She put witch hazel on his swollen neck. . . . She kissed his mouth. He touched her face. She said please come back. He said I'll see you tonight.[34]

Both scenes express sensuality and a caretaking which heals or, in Hélène Cixous' words, "a love that rejoices in the exchange that multiplies."[35]

Like Hilda and Kenyon, Will and Allie respond to each other's loneliness, but their relationship will not be exactly a solitude of a united two. With the money he has inherited, Will is determined to found a community on a piece of property Allie has inherited; it will consist of two crippled builders, a gardener, and an assortment of social outcasts. They will inhabit Allie's greenhouse, and they will grow fruits and vegetables. This pastoral retreat, reminiscent of the endings of both *Lancelot* and *The House of the Seven Gables*, coupled with the promise of love and marriage, constitutes no doubt Percy's alternative to stagnant existence ("the living death") and social corruption. Furthermore, the last paragraphs of the book clearly establish its religious context.

To grasp the meaning of these last paragraphs, we must resort to the scene which pivots *The Last Gentleman* as it not only alludes to the conclusive episode in *The Moviegoer*, where Lonnie's death creates a theological focus of the novel, but also anticipates an exchange between Will and an Anglican priest, Weatherbee, at the end of *The Second Coming*. The three scenes testify to Percy's indebtedness to Kierkegaard's notion of an "apostle." In *The Last Gentleman*, the Catholic priest hastily summoned to baptize the dying boy asks Jamie to accept the creeds of faith. Jamie wants to know if what the priest has told him is true and why he should believe it. The priest says:

> "It is true because God Himself revealed it as the truth."
>
> Again the youth's lips moved and again the priest turned to the interpreter.
>
> "He asked how, meaning how does he know that?"
>
> The priest sighed. "If it were not true," he said to Jamie, "then I would not be here. That is why I am here, to tell you."[36]

This is the closest Percy ever gets to paraphrasing Kierkegaard's insight. Will misses the import of this scene (just as Kate Cutrer-Bolling misses the deeper meaning of the exchange between Binx and the children, following Lonnie's death) but senses its importance because he asks Sutter to interpret it for him. As if requiring to emphasize his protagonist's transformation in *The Second Coming*, Percy mirrors the preceding scene in Father Weatherbee's recollection of how he brought faith to some villagers on the coast of the Pacific:

> They believed me! They believed the Gospel whole and entire, and the teachings of the church. They said that if I told them, then it must be true or I would not have gone to so much trouble. (359)

Deeply moved, Will addresses a query to the priest, believing in the latter's authority to answer it:

> "Right!" cried Will Barrett. In his excitement he had risen from his chair and started around the desk. "Tell me something, Father. Do you believe that Christ will come again and that in fact there are certain unmistakable sings of his coming in these very times?" (359-60)

The priest only nods and smiles but Will grasps the "unspeakable" in a flash of insight (a *syneidesis*). The three alternatives suggested in *The Last Gentleman*: faith, sex, and intersubjectivity, are reconciled in *The Second Coming* and, for Will, Allie fulfills all three. This is to say that Percy's hero no longer needs to gamble on faith. In gaining both Allie's "dearest heart" and her "dear ass, which is the loveliest in all of Carolina," Will not only has his existence provided for but, in addition, has the existence of God proved to him, once and for all, by the act of giving. The last paragraph makes this quite clear, even as it alludes to the idea of male and female messiahship inherent in the Shakers' doctrine:

> Will Barrett thought about Allie in her greenhouse, her wide gray eyes, her lean muscled boy's arms, her strong quick hands. His heart leapt with a secret joy. What is it I want from him, he wondered, not only want but must have? Is she a gift and therefore a sign of a giver? Could it be that the Lord is here, masquerading behind this simple silly holy face? Am I crazy to want both, her and Him? No, not want, must have. And will have. (360)

This conclusion elicited considerable objection from a number of critics, again reminding one of the critical condescension toward the sentimental ending of *The Marble Faun*. Brinkmeyer, for instance, writes *à-propos* the conclusion of *The Second Coming*, "[it] weakens the point Percy is making about Will's movement toward the Church," and he notes that, after Will and Allie's previous anguish, the apparent ease with which they "start afresh seems artificial and unduly romantic."[37] Similarly, Doreen Fowler, in her analysis of the ambiguities of the novel, protests that the crucial issue Percy attempts to communicate is not "a feasible one, given the world Percy has created."[38]

Percy, we remember, has called *The Second Coming* his first unalienated novel. To grasp the meaning of this opinion we must once again return to his criticism of Kierkegaard's subjectivity and his implied juxtaposition of what he calls the "trap of inwardness" with Marcelian intersubjectivity. Arguably, nowhere before *The Second Coming* does Percy articulate intersubjectivity closely. Admittedly, all of his novels end on a hopeful note, but it is in *The Second Coming* that the hope Percy's vision embraces is expressed in truly Marcelian terms. This hope, to Marcel, is "essentially the availability of a soul which has entered intimately enough into the experience of communion to accomplish in the teeth of will and knowledge the transcendent act—the act establishing the vital regeneration of which this experience affords both the pledge and the first-fruits."[39] While Binx Bolling does achieve transcendence at the end of *The Moviegoer*, the Postscript makes it clear that his transcendence works solely in Kierkegaardian terms. Binx closes his business in Gentilly, marries Kate, on Aunt Emily's prompting enters medical school, moves with his wife to the cottage in the vicinity of Emily's house, and becomes a kind of family clown.[40] Binx's mental peace rests mainly in what Kierkegaard calls "infinite resignation." Nothing in the book suggests that Binx's union with Kate goes beyond a mere ethical choice, even as there is nothing in Kierkegaard's conception of marriage to suggest that it can be conceived in other than ethical terms. Ostensibly, such a solution could have been enacted in *Lancelot*, but the book ends prior to it. *Lancelot*, however, paves the way for *The Second Coming* for a number of reasons, the most crucial of which is that the vision embraced in *The Second Coming* seems to arise ultimately through the enactment of the *cathartic* principle in terms of Percy's art. Like Marcel's *homo viator*, and like Hawthorne's American couple in *The Marble Faun*, Allie and Will finally arrive home.

NOTES

1. Jan Nordby Gretlund, "Laying the Ghost of Marcus Aurelius?" in *Conversations with Walker Percy*, ed. Lewis A. Lawson and Victor A. Kramer (Jackson: Univ. Press of Mississippi, 1985), p. 215.

2. Gabriel Marcel, *The Existential Background of Human Dignity* (Cambridge: Harvard Univ. Press, 1963), p. 96.

3. Jo Gulledge, "The Reentry Option: An Interview with Walker Percy," in *Conversations with Walker Percy*, p. 300.

4. See Harriet Doar, "Walker Percy: He Likes to Put Protagonist in Situation," ibid., p. 5.

5. See James Atlas, "An Interview with Walker Percy," ibid., p. 183.

6. Walker Percy, *The Second Coming* (New York: Farrar, Straus and Giroux, 1980), p. 280. All subsequent references are to this edition. All emphases in the quoted material throughout this chapter are mine.

7. See Linda Whitney Hobson, "The Study of Consciousness: An Interview with Walker Percy," *Conversations with Walker Percy*, pp. 219-20.

8. Blaise Pascal, *Pensées*, trans. A. J. Krailsheimer (New York: Penguin Books, 1987), p. 72.

9. Ibid., p. 48.

10. Walker Percy, *The Last Gentleman* (New York: Farrar, Straus and Giroux, 1966), p. 158.

11. Jan Miel, *Pascal and Theology* (Baltimore and London: The Johns Hopkins Univ. Press, 1969), p. vii.

12. Cited from Linda Whitney Hobson, *Understanding Walker Percy* (Columbia: Univ. of South Carolina Press, 1988), pp. 114-15.

13. *Pensées*, p. 136.

14. Miel, p. 180.

15. *Pensées*, p. 152.

16. Walker Percy, *Lancelot* (New York: Farrar, Straus and Giroux, 1977), p. 139.

17. Lewis A. Lawson, *Another Generation. Southern Fiction Since World War II* (Jackson: Univ. Press of Mississippi, 1984), p. 140.

18. Walker Percy, *The Moviegoer* (New York: Alfred A. Knopf, 1960), p. 162.

19. See Stephen C. Levinson, *Pragmatics* (Cambridge: Cambridge Univ. Press, 1983), pp. 101-02.

20. Robert H. Brinkmeyer, Jr., *Three Catholic Writers of the Modern South: Allen Tate, Caroline Gordon, Walker Percy* (Jackson: Univ. Press of Mississippi, 1985), p. 15.

21. Mary Jacobus, *Reading Woman. Essays in Feminist Criticism* (New York: Columbia Univ. Press, 1986), p. 29.

22. Elizabeth Meese, *Crossing the Double-Cross. The Practice of Feminist Criticism* (Chapel Hill and London: Univ. of North Carolina Press, 1986), p. 120.

23. See Donna Kelleher Darden, "Southern Women Writing about Southern Women: Jill McCorkle, Lisa Alther, Gail Godwin, Ellen Gilchrist, and Lee Smith," in *Southern Women*, ed. Caroline Matheny Dillman (New York and London: Hemisphere Publishing Corporation, 1988), pp. 215-20.

24. John Edward Hardy, *The Fiction of Walker Percy* (Urbana and Chicago: Univ. of Illinois Press, 1987), p. 190.

25. Dorothy E. Smith, "Ideological Structure and How Women Are Excluded," *Canadian Review of Sociology and Anthropology* vol. 12, no. 4 (1975), p. 367.

26. *Pensées*, pp. 215 and 225.

27. This device supports William Rodney Allen's insightful observation about the metafictional quality of *The Second Coming*. Allen says that Percy's procedure in *The Second Coming* is reminiscent of Kurt Vonnegut's and John Fowles' metafictional play. See *Walker Percy. A Southern Wayfarer* (Jackson: Univ. Press of Mississippi, 1986), pp. 135-36.

28. Walker Percy, "Herman Melville," *The New Criterion* 213 (November 1983), p. 42.

29. Edward Deming Andrews, *The People Called Shakers* (New York: Dover Publications, Inc., 1963), p. 5.

30. This passage contains a very eloquent and value-laden simile, "like a parrot shot by the poisoned arrow of a pygmy's blowgun." "Parrot" signifies a *higher* species, domesticated by humans, whereas "pygmy" signifies a *small* reduced being, wreaking violence through foul means (poison). The simile conveys the general sense of *insignificant*.

31. Dukhipoor, in effect, imposes Masterplot on Allie's experience. See Peter Brooks, *Reading for the Plot. Design and Intention in Narrative* (New York: Alfred A. Knopf, 1984), pp. 90-113.

32. See David R. Lamson, *Two Years' Experience Among the Shakers . . .* (1848; rpt. New York: AMS Press, 1971), p. 81.

33. For the discussion of Eros and Thanatos in *The Second Coming*, see Allen, pp. 131-51.

34. Toni Morrison, *Song of Solomon* (New York: Alfred A. Knopf, 1977), p. 285.

35. Hélène Cixous, "The Laugh of the Medusa," *Signs. Journal of Women in Culture and Society*, vol. 1, no. 4 (Summer 1976), p. 887.

36. *The Last Gentleman*, p. 388.

37. Brinkmeyer, p. 168.

38. Doreen Fowler, "Answers and Ambiguity in Percy's *The Second Coming*," *Critique* 23, no. 2 (1981-82), p. 16.

39. Gabriel Marcel, *Homo Viator. Introduction to a Metaphysic of Hope*, trans. Emma Craufurd (New York: Harper and Brothers/Harper Torchbooks, 1962), p. 67.

40. He says, "Both women find me comical and laugh a good deal at my expense." See *The Moviegoer*, p. 237.

Bibliography

Primary Sources

Works by Nathaniel Hawthorne

The Centenary Edition of the Works of Nathaniel Hawthorne, ed. William Charvat, Roy Harvey Pearce, Claude M. Simpson, Thomas Woodson, Fredson Bowers, L. Neal Smith, and James Rubino, 18 vols. Columbus: Ohio State Univ. Press, 1962-87.

First Editions of the Works of Nathaniel Hawthorne together with Some Manuscripts, Letters, and Portraits. New York: The Gollier Club, 1904.

Works by Walker Percy

"Herman Melville." *The New Criterion* 213 (1983).

"Naming and Being." *Personalist* XLI (1960).

Lancelot. New York: Farrar, Straus and Giroux, 1977.

The Message in the Bottle. New York: Farrar, Straus and Giroux, 1975.

The Last Gentleman. New York: Farrar, Straus and Giroux, 1966.

The Moviegoer. New York: Alfred A. Knopf, 1960.

The Second Coming. New York: Farrar, Straus and Giroux, 1980.

Secondary Sources

Allen, E. L. *Existentialism from Within*. London: Routledge and Kegan Paul, Ltd., 1953.

Allen, William Rodney. *Walker Percy. A Southern Wayfarer*. Jackson: Univ. Press of Mississippi, 1986.

Andrews, Edward Deming. *The People Called Shakers*. New York: Dover Publications, Inc., 1963.

Auden, Wynstan Hugh, ed. *The Living Thoughts of Kierkegaard*. New York: David McKay Company, Inc., 1952.

Ayo, Nicholas. "The Labyrinthine Ways of 'Rappaccini's Daughter'." *Research Studies* 42, 1974.

Baym, Nina. "Hawthorne's Women: The Tyranny of Social Myths." *Centenary Review* 15, 1971.

———."Thwarted Nature: Nathaniel Hawthorne as Feminist," in *American Novelists Revisited: Essays in Feminist Criticism*, ed. Fritz Fleishmann. Boston: G. K. Hall & Co., 1982.

Bednarowski, May Farrell. "Outside the Main Stream: Women's Religion and Women Religious Leaders in Nineteenth-Century America." *JAAR* XLVIII, 1980.

Breisach, Ernst. *Introduction to Modern Existentialism*. New York: Grove Press, Inc., 1962.

Bretall, Robert, ed. *A Kierkegaard Anthology*. New York: The Modern Library, 1938.

Breuer, Josef and Sigmund Freud. *Studies on Hysteria*, trans. and ed. James Strachey. New York: Basic Books, Inc., Publishers, 1957.

Bridgman, Richard. "As Hester Prynne Lay Dying." *English Language Notes*, vol. II, no. 4, June, 1965.

Brinkmeyer, Robert H., Jr. *Three Catholic Writers of the Modern South: Allen Tate, Caroline Gordon, Walker Percy*. Jackson: Univ. Press of Mississippi, 1985.

Brooks, Peter. *Reading for the Plot. Design and Intention in Narrative*. New York: Alfred A. Knopf, 1984.

Broughton, Panthea Reid, ed. *The Art of Walker Percy. Stratagems for Being*. Baton Rouge: Louisiana State Univ. Press, 1979.

Brown, Gillian. "The Empire of Agoraphobia." *Representations* 20, Fall 1987.

Campbell, Joseph. *The Hero with a Thousand Faces*. Princeton: Princeton Univ. Press, 1968.

Camus, Albert. *The Myth of Sisyphus and Other Essays,* trans. Justin O'Brien. New York: Vintage Books, 1955.

Cixous, Hélène. "The Laugh of the Medusa." *Signs. Journal of Women in Culture and Society*, vol. 1, no. 4, Summer 1976.

Cixous, Hélène and Catherine Clement. *The Newly Born Woman*, trans. Betsy Wing. Minneapolis: Univ. of Minnesota Press, 1986.

Coles, Robert. *Walker Percy. An American Search.* Boston and Toronto: Little, Brown and Company, 1978.

Collins, James. *The Mind of Kierkegaard.* Chicago: Henry Regnery Company, 1965.

Crews, Frederick. *The Sins of the Fathers. Hawthorne's Psychological Themes*. New York: Oxford Univ. Press, 1966.

Darden, Donna Kelleher. "Southern Women Writing about Southern Women: Jill McCorkle, Lisa Alther, Gail Godwin, Ellen Gilchrist, and Lee Smith," in *Southern Women*, ed. Caroline Matheny Dillman. New York and London: Hemisphere Publishing Corporation, 1988.

DeSalvo, Louise. *Nathaniel Hawthorne*. Atlantic Highlands: Humanities Press International, Inc., 1987.

Donohue, Agnes McNeill, ed. *A Casebook on the Hawthorne Question*. New York: Thomas Y. Crowell Company, 1963.

———. *Hawthorne. Calvin's Ironic Stepchild.* Kent: The Kent State Univ. Press, 1985.

Dostoyevski, Fyodor. *The Brothers Karamazov*, trans. Constance Garnett. New York: New American Library, 1957.

Dryden, Edgar. *Nathaniel Hawthorne. The Poetics of Enchantment.* Ithaca and London: Cornell Univ. Press, 1977.

Elrod, John W. *Being and Existence in Kierkegaard's Pseudonymous Works*. Princeton: Princeton Univ. Press, 1975.

Fairbanks, Henry G. *The Lasting Loneliness of Nathaniel Hawthorne. A Study of the Sources of Alienation in Modern Man.* Albany: Magi Books, Inc., 1965.

Finkelstein, Sidney. *Existentialism and Alienation in American Literature*. New York: International Publishers, 1965.

Fowler, Doreen. "Answers and Ambiguity in Percy's *The Second Coming*." *Critique*, vol. 23, no. 2, 1981-82.

Freud, Sigmund. *The Standard Edition of the Complete Psychological Works of Sigmund Freud*, trans. and ed. James Strachey. London: Hogarth Press, 1953-74.

Frye, Northrop. *The Great Code. The Bible and Literature*. San Diego: Harcourt Brace Jovanovich, Publishers, 1982.

Gallop, Jane. *The Daughter's Seduction. Feminism and Psychoanalysis*. Ithaca and London: Cornell Univ. Press, 1982.

———. *Reading Lacan*. Ithaca and London: Cornell Univ. Press, 1985.

Girad, René. *Violence and the Sacred*, trans. Patrick Gregory. Baltimore: The Johns Hopkins Univ. Press, 1977.

Goethe, Johann Wolfgang. *Faust*, trans. Walter Kaufman. Garden City: Anchor Books, 1961/63.

Gollin, Rita K. *Nathaniel Hawthorne and the Truth of Dreams*. Baton Rouge and London: Louisiana State Univ. Press, 1979.

Green, Calvin. *A Summary View of the Millennial Church, or United Society of Believers, Commonly Called Shakers*. Albany: C. van Benthusyen, 1823.

Hanley, Katherine Rose. *Dramatic Approaches to Creative Fidelity. A Study in the Theater and Philosophy of Gabriel Marcel (1889-1973)*. Lanham: Univ. Press of America, 1987.

Hardy, John Edward. *The Fiction of Walker Percy*. Urbana and Chicago: Univ. of Illinois Press, 1987.

Harris, Kenneth Marc. *Hypocrisy and Self-Deception in Hawthorne's Fiction*. Charlottesville: Univ. Press of Virginia, 1988.

Hobson, Linda Whitney. *Understanding Walker Percy*. Columbia: Univ. of South Carolina Press, 1988.

Howells, William Dean. *Heroines of Fiction*. New York and London: Harper and Brothers Publishers, 1901.

Jacobus, Mary. *Reading Woman. Essays in Feminist Criticism*. New York: Columbia Univ. Press, 1986.

Kelly, Dorothy. *Fictional Genders. Role and Representation in Nineteenth-Century French Narrative*. Lincoln and London: Univ. of Nebraska Press, 1979.

Kierkegaard, Sören. *Concluding Unscientific Postscript*, trans. David F. Swenson. Princeton: Princeton Univ. Press, 1941.

———.*The Journals of Sören Kierkegaard*. trans. Alexander Dru. New York: Oxford Univ. Press, 1938.

———.*The Present Age and of the Difference Between a Genius and an Apostle*, trans. Alexander Dru. New York: Harper and Row, 1962.

———.*Sören Kierkegaard's Journals and Papers*, trans. Howard V. Hong and Edna H. Hong. Bloomington: Indiana Univ. Press, 1967-1970.

———.*Stages on Life's Way*, trans. Walter Lowrie. Princeton: Princeton Univ. Press, 1944.

Krieger, Murray. *Visions of Extremity in Modern Literature*. Vol. I: *The Tragic Vision. The Confrontation of Extremity*. Baltimore: The Johns Hopkins Univ. Press, 1973.

Lacan, Jacques. *Écrits. A Selection*, trans. Alan Sheridan. New York: W. W. Norton and Company, Inc., 1977.

Lamson, David R. *Two Years' Experience Among the Shakers . . .* (1848), rpt. New York: AMS Press, 1971.

Lasch, Christopher. *The Culture of Narcissism. American Life in an Age of Diminishing Expectations*. New York: Warner Books, 1979.

Lawson, Lewis A. *Another Generation. Southern Fiction Since World War II*. Jackson: Univ. Press of Mississippi, 1984.

———."Walker Percy's Indirect Communication." *Texas Studies in Literature and Language* 11, 1969.

Lawson, Lewis A., and Victor A. Kramer, eds. *Conversations with Walker Percy*. Jackson: Univ. Press of Mississippi, 1985.

Levinson, Stephen C. *Pragmatics*. Cambridge: Cambridge Univ. Press, 1983.

Lischer, Tracy Kenyon. "Walker Percy's Kierkegaard. A Reading of *The Moviegoer*." *The Cresset*, vol. XLI, no. 10, October 1978.

Lloyd-Smith, Allan Gardner. *Eve Tempted. Writing and Sexuality in Hawthorne's Fiction*. Totowa: Barnes and Noble Books, 1984.

Male, Roy R. *Hawthorne's Tragic Vision*. New York: The Norton Library, 1957.

Marcel, Gabriel. *The Existential Background of Human Dignity*. Cambridge: Harvard Univ. Press, 1963.

———.*Homo Viator. Introduction to a Metaphysic of Hope*. trans. Emma Craufurd. London: Victor Gollancz Ltd., 1951.

———.*Homo Viator. Introduction to a Metaphysic of Hope*, trans. Emma Craufurd. New York: Harper & Brothers, 1962.

———.*The Mystery of Being*, trans. G. S. Fraser and R. Hague. Chicago: Gateway Edition. Henry Regnery Company, 1960.

———.*The Philosophy of Existence*, trans. Manya Harari. New York: Philosophical Library, 1949.

McPherson, Hugo. *Hawthorne as Mythmaker*. Toronto: Univ. of Toronto Press, 1969.

Meese, Elizabeth. *Crossing the Double-Cross. The Practice of Feminist Criticism*. Chapel Hill and London: Univ. of North Carolina Press, 1986.

Mellow, James R. *Nathaniel Hawthorne in His Times*. Boston: Houghton Mifflin Company, 1980.

Miel, Jan. *Pascal and Theology*. Baltimore: The Johns Hopkins Univ. Press, 1969.

Moi, Toril. *Sexual/Textual Politics: Feminist Literary Theory*. London and New York: Methuen & Co. Ltd, 1985.

Monegal, Emir Rodrigues, and Alastair Reid, eds. *Borges. A Reader. A Selection from the Writings of Jorge Luis Borges*. New York: E. P. Dutton, 1981.

Morrison, Toni. *Song of Solomon*. New York: Alfred A. Knopf, 1977.

Mounier, Emmanuel. *Existentialist Philosophies. An Introduction*, trans. Eric Blow. London: Rockliff, 1948.

Muller, John P. and J. William Richardson. *Lacan and Language. A Reader's Guide to Écrits*. New York: International Universities Press, Inc., 1982.

The New English Bible with an Apocrypha. Cambridge: Cambridge Univ. Press, 1970.

Normand, Jean. *Nathaniel Hawthorne. An Approach to an Analysis of Artistic Creation*, trans. Derek Coltman. Cleveland and London: The Press of Case Western Reserve University, 1970.

Oleksy, Elżbieta H. "Hawthorne's Monstrous Doubles." *The Nathaniel Hawthorne Review* (in press).

———."Ostatni dżentelmen z Luizjany—rozmowa z Walkerem Percy." *Literatura na świecie* 5-6, 1987.

O'Malley, John B. *The Fellowship of Being. An Essay on the Concept of Person in the Philosophy of Gabriel Marcel*. The Hague: Martinus Nijhoff, 1966.

Pascal, Blaise. *Pensées*, trans. A. J. Krailsheimer. New York: Penguin Books, 1987.

Person, Leland S., Jr. *Aesthetic Headaches. Women and a Masculine Poetics in Poe, Melville, and Hawthorne*. Athens and London: Univ. of Georgia Press, 1988.

Prunty, Wyatt. "Querns, Queries, and Quahogs: Walker Percy's Reviewers on Review." *The Georgia Review*, vol. XXXV, no. 1, Spring 1981.

Rigney, Barbara Hill. *Lilith's Daughters. Women and Religion in Contemporary Fiction*. Madison: Univ. of Wisconsin Press, 1982.

Scholes, Robert. *Fabulation and Metafiction*. Urbana: Univ. of Illinois Press, 1979.

Schriber, Suzanne. *Gender and the Writer's Imagination from Cooper to Wharton*. Lexington: Univ. Press of Kentucky, 1987.

Smith, Dorothy E. "Ideological Structure and How Women Are Excluded." *Canadian Review of Sociology and Anthropology*, vol. 12, no. 4, 1975.

Solomon, Robert C. *Introducing the Existentialists. Imaginary Interviews with Sartre, Heidegger and Camus*. Indianapolis and Cambridge: Hackett Publishing Company, 1981.

Tharpe, Jac. *Nathaniel Hawthorne. Identity and Knowledge*. Carbondale and Edwardsville: Southern Illinois Univ. Press, 1967.

———, ed. *Walker Percy: Art and Ethics*. Jackson: Univ. Press of Mississippi, 1980.

Todd, Janet. *Feminist Literary History*. New York: Routledge, 1988.

Tyner, Paul. "The Christ Ideal in Shakerism." *The Manifesto*, vol XXVI, no. 6, 1896.

Waggoner, Hyatt H. *Hawthorne: A Critical Study*. Cambridge: Harvard Univ. Press, 1955.

Warnock, Mary. *Existentialist Ethics*. London: MacMillan St. Martin's Press, 1970.

Warren, Joyce W. *The American Narcissus. Individualism and Women in Nineteenth-Century American Fiction*. New Brunswick: Rutgers Univ. Press, 1984.

Weston, Jessie L. *From Ritual to Romance.* New York: Doubleday Anchor Books, 1957.

Winnett, Susan. "Coming Unstrung: Women, Men, Narrative, and Principles of Pleasure." *PMLA*, vol. 105, no. 3, May 1990.

Young, Thomas, Daniel. "A New Breed: Walker Percy's Critics' Attempts to Place Him." *The Mississippi Quarterly*, vol. XXXIII, no. 4, Fall 1980.

Zimmer, Heinrich. *The King and the Corpse. Tales of the Soul's Conquest of Evil*, ed. Joseph Campbell. Princeton: Princeton Univ. Press, 1956.

Index